To Phil

Queer Fish

Best - [signature]

In Christian art and literature the fish is a symbol of Christ, also
sometimes of the newly baptized and of the Eucharist
. . . *ichthus*, the Greek for 'fish' was once a secret
christological acronym: *Ië-sous Christos Theou
Huios Sötër* ('Jesus Christ Son of God, Saviour')
(*The Oxford Dictionary of the Christian Church*)

'Look out, fellow Christians,
particularly you that lodge in Queer Street!'
(Charles Dickens, *Our Mutual Friend*, 1865)

Odd unexpected people turned up; an artist sometimes;
sometimes a writer; queer fish in that atmosphere.
(Virginia Woolf, *Mrs Dalloway*, 1925)

In the vivid phrase, he did indeed live in Queer Street
and was acquainted with very queer fish.
(G. K. Chesterton, *Charles Dickens*, 1906)

What are all these fish that lie gasping on the strand?
(W. B. Yeats, 'Three Movements', 1933)

Queer Fish

Christian Unreason from Darwin to Derrida

JOHN SCHAD

sussex
ACADEMIC
PRESS

BRIGHTON • PORTLAND

Copyright © John Schad 2004

The right of John Schad to be identified as author of this work has been asserted in accordance with the Copyright, Designs and Patents Act 1988.

2 4 6 8 10 9 7 5 3 1

First published in 2004 in Great Britain by
SUSSEX ACADEMIC PRESS
PO Box 2950
Brighton BN2 5SP

and in the United States of America by
SUSSEX ACADEMIC PRESS
920 NE 58th Ave   Suite 300
Portland, Oregon 97213-3786

British Library Cataloguing in Publication Data
A CIP catalogue record for this book is available from the British Library.

Library of Congress Cataloging-in-Publication Data
Schad, John, 1960.
    Queer fish : Christian unreason from Darwin to Derrida /
John Schad.
    p.   cm.
    Includes bibliographical references and index.
    ISBN 1-84519-019-X (alk. paper)—ISBN 1-84519-020-3
    (pbk. alk. paper)
    1. Christianity and culture—History—19th century.
2. Intellectual life—History—19th century. 3. Christianity and
culture—History—20th century. 4. Intellectual life—History—
20th century. I. Title.
    BR115.C8S264 2004
    70.8—dc22
                                                          2004001084
                                                          CIP

Typeset and designed by G&G Editorial, Brighton
Printed by The Cromwell Press, Trowbridge, Wiltshire
This book is printed on acid-free paper.

Contents

Contents

Illustrations

Jacket, cover and chapter images: *All Round the Fish* (1926), by Paul Klee. Digital image © 2003 The Museum of Modern Art/Scala, Florence; © SCALA, Florence.

'Moses Getting a Back View' from the *Freethinker*, © 1882. By permission of the British Library, p. 32.

'A New Life of Christ', from the *Freethinker*, © 1882. By kind permission of the British Library, p. 33.

'The man in white paper', by John Tenniel, from *Through the Looking Glass* (1871). By permission of the British Library, p. 56.

Drawing of Oscar Wilde by Toulouse-Lautrec (1895), from *La Revue Blanche* (1895). Cliché Bibliothèque nationale de France, Paris, p. 100.

Acknowledgements

I should like to thank the following for reading and commenting on earlier drafts of part of this book and/or supporting me in the process of writing it: David Amigoni, Andrew Bennett, Valentine Cunningham, Bryan Cheyette, Jonathan Dollimore, Ellis Hanson, Geoffrey Hartman, Willy Maley, Laura Marcus, Kevin Mills, Michael Payne, Jean Michel Rabaté, and Nick Royle. Equally important has been the encouragement of all my colleagues in the Department of English and Drama at Loughborough; I must, though, make special mention of Andrew Dix, Clare Hanson, Brian Jarvis, Simon King, Marion Shaw, Jonathan Taylor and, indeed, Roger Ebbatson who nobly took it upon himself to read the whole of what he still calls *Fishy Extremities*, an experience from which, I fear, he may not have recovered. Also crucial was the encouragement provided by Jacques Derrida, Frank Kermode, and Christopher Norris, each of whom took part in the 'life.after.theory' conferences here at Loughborough. Talking of conferences, or at least of universities, I should also thank those who heard and commented upon early drafts of various parts of the book – particularly helpful were audiences at Birkbeck, Birmingham, Boston, Bristol, East Anglia, Glasgow, Keele, Leicester, Reading, Royal Holloway, and Sussex. In the end, of course, one needs a publisher – here I must thank the wonderful Anthony Grahame. Neither he, though, nor any of the above, could have managed any of the errors or weaknesses in what follows without my assistance.

Earlier, shorter versions of two of the chapters in this book have appeared in print before – chapters four in Schad (ed.), *Dickens Refigured* (Manchester University Press), and chapter six in Schad (ed.), *Writing the Bodies of Christ* (Ashgate). I am grateful to both the presses concerned.

This still leaves, of course, the question of how one thanks those who have not read a single word of what follows and yet have made it (or rather me), possible – namely, Katie and the twins, Bethan and Thomas.

Loughborough
December 2003

For Katie

You, you carry the rejected stone.
By me it is now also kept,
Like Zacheriah's silence.
So wait, wait till we dumb found sense.

The Sea of Faith
Was once, too, at the full, and round earth's shore
Lay like the folds of a bright girdle furled.
But now I only hear
Its melancholy, long, withdrawing roar,
Retreating, to the breath
Of the night-wind, down the vast edges drear
And naked shingles of the world.

(Matthew Arnold, 'Dover Beach', 1867)

'Dover Beached'

> The great theme of the madness of the Cross, which belonged so intimately to the Christian experience of the Renaissance, began to disappear in the seventeenth century despite . . . Pascal. . . . Christian unreason was [then] relegated by Christians themselves into the margins of . . . reason . . . [and] men would have to wait two centuries – until Dostoyevsky and Nietzsche – for Christ to regain the glory of his madness, for scandal to recover its power as revelation.
>
> (Michel Foucault, *Madness and Civilisation*)[1]

This book began, quite simply, when I came across this startling and neglected passage. I was immediately intrigued; in part because Foucault's claim is almost as eccentric as the 'tradition' it identifies, and in part because I am, I confess, one of his unreasonable Christians. For Foucault, of course, the mad, unreasoning Christian has only re-emerged since the age, or 'moment' of Dostoyevsky and Nietzsche. Hence the scope of my book, which works on and around this later-nineteenth-century moment. It is a moment in which Christianity, or rather, certain forms of Christianity do indeed seem to become, once more, an affront to reason and its various, though often occasional, partners – such as truth, knowledge, science, sense, thought, Enlightenment, consciousness, seriousness, even the academy.

There has never, of course, been any happy marriage of faith and knowledge, or religion and reason; but with the Victorians there is a new tension, or friction. Consider, for example, that in 1695 John Locke could write *The Reasonableness of Christianity*, in 1793 Immanuel Kant could write *Religion within the Limits of Reason Alone,* and even in 1873 Matthew Arnold could talk of 'the method and secret and sweet reasonableness of Jesus'.[2] If, though, it is 'secret', the reasonableness of Jesus is already becoming *un*reasonable, even perverse. As well it might, for alongside the huge growth of rationalist, demythologized

1

Protestantism, the nineteenth century witnessed a whole number of very different Christian creeds all insisting on the irrational, or non-rational – all echoing what St Paul calls the 'foolishness of God'.[3] For example, stressing the impossibility of lived, or experiential Christianity, Søren Kierkegaard writes: 'I who, in fear and trembling, scarcely dare call myself a Christian, I am mad, am eccentric'; again, stressing Christianity's mystical dimension, Gustave Flaubert has St Anthony, the third-century hermit, declare that even 'God is delirious'; yet again, drawing on the memory of Romanticism, John Henry Newman laments that 'the Rationalist makes *himself* his own centre, not his Maker [and so] the notion of half views . . . of guesses, surmises [and] isolated facts . . . , in a word, the idea of Mystery, is discarded.'[4] Newman speaks here for the High Anglican Oxford Movement, which began in 1833 as, in part, a reaction to the rationalist ideas of liberal Protestantism. The same may be said of the various forms of evangelical revivalism which, with their stress upon dramatic physical experiences of God, erupted at various points throughout the nineteenth century. As for Catholicism, its opposition to the growth of scientific rationalism may be measured by the fact that it was only in the second half of the century that Rome elevated to the status of dogma the Immaculate Conception of Mary and the infallibility of the Pope.[5]

All this is not to deny the existence of many sorts of Christian unreason in the seventeenth, eighteenth and early nineteenth centuries. For a start, as Foucault points out, there was Blaise Pascal with his famous claim that, as regards faith, 'the heart has its reasons of which reason knows nothing',[6] a claim which anticipates that vast explosion of largely secular unreason we call Romanticism. Clearly, we are now beginning to glance, and only glance, at what is an enormous and complex history. Nevertheless, it *is* possible to say that there was something peculiarly sustained and dramatic about the Christian flight from reason in the mid-to-late nineteenth century; witness the words of Charles Kingsley, the self-appointed spokesman for commonsensical Victorian Anglicanism: writing in 1870 he declares that 'Christianity was swamped by [hysteria] from at least the third to the sixteenth century and . . . we [must now] . . . save ourselves from the same terrible abyss.'[7] Kingsley anticipates Foucault, but both err in the sense that the Christian turn to madness was not just a re-turn, a re-run of older forms of holy idiocy, but also a new departure, an effect of that peculiarly modern phenomenon, secularization. As unbelief became the norm among not only the intellectuals but 'the masses', so Christianity became, in some senses and in some instances, marginal and othered. Christianity's ancient, inherent disposition to unreason was redoubled by a new, cultural positioning as the other of secular modernity. It was now – or rather, now and again – something eccentric, odd, even queer.

'Queer' is certainly the word for Charles Dickens, or rather for Fascination Fledgeby who, in *Our Mutual Friend* (1865), utters the astonishingly resonant words: 'Look out, fellow-Christians, particularly you that lodge in Queer Street!'[8] To lodge in Queer Street here means to be in debt, but the more general sense of being odd, or peculiar clearly haunts Fledgeby's ominous cry. It certainly haunts Trollope's *The Way We Live Now* (1875), where 'talking about the Bible . . . [is thought] very queer'; or again, Edmond Gosse's *Father and Son* (1907), where Gosse recalls his own 'queer reputation for sanctity'; or yet again, James Joyce's *Ulysses* (1922), where Bloom remarks, of one particular Dublin church, 'Queer the whole atmosphere'.[9] There is also Dostoyevsky's *The Idiot* (1868), where the Idiot himself, the holy fool, is known as 'that queer fellow'.[10] Another queer fellow, Oscar Wilde – he who converts on his death-bed – is an important figure in this book; in Wilde's case, of course, the epithet 'queer' entails the homosexual significance that enters English slang around 1900.[11] Wilde is a Christian who lodges in a street that is queer in all senses of the word; since Wilde was a frequent debtor this includes the Victorian sense of being in debt. We must not forget that Queer Street was a street for those who have a debt to pay – in some cases, a debt to society (note that by 1886 Robert Louis Stevenson's notorious Dr Jekyll is also said to live in 'Queer Street').[12] Make no mistake, in the book that follows, Christians often stand accused; it is no accident that those that lodge in Queer Street are told to 'Look out!' As Wilde once wrote, 'the soul . . . has memories of curious sins', and this book of queer Christian souls, running as it does from Darwin to Derrida, cannot avoid some terrible Christian memories, among them: slavery, forced conversion, anti-Semitism, Fenian bombs, the Great War, and even Hiroshima.[13] Perhaps, though, the most terrible Christian memory of all is the Holocaust and this too cannot be avoided, if only because anti-Semitism acquired a new impetus from that highly sophisticated instance of Christian insanity, nineteenth-century racial science. It is no accident that in 1881 Nietzsche – the exponent as well as exposer of Christian unreason – delightedly announces that 'the ship of Christianity threw overboard a good part of the Jewish ballast'.[14]

Nietzsche refers, specifically, to what he sees as the Christian annihilation of the Jewish law; and ballast, of course, is the weighty material that gives stability to a ship. Thus, what Nietzsche sees, and almost celebrates, is a lawless and anarchic ship that is heading for disaster. Nietzsche is right; by the end of the nineteenth century the ship of Christianity *is*, in a sense, wrecked, or beached. This is most famously expressed in Matthew

Arnold's 'Dover Beach' (1867), where Arnold stands on the shore as 'the Sea of Faith' goes out: 'it was once . . . at the full . . . / But now I only hear its long withdrawing roar.'[15] The Christian, it seems, is Dover beached – an intuition shared by Christina Rossetti, who writes that 'a Christian resembles a sea anemone . . . But what will become of it in a world where there shall be no more sea?'[16]

Christians, of course, have long identified with sea-life, ever since the fish was used as a secret Christian symbol; once, though, the Christian fish is Dover beached, it is a fish out of water, an odd or queer fish. And this strange, dripping-wet figure of a Christian keeps returning to the book. In this sense, the book is all at sea. It begins with Darwin's voyage to South America, or what he calls 'the extreme point of . . . Christendom', and ends with Joyce and Derrida 'in the same boat', the ruined but sea-going boat that is the Church. In between, Marx is to be found in 1848 watching the 'waves of . . . revolution' withdraw in Berlin, Freud stands incredulous by the shore of Loch Ness, Wilde is laughed at in the rain at Clapham Junction, and Dickens visits a church for ship-wrecked corpses. Revisiting 'Dover Beach' is sometimes an appalling event, an event of death; sometimes it is comic or even absurd – never more so than when the dripping Christian turns into Joyce's 'man in the macintosh', or even into the church-going umbrella that is passed like a surreal baton from Dickens to Wilde, via the forgetful Nietzsche.

At moments like these the 'tradition' of holy idiocy reveals the secret history, or histories of Christian involvement in such radical movements and developments as Anarchism, Surrealism, the Absurd, deconstruction and even quantum physics. Indeed, it is these same secret histories that haunt, disrupt and even terrorize the writers and thinkers of Part I of this study: namely, Darwin, Marx and Freud, those most likely suspects of secular modernity, each of whom seeks a serious science of Man that will control, or even banish the dangerous forces of Christian unreason. These same forces are, though, set in play by the writers and thinkers of Part II: namely, Dickens, Wilde, Joyce and Derrida. As Kierkegaard writes, 'what Christianity needs is traitors',[17] and that is exactly what it gets with Dickens *et al.* Insofar as they are Christians they are treacherous Christians; in their case, Christian unreason is not so much the external other of secular modernity as the internal other of Christian orthodoxy. They offer what Derrida himself calls an 'internal critique of Christianity [that is] at once heretical and evangelical'.[18] To borrow some words of Hélène Cixous', they put us 'in strange Christian moods'.[19]

There is, I confess, something arbitrary about my selection of these four heretical evangelists; there could have been others, many others: for example, Emily Dickinson, Florence Nightingale, Gerard Manley

Hopkins, Lewis Carroll, T. S. Eliot, Samuel Beckett Julia Kristeva, Kierkegaard and – of course – Foucault's odd couple, Dostoyevsky and Nietzsche. The latter three do, in fact, provide a recurring frame of reference, a net to catch queer fish, but they could so easily have been the fish themselves.

In contrast to all this, secular modernity has the relatively fixed, even trinitarian, genealogy of Marx – Darwin – Freud. It is ironic that thinkers who have so often become aligned with doubt, uncertainty and indeterminacy, should themselves be part of what Derrida calls 'a *certain* . . . anti-religious . . . filiation . . . a [quite] determinate heritage . . . of critical . . . reason'.[20] This heritage or history is familiar and well-told, but then history *is* written by the winners. Those losers, the unreasonable Christians, have *no* official history, no history of their own; indeed, theirs is a 'tradition' that refuses tradition, that takes many forms, and that emerges when and where it is least expected. Above all, it is often a church invisible, even to itself. Derrida once asked, 'How can we speak of a history of Christianity . . . for at the heart of this history there is an abyss?';[21] one name for this abyss, or hole in Christian history is 'Christian unreason' – it is all the madness, cruelty, blood, sweat, prayers and tears that make impossible a smooth and followable history of Christianity.

No surprise, then, that the book which follows does *not* follow; it is *not* a general overview of Christian unreason in the age of secularization. As Kierkegaard writes, 'philosophy should use very local maps for Christianity'[22] – here, I would like to think that the local map is the individual chapter, or rather the Newmanesque 'guesses, surmises . . . and . . . isolated facts' that constitute each chapter. This self-congratulatory thought is, however, countered by a memory of Wilkie Collins's *The Moonstone* (1868), where Gabriel Betteredge asks: 'when Christians take leave of their senses, who is to expect that pencils will keep their points?'[23] Since I have penned, or pencilled a book about Christians losing what senses they ever had, who is to expect that my book will not lose *its* point? But then that may yet *be* the point, certainly if this book has any claim to academic knowledge, and thus to science; for, as Flaubert's St Anthony rudely declares, 'after Jesus, science is pointless'[24] – *truly* pointless, I must hope.

Part I

Three Moderns

My men, my modern Christs,
Your bloody agony confronts the world.
(Herbert Read, 'My Company', 1917)

Not a Christian . . . and yet leading others to Christianity.
(Søren Kierkegaard, *The Point of View*, 1859)

Let us see what sort of a look it is, this look of faith.
(Anthony Trollope, *Framley Parsonage*, 1861)

chapter one

Boat Memory

Darwin's Strange Sea of Faith

Dead fish

We no longer look at an organic being as a savage looks at a ship.

(The Origin of Species)[1]

In December 1831 *HMS Beagle* set sail from Plymouth; on board was Charles Darwin and three converted Fuegians whose strange, Christianized names were York Minster, Fuegia Basket and Jemmy Button. There should have been a fourth; however, he died before the ship ever set sail – his name was Boat Memory.[2] When Darwin speaks of a savage and a ship his analogy is haunted by another boat memory, the memory of Jemmy Button canoeing towards the *Beagle* a year after being returned to Tierra del Fuego:

> a canoe was approaching . . . in it was a thin haggard savage . . . [who] turned his back to the ship.[3]

We have, then, two 'savages': one analogical, one actual; however, whilst the analogical savage *looks* at a ship, the actual savage chooses not to. It is ironic that Darwin should elsewhere recall Jemmy's distinctive look-out cry: '"me see ship."' In this instance, 'me' *refuses* to see 'ship' and, in so doing, disrupts Darwin's analogy – with his back turned to the *Beagle*, Jemmy just does not look as a savage should.[4]

Indeed, this converted Fuegian does not look as a *Christian* should; the savage in the canoe has 'long disordered hair, and [is] naked, except [for] a bit of a blanket round his waist'.[5] This, though, is only to be expected: in these parts, as Darwin himself remarks, mankind 'does not look like the Lord of all'.[6] The complete sentence is, I confess, 'the Lord of all *he surveys*', but in the case of Jemmy both senses, intended and *un*intended, obtain; for he neither looks *like* the Lord of all that is the genteel Christ of Victorian art nor *looks* – that is, sees – like that new Lord of all, the evolutionist.[7] Darwin claims to be 'looking not to any one time, but to all time', 'I . . . look back thousands on thousands of generations.'[8] For Darwin to say 'we no longer look as a savage looks' is an understatement – we are a world away from Jemmy's 'me see ship'. Jemmy, however, is in this respect just like those first Christian readers of the *Origin* who still saw 'man [as] . . . a separate act of creation'; such readers, writes Darwin, are 'content to look, *like a savage*, at the phenomena of nature'.[9] For 'Christian savages' – namely, the converted Fuegians – read 'savage Christians'; in Darwin, it seems, there is a slippage. Indeed, his Christian reader does not only *look* like a savage but also looks *like* a savage. In the *Descent* we read that 'he who rejects with scorn [that we descend from apes] . . . will reveal by sneering the line of his descent. For . . . he will unconsciously retract his "snarling muscles."'[10]

Though Darwin's creationist reader may be snarling, so too, in this instance, is Darwin; here his own image can be seen in the face of the savage Christian. There is, for many, something familiar about this; after Gillian Beer's work on Darwin and the Fuegians it is difficult *not* to see Darwin's image in the figure of the undressed Jemmy, the absence of his Western clothes mirroring the process of deconversion upon which Darwin is, by now, embarked.[11] However, the figure with 'long disordered hair and naked, except [for] a bit of a blanket around his waist' is also suggestive of John the Baptist, the savage, locust-eating believer who wore only 'a leathern girdle about his loins' and, as a Nazarite, grew his hair long.[12] The semi-naked Jemmy is suggestive of a Christianity outside Christianity; this is not what George Eliot calls 'the genteel Christianity of the nineteenth century' but a Christianity without clothes and grown wild, and that is precisely what Darwin encounters throughout his voyage to what he calls 'the extreme point of . . . Christendom'. In Chile, Darwin witnesses atrocities that he describes, with searing irony, as acts of '*Christian* humanity'.[13] In Argentina, Darwin describes how the indigenous Indians are brutally corralled by the Catholic government into what he calls a 'Christians' zoo'.[14] The Christians, it is clear, should be *in* the zoo.

And so they are, in the broader, historical sense that the conventional equation of Christianity with civilization is beginning to be challenged. One reason for this is, of course, the increasing exposure to non-European Christianity, as in the case of Darwin. Moreover, with the first flickers of secularization, Christians were just beginning to move beyond the pale: evangelical Methodists called themselves 'Primitives'; charismatic revivalists were said to 'gobble like turkey cocks' and 'bark . . . [like] dog[s]'; Ritualist riots were condemned as 'zoo and horror'; the Christian oath sworn by new Members of Parliament was compared to 'the Mumbo Jumbo [of] . . . African savages'; and the 'Christian mobs' that disrupted Secularist lectures were not just 'savage' but 'wild beasts'.[15] This, broadly speaking, is the context that begins to make sense of the strange and cryptic ways by which, in contemporary writing, Christians begin to go native (note the 'Christian Carnivora' of *Middlemarch*), begin to go naked (note the 'flesh-coloured Christians' of *Pickwick Papers*), and begin even to go on all fours. In 1839 Bill Sykes' savage dog is compared to 'an out and out Christian', in 1841 the wind in *Barnaby Rudge* is 'howling like a Christian', and by 1883 the Salvation Army is said to be, quite literally, 'Creeping for Jesus', a spiritual exercise in which 'men and women . . . crawl[ed] upon the floor . . . in . . . darkness'.[16] Nietzsche, it seems, speaks for many when, in 1888, he declares that 'Christian[s are possessed by a] hatred towards everything that stands erect.'[17] This is certainly the case in Charles Kingsley's *Hypatia* (1853), where the Christians of Alexandria are depicted as 'hellhounds', or 'wild beasts' literally tearing to pieces the eponymous female philosopher.[18]

Just seven years later this scene is almost re-imagined when Darwin the 'philosopher' (his nickname on the *Beagle*), declares that the *Athenaeum*'s hostile reviewer of the *Origin* 'would set . . . the priests at me . . . He [himself] would [not] . . . burn me, but he will get the wood ready, and tell the black beasts [the priests] to catch me'.[19] For Darwin, Christians are wild; indeed, in 1859 they are not only wild about the *Origin* but wild with the revivals of that year – within less than twelve months of Darwin's natural history the atheist John Chapman publishes the pointedly titled *Christian Revivals: History and Natural History*.[20] Just as the early Christians belonged with the lions in the amphitheatre so, for Chapman, contemporary Christians belong to what Darwin so nearly called the Christian zoo. In 1838 Darwin complains that 'zoology is [still] . . . purely theolog[y]', but by 1860 the reverse is almost the case.[21] Either way, in Darwin's writing the two can never be fully disentangled. To be more precise, the *Origin* can never fully escape what Darwin calls his 'queer' and 'uncertain ship-letters', his 'outlandish' writing of his voyage to the extreme of Christendom.[22] This (un)holy voyage is, in Derrida's terms, the 'non-full, non-simple . . . origin' of the *Origin*; or what Derrida calls, 'The Supplement of (at), the Origin'.[23] In short, Darwin's boat memory persists, his memory of that ship of '76 souls' which carried converted Fuegians, was captained by the evangelical Fitzroy, and had set sail with a young Darwin who, fresh from Cambridge, was still 'a sort of Christian' and destined for the Church.[24] For the older, agnostic Darwin the memory of faith is always, in part, a boat memory; in this respect he sails not only the Atlantic but also

Matthew Arnold's 'Sea of Faith', the sea that was always already 'withdrawing', always already a memory.

The sound of this sea is unwittingly echoed in Darwin's talk of the 'influence [literally, the in-flow] of my former belief'.[25] That in-flow is still a force in the *Descent*. In advancing the 'monstrous' 'belief' that 'vertebrate[s] . . . are derived from some fish-like animal', Darwin recovers a marine pre-existence that chances upon not only his own, half-remembered Christian past but the half-remembered past of Christianity itself, a past in which Christianity was also a monstrous belief in fish.[26] Drawing, *inter alia*, on the Flood, Jonah, baptism and the sea of Galilee, the early Christians depicted both themselves and Christ as fish – a depiction that modern Christianity often seeks to erase.[27] It often seeks, in Lewis Carroll's riddling words, to 'Un-dish-cover the fish'.[28] The Victorians, however, at times *re*-dish-cover the fish. For example, Swinburne sees Christ as a sea-born 'Galilean serpent', whilst Christina Rossetti writes that 'a . . . Christian resembles a sea anemone'.[29] Darwin's role in this re-dish-covery is unwitting but crucial. According to Stanley Edgar Hyman, Darwin's work is entangled with the story of Jonah, or Jonas, he who was 'reborn out of the belly of the great fish' – a re-birth or progress through the guts of a fish that is echoed by Christ when he compares his resurrection to the miracle, or 'sign of . . . Jonas'.[30] Christianity once thought of itself as progress through the guts of a fish.

Darwin makes similar progress when researching the dissemination of plant seeds:

> I forced many kinds of seeds into the stomachs of dead fish, and then gave their bodies to fishing-eagles, storks, and pelicans; these birds after an interval of many hours . . . passed [the seeds] . . . in their excrement . . . several of the seeds retained their power of germination.[31]

Unlike Christ, Darwin thinks new life through the guts of a *dead* fish but then, in a strange sense, he is himself such a fish. In one particular ship-letter Darwin asks the question, 'Am I a ship?'; in another, written a month or two before, he observes 'our . . . ship was . . . like a fish'[32] – the buried question, 'Am I a *fish*?' will, in effect, be answered in the *Descent* as 'I used to be, for we were *all* once fish'. Indeed, Darwin himself is also a dead, or dying fish in the sense that the only treatment for the mysterious illness that forever beset him after the voyage was 'the Water Cure', a punishing regime of wet compresses and dowsing in water. It was during one particularly intense phase of this treatment that the Darwinian Joseph Hooker, upon returning in 1860 to High Anglican Oxford, complains to Darwin of 'feeling like a fish out of water'.[33] Hooker speaks better than he knows, speaking as he does for both the soaked, water-curing Darwin and a whole generation of Victorians for whom, like Arnold, the 'Sea of Faith' had withdrawn.[34] It had withdrawn almost literally in the sense that Charles Lyell's geology had argued away the biblical Flood; many a Victorian believer felt stranded, Dover-beached. To quote Rossetti again, 'a Christian resembles a sea anemone . . . But what will become of it in a world where there shall be no more sea?'[35] Rossetti's question is, in a sense, anticipated by that stranded Jesuit, Gerard Manley Hopkins. Amongst papers recently discovered we find the cryptic story of a 'talking fish' who 'suffer[ed] . . . from too much soul', was removed from the sea, and exhibited in a museum where he 'suffer[ed] . . . from too little water'.[36] This story is itself anticipated by yet another queer fish, Søren Kierkegaard; he too is beached, or at best floundering when, in *Fear and Trembling* (1843), he compares faith to swimming:

> I can describe the movements of faith but when I am thrown into the water, although I may be said to be swimming . . . I make other movements.[37]

With a hammer

> I hardly know what I am writing . . .
> (Darwin, 1836)
> My species theory is all gospel . . .
> (Darwin, 1848)[38]

For Kierkegaard, 'the movements of faith' must 'be made . . . on the strength of the absurd' and so have nothing, he presumes, to do with the contemporaneous movements of such as Darwin: 'people commonly travel the world . . . to see rivers and mountains . . . garish birds, freakish fish [and] grotesque breeds of humans . . . I am not concerned with this'.[39] For Darwin, however, to travel the world *is*, eventually, to go the way of the absurd: 'to suppose that the eye, with all its . . . contrivances . . . could have been formed by natural selection, seems, I freely confess, absurd.'[40] No wonder that, in 1856, Darwin concludes one letter with: 'Adios. Your insane and perverse friend.' *Adios*, or '*A Dios*' as Darwin writes it elsewhere, transliterates, of course, as 'to God'.[41] Kierkegaard might just smile, for it is as if the sheer absurdity of evolutionary theory returns the middle-aged and agnostic Darwin to the language of his South American voyage, a language still marked by the movement of faith: to God.

It is not only in Darwin that the absurdity of evolution is entangled with Kierkegaardian movements of faith. Something of Kierkegaard's 'leap', or 'fall' of faith is also at work when, in 1851, John Ruskin describes the Victorian experience of reading the Bible: 'those dreadful geologists' hammers! I hear them at the end of every cadence' – literally, every 'falling away'.[42] Ruskin reads his Bible to the noise of evolutionary science; for him, the falling movement of faith coincides with the hammers of geology. Curiously, this strange scenario is almost enacted by Darwin himself:

> Towards the close of our voyage I received a letter whilst [on the island of] ...Ascension...which...told me that Sedgwick had...said that I should take a place among the leading scientific men....After reading this letter I clambered over the mountains of Ascension with a bounding step and made the volcanic rock resound under my geological hammer![43]

On an island named after Christ's final leap Darwin performs his own leap of science through the bound of his step and the fall of his hammer. 'Nature', he reminds us, 'can never take a leap' – Darwin, however, *can* and does.[44] But then the author of the *Descent* descends from 'a falling Christian', walks 'knife-edge ridges . . . [over] profound ravines', is fascinated by a 'young woman [who] threw herself from [a mountain]', and lives for forty years in a place he calls the 'extreme verge of [the] world'.[45] In the same year as Blondin walks a tightrope across Niagara Falls, the *Origin* is published. This, though, is a book that is perilously *im*balanced: 'a fair result', writes Darwin, 'can be obtained only by . . . balancing the . . . arguments on both sides . . . [but] this cannot possibly be here done'.[46] It is no surprise that, earlier, Darwin '*leans* toward the side of change' and is '*inclined* to believe'.[47] Later in the *Origin* we are reminded that 'throw up . . . feathers and all must fall'; Blondin, however, does not fall and neither, finally, does Darwin.[48] The origin of 'origin' is, of course, *oriri* meaning 'rise' and the *Origin* does, in the end, take off; the very last words combine a triumphant faith in evolution with an acknowledgment that all must *not* necessarily fall:

> whilst this planet has gone cycling on according to the fixed laws of gravity, from so simple a beginning endless forms most beautiful and most wonderful have been, and are being, evolved.[49]

In this final moment of weightless evolutionary confidence Darwin is once again on the top of Ascension leaping a leap of faith that has no descent. But that was Darwin in 1836 as described by Darwin in 1876, and these are both historical moments when the idea, or trope of gravity is more generally in question. In 1832 political reform was compared 'to suspend[ing] the principle of gravitation', whilst in 1883 Nietzsche's Zarathustra declared, '"Come, let us kill the spirit of Gravity!"'[50]

Nietzsche once wrote that 'without Hegel there could have been no Darwin' but, strange though it may seem, the Darwin of Ascension is almost unthinkable without Nietzsche.[51] For there Darwin defies gravity in both senses of the word; moreover, he does so, like Nietzsche, with a hammer in his hand. Nietzsche claims to teach 'How to Philosophise with a Hammer', Darwin does so with a *geological* hammer: geology, for Darwin, is 'thinking and hammering'.[52] Sometimes this is an 'impetuous hammering', at other times the hammering takes on almost insane force: both on board – 'the cawkers . . . hammering above my head [are] veritable devils'; and on shore – 'surrounded . . . by birds . . . [I took out] my hammer . . . and the . . . slaughter began'.[53] At such times Darwin's hammer is not so much *geo*logical as *il*logical. But then, in the 1830s, geology is itself on the edge of conventional wisdom. As the newest and most daring branch of science, geology is, for the voyaging Darwin, a 'much larger field for thought'.[54] As he later recalls, 'the investigation of . . . geology . . . was far more important, as reasoning here comes into play.' Indeed, it here comes into 'play' in a Derridean sense, since for Darwin geology is the groundless science of the ground: he compares it to 'gambling' and builds 'geological castles *in the air*'.[55] When Darwin writes of 'the geological structure of the world', a structure riven with 'metamorphic schists', he comes close to what Derrida calls 'the structurality of structure', the play or movement that must, for Derrida, haunt all structures.[56]

This play, in the case of nineteenth-century geology, goes by various names. In Kierkegaard it goes by the name of belief: what 'move[s] mountains', he reminds us, is 'faith'.[57] In Darwin it goes by the name of history. Here what disrupts the geological structure of the world is, strangely, the history of the world: 'the . . . geological record', writes Darwin, '[is] a history of the world imperfectly kept', a 'story . . . told by faults'.[58] This is true in the twisted, unintended sense that, within Darwin's *own* geological records, world history is a story told *with* faults, a narrative imperfectly kept in place. This is most conspicuous in Darwin's *Beagle Diary* where the scientific narrative is repeatedly ambushed by the most peculiar scraps of history: first, Darwin remarks, of the Valdivians, that 'the long hair [and] . . . grave . . . features . . . called to mind . . . Charles the First'; later he writes of a giant tortoise that had 'various dates carved on its shells; one was 1786'; still later, when on St Helena, Darwin's 'examin[ation] . . . of . . . geolog[y]' cannot keep out references to both 'Napoleon's tomb' and 'the wantonly disfigured' house in which he 'died'.[59] Charles the First, 1786, Napoleon – this *is* a history of revolution itself wantonly disfigured; the chronological sequence is right but 1786 'should' read 1789, the year of the revolution that leads to Napoleon's rise. This is, of course, a purely accidental history, a history of revolution imperfectly kept by Darwin's political unconscious; nevertheless, the voyaging Darwin did read of the fear of revolution in 1830s Britain and write of the fact in South America.[60]

The fact, as Darwin knew, was very bloody, for the history of revolution belongs to the history of killing, a history in which Darwin's work is also entangled if only because of his famous remark that arguing for evolution is 'like confessing a murder'.[61] Darwin's simile is striking; especially since there is one moment in that imperfectly kept history, the *Beagle Diary*, which does read like such a confession:

> he allowed me to walk behind him and actually kill him with my geological hammer.[62]

Darwin refers to a fox that is now, he adds, 'in the museum of the Zoological Society' – Darwin is here merely being the natural philosopher; this, though, is philosophy with a hammer, with a brutality that kills. And, indeed, there is something about this particular moment in the history of killing which *is* akin to making a human sacrifice; not only is the victim strangely acquiescent – 'he allowed me . . . to kill him' – but the killing takes place, very precisely, at 'the extreme of Christendom'. And that, according to Kierkegaard just a few years later, is exactly where murder might always take place. In *Fear and Trembling* Kierkegaard cites Abraham's terrible willingness to kill his own son as the model of a 'faith that draws its strength from the absurd'. This is what Foucault would call 'Christian unreason', the nineteenth-century re-emergence of a faith that lays bare the impossibility of philosophy and, in particular, moral philosophy, or ethics; if Abraham's relationship to God means he is prepared to kill, the lesson, as Derrida observes, is that

> As soon as I enter into a relation with the other . . . I know that I can respond only by sacrificing ethics . . . by sacrificing whatever obliges me to also respond, in the same way, in the same instant, to all the others.[63]

Precisely this Kierkegaardian dilemma besets Darwin; as he enters into relation with the other that is nature he is, at times, haunted by all he must sacrifice. When Alfred Wallace argues, in 1869, that a spiritual power is at work within natural selection Darwin declares 'You have murdered your own and my child';[64] and that, strangely, is almost how Darwin elsewhere imagines the cost of his researches, or at least, his study of pigeon skeletons. In 1855 he writes of his pigeons, 'I love them to that extent that I cannot bear to kill . . . them.' A little later he writes, 'I have done the black deed and murdered an angelic little Fan-tail . . . at 10 days old.'[65] Darwin, it seems, is already confessing to murder; but what makes this doubly confessional is that, only four years before, his daughter Annie had been struck by a fever which 'carried her off . . . [like] a little angel' in just '10 days' – she was, at the time, 10 *years* old.[66] It is almost as if the pigeon-killing Darwin imagines he has murdered his own angelic little child. He later writes, 'I would as soon be descended from . . . [a] monkey . . . as from a savage who . . . practices infanticide';[67] Darwin cannot, however, escape this savage for he is, as Kierkegaard points out, part of our religious legacy and his name is not only Abraham but God, the Father that sacrifices the Son.

The death of Darwin's child is an insistent subtext, never more so than when he observes a 'desolated' ants' nest – Darwin writes of 'ants carrying the dead bodies' of others before remarking that one particular ant was 'perched motionless with its own pupa in its mouth on the top of a spray of heath, an image of despair, over its ravaged home'.[68] For the pupa (Latin for 'girl' or 'doll'), read 'Annie'? If so, the parent ant is an image of *Darwin's* despair – he is away with Annie when she dies, the pregnant Emma being confined to Down. Even as Darwin analyses the activities of ants he seems to stare at the tiny image of Annie's death: the word 'pupa' is related to 'pupil', that part of the eye in which we see a tiny, doll-like image of ourselves. Annie, who elsewhere becomes a dead fan-tail, here becomes a dead ant; her *human* death thus enters into a chain of analogous *animal* deaths, a chain which mimics that 'long succession of . . . death[s]' which is, for Darwin, evolution.[69] It is, of course, a democratic succession in which there are no privileged, or special deaths – not even the death of Annie.

This, in a sense, is anticipated in the *Voyage* – where, stressing the dangers that beset him, Darwin remarks how:

> [just] the day before, a traveller . . . had been found, with his throat cut, lying dead on the road – it happened close to a cross, a record of a former murder.[70]

One murder takes place upon the site of another, whilst the cross, of course, represents yet another 'former murder', the murder of Christ; Darwin, though, seems oblivious to this originary murder. Christ's death thus vanishes into a series, or regression of deaths. And that is almost the point that Darwin seeks to make in the *Descent* where, to demonstrate that morality is not uniquely human, he cites the example of the 'heroic . . . monkey' who, upon seeing his friend the zookeeper attacked by 'a fierce baboon, . . . rushed to the rescue [thereby] . . . running great risk . . . of his [own] life'.[71] The monkey, implies Darwin, is as capable as any man of laying down his life for his friend. If this heroic monkey is, for Darwin, a kind of Christ then so too is 'the dog suffering under vivisection, who licked the hand of the operator' – shades here of Christ's death-cry: 'Father, forgive them; for they know not what they do.'[72] In 1860 Florence Nightingale dares to propose that 'the next Christ will perhaps be . . . female' – just eleven years later Darwin, almost without knowing it, imagines a Christ that might perhaps be animal. As Beer suggests, Darwin anticipates the bestial Christ of W. B. Yeats – that 'rough Beast [who] . . . / Slouches towards Bethlehem to be born.'[73]

In Darwin, however, the animal Christ is marked not by birth but death; in this respect Darwin anticipates Swinburne who, revolted by the very idea of the crucifixion, asks, 'Shall God then die as the beasts die?'[74] For Swinburne, like Darwin, the cross is the site of merely *just another death*; the cross, it seems, can be crossed out, erased from Victorian memory. And indeed the *Origin* is testimony to this; for there is something remarkable about the fact that, in a culture still saturated by religious imagery, Darwin is able to write a best-selling work of popular science which repeatedly employs the word 'cross' – as short-hand for 'cross-breed' – without any apparent fear of Christian connotation. In the *Origin* he writes, variously, of 'occasional crosses', 'the sterility of . . . crosses', 'a reciprocal cross', 'ancient crosses' and even, more than once, 'the first cross'.[75] Elsewhere, Darwin writes that 'my object always has [been] to avoid writing on religion' and, remarkably, in the case of the cross he is successful.[76]

This is not, though, just a trick of newly secularized science; it also has to do with Victorian Christianity's own movement away from the crucified Christ. The new liberal theology is at the root of Matthew Arnold's cry, 'Leave then the Cross!'; whilst amongst even Dissenters there is, as Robin Gilmour remarks, 'a slow shift from the Atonement to the Incarnation, from Christ's death to his humanity.'[77]

Darwin's animal Christ is, in a sense, just an extension of this shift towards a human and immanent Christ. 'Christ plays in ten thousand places', writes Hopkins; the logic of the Incarnation, of Christ's radical identification with suffering flesh, is that he might also *die* in ten thousand places, or forms.[78] Christ the lamb, or scapegoat, dies not only *for* us but also *with* the lamb, *with* the goat. In the wilderness 'Jesus', we read, 'was *with* the . . . beasts'.[79] Darwin's new evolutionary science is curiously paralleled by Christianity's newly human Christ.

Galilean space

> O pale Galilean the world grows grey from thy breath.
> (Swinburne, 1867)
> It appears most strange . . . to stand in the court of Christ.
> (Darwin, 1836)[80]

Darwin and the Victorian Christ again cross paths as and when Darwin believes himself persecuted, or martyred. Witness his transition from

Galileo to Christ: in 1838 Darwin identifies with the 'persecution of the early Astronomers', whilst in 1859 he writes of the *Origin*, 'if you read it . . . how you will . . . crucify me.'[81] Even as Darwin imagines himself as a kind of Galileo, and in *that* sense a Galilean, so he is also haunted by the Galilean that is Christ. The Victorian Christ is, though, a Galilean who is not a Galilean: 'the carpenter's son', writes Nightingale, 'did not know that the earth moved round the sun.'[82] The two Galileans represent very different accounts of space; both accounts, however, shape the *Origin*. On the one hand, we are made mindful that evolving time takes place within *r*evolving space: 'planets revolve . . . round the sun', 'this planet . . . go[es] . . . cycling on.'[83] On the other hand, we are also made mindful of fixed, and local space – having been forced to reduce his original manuscript to what he considered merely an 'Abstract', Darwin repeatedly draws attention to the book's 'want of space'.[84]

The two kinds of Galilean space particularly inform the *Origin*'s seeming compulsion to confess. Both Galileo and Christ are, for Darwin, primarily figures of prosecution, or trial; and this book that felt 'like confessing to a murder' and is so full of confession – 'I freely confess', 'it must be confessed', 'I am bound to confess' – implies a space of confession that is, at times, turning or circling but, at others, all too fixed.[85] On the one hand, there is the circuitous space of what Derrida calls '*circumfession*'; this is when going in circles is what Darwin almost confesses to: 'how liable we are to argue in a circle'.[86] On the other hand, there is the rigid and confined space of the confessional, or the prison. This is when it is the lack of space that Darwin almost confesses to: 'I *regret* th[e] . . . want of space . . . '[87] In such moments the *Origin* is locked into a carceral topology. Speaking of bees, Darwin writes 'I . . . examined the cell'; speaking of the skull, Darwin asks, 'Why should the brain be enclosed in a box?'[88] Darwin once remarked that writing the *Origin* 'cost . . . thirteen months *hard labour*' – the Galilean space of Darwin's writing is, in one sense, the confined space of the prison.[89]

It is, though, more precisely, the ambiguous space of the ship – in particular, the *Beagle*. The *Origin*'s strangely double sense of both 'how large the world is' and yet also of an acute 'want of space' derives, in part, from the tiny ship from which Darwin saw so much of the world – in his letters written from the *Beagle* he complains of an 'absolute want of room'.[90] The *Origin*, at once both spacious and cramped, is a ship-shape book; like Ascension Island, it 'may be compared to [a] . . . Ship'.[91] This book that so depends upon the findings of Darwin's voyage has its own secreted boat memory. When he is at sea Darwin writes, 'everything is topsy turvy [but] . . . my memory is in its right place.' In the *Origin*, however, his memory is all at sea: 'we now', he writes, 'very seldom hear the action of the . . .

waves'.[92] I must confess the full sentence is 'we now [after Lyell] very seldom hear the action of the . . . waves *called trifles*.' Here the boat memory is a false memory; nevertheless, the reader *has* heard and cannot forget the sound of one who can no longer hear the waves. Though the waves are now inaudible we can still hear in the *Origin* the noise of what Darwin himself calls 'a most unquiet ship'.[93] In the *Origin* Darwin 'turn[s] . . . to the sea'; this he does both literally – 'it is good to wander along . . . [the] sea-coast' – and rhetorically, the sea is not just a part of his argument but a source of metaphor: 'a mountain', he writes, 'is an island on the land'.[94] At such moments it seems that all the world is a sea.

For Darwin, however, the sea is not always and forever the sea; by the end of the *Beagle Diary* the absolute space of the sea becomes a desert: 'What', asks the weary Darwin, 'are the boasted glories of the illimitable ocean? A tedious waste, a desert of water.'[95] In moving from sea to desert Darwin curiously anticipates his own evolutionary narrative. Moreover, at the same time he rehearses the biblical narrative of escape from slavery: 'all our fathers', writes St. Paul, 'passed through the sea, and . . . [entered] the wilderness'.[96] Once again, at the level of both plot and rhetoric, Darwin – whose 'theory', of course, 'is all gospel' – unwittingly maps something of the strange ways of biblical faith.

Darwin thus replaces boat memory with desert memory. In Patagonia he asks: 'Why . . . do these arid wastes take so firm a possession of the memory?'[97] The answer, it seems, is that the desert is a way of remembering not only the past but the future: 'these . . . wastes', he continues, 'bear the stamp of . . . ages, . . . and there appears no limit to their duration through future time.' 'It is very un-Sailor-like', writes Darwin, 'to think of the Future' – whoever travels the desert cannot, though, avoid it.[98] 'In the . . . future', declares Darwin, 'I see open fields', but it is through the absolutely open field of the desert that he seems to see the future itself. 'The absolute desert', as Darwin calls it, represents an extreme, or outer limit that gestures toward the future:

> Not until we reach the extreme confines of life . . . on the borders of an utter desert, will competition cease.[99]

Here Darwin chances upon those familiar biblical futures in which 'wars . . . cease' and 'the leopard shall lie down with the kid'.[100] But this utopian glimmer, so typical of the *Origin*, is counterpointed by an equally characteristic anxiety; for a desert where competition will cease is a place unregulated by what Darwin goes on to call the 'one general law . . . namely . . . let the strongest live and the weakest die.'[101] 'Turning to the sea', writes Darwin, 'we find the same law'; but turning to the desert he sees, for a moment, something radically other: not only a utopia but also a dystopia, a place without law. Darwin is well aware of the anarchic potential of his ideas; in the *Descent* he finds it necessary to state that 'any government is better than anarchy'.[102] Nevertheless, he cannot avoid formulations that do naturalise a state of anarchy: 'I believe . . . in no law', writes Darwin – 'no law of necessary development', he continues, but the damage has been done.[103] And it has always already been done in the sense that Darwin's one great law – let the strongest live and the weakest die – is no more than the law of lawlessness. Turning to the desert we *do*, then, in a paradoxical sense, see the same law of lawlessness, or at least absence of law. Darwin's desert beyond the sea, the desert that for a moment in the *Origin* promises so much, finally turns out to be a false horizon, to be not an-other place at all, but simply more of the same, the same absence of law that so dominates the world according to Darwin.

Absence itself is the primary feature of Darwin's desert. Darwin writes that the desert of Patagonia 'can be described only by negative characters', by what is *not* there. This is 'desert in the strictest sense', 'desert' as in deserted, forsaken, nothing – a place that is, more properly, *space* or, more *im*properly, outer space.[104] This is certainly the link that Darwin makes, or recalls: 'the ancients', he writes, 'supposed the . . . earth was surrounded by . . . deserts.'[105] So too, in fact, does Darwin's disciple Winwood Reade; for Reade, writing in 1872, the evolution of mankind implies an inevitable ascent into the desert that is space: 'the earth being small', he writes, 'mankind will migrate into space, and will cross the airless Saharas which separate planet from planet.'[106] Just as Darwin's sea becomes desert so desert becomes space. Writing to Darwin in 1870, Adam Sedgwick declares, 'You have deserted . . . the true method of induction and started in machinery as wild as Bishop Wilkins' locomotive that was to sail to the moon.'[107] Sedgwick is right – Darwin's method is, in a sense, that of the space traveller: to make the point of sexual selection he asks what 'an inhabitant of another planet' would make of 'a number of . . . rustics . . . quarrelling over a pretty girl'; likewise, of the Galapagos Islands he remarks that 'the leafless shrubs & large Cacti . . . appeared [like] . . . inhabitants of some other planet.'[108] This is in September 1835, the month in which the *New York Sun* newspaper created an international sensation by running a series of articles claiming that Sir John Herschel had, from his observatory, discovered on the moon not only plants but 'creatures like human beings'.[109] The very moment that Darwin is encountering life on 'planet' Galapagos, Herschel is said to encounter life on the moon. Darwin's science coincides, it seems, with a mid-century dream of life-out-there, of an outer space that is not just space. Indeed, in the Galapagos, Darwin almost makes this dream come true. In a sense the *New York Sun* is correct, there *is* human life on the moon in 1835: Darwin's. Of the

Galapagos vegetation he remarks, 'I know no more about [it] . . . than the Man in the Moon.'[110] He also remarks, about this time, that 'a blue sky . . . tell[s] one there is a . . . something beyond the Clouds';[111] and if Darwin can visit 'another planet' there is the possibility of not just some*thing* beyond the clouds but some*one*.

By 1838, however, Darwin is sceptical of blue-skied heavens, declaring that 'man with divine face, turned towards heaven, . . . his end . . . will come.'[112] This claim of Darwin's proves not just philosophical but experiential, something that issues from the experience of writing the *Origin*: 'my life', he laments, 'is now measured by volume, chapters & sheets & has little to do with the sun'.[113] For Darwin, the space of writing is *not* the space of outer space, the heliocentric space of Galileo; it is instead the intensely *geo*centric space of 'Down House' in Down, the Kentish village where Darwin writes himself (down), into the ground, or earth – here he writes his book on worms and, once this is done, declares 'I . . . look forward to Down graveyard, as the sweetest place on earth.'[114] Though Darwin styles himself as a heliocentric Galilean he becomes, more precisely, as writing separates him from the sun, Swinburne's *pale* Galilean.

Darwin and this sea-of-Galilee Galilean (the Galilean fisher of men), are also related via the mysterious and mythical figure of the Fisher King.[115] In the mid-nineteenth century there was renewed interest in the Grail legend, an interest pursued by Darwin's long-time neighbour, friend and folklore enthusiast Sir John Lubbock;[116] the *Origin*, we should note, is published in the same year as the first installment of the *Idylls of the King*, which Darwin quotes in the *Descent*. Indeed, the myth of knightly quest has always haunted both Darwin and the *Origin*: in 1833 he laments the loss of even the 'remains of chivalry'; in 1867 the King of Prussia makes Darwin a knight; whilst in 1860, in a review of the *Origin*, Asa Gray writes of 'Darwin's *cheval de bataille*' and declares that he 'advances on his perilous way . . . grappl[ing] manfully with . . . formidable difficulties.'[117] In the *Origin* Darwin makes a veiled attempt to escape any such quest myth: he remarks, of the term 'species', that 'we shall . . . be freed from the vain search for the undiscovered and undiscoverable essence.'[118] We are not, however, freed from the shadow of the Fisher King. Earlier in the *Origin* he writes, of South America,

> I have often watched a tyrant flycatcher . . . standing stationary on the margin of the water, and then dashing like a kingfisher at a fish.[119]

In the *Voyage*, Darwin remarks of precisely the same scene that,

> the curse of sterility is on the land, and the water partakes of the same curse.[120]

If this, in a sense, is the cursed land of the sterile Fisher King then the promised stranger who will, by asking questions, redeem the land is most nearly named as Darwin's 'desired character' – 'the long-lost [but 'reappear'-ing] character' 'who' is an accident of Darwin's tendency to speak not of characteristics but *characters*: when speaking of an inherited characteristic Darwin talks, almost like a novelist, of the return of a 'long-lost character'.[121] The returning stranger of the Fisher King myth, the stranger who redeems the land by his questions, is, indeed, Darwin's own shadow; for in 1836, at the end of his voyage, Darwin *is* the long-lost character who, as we read in his letters, 'returns a stranger' with a 'list of . . . questions'.[122] In these same ship-letters Darwin twice imagines himself as a future revenant: the first time as a scientist still asking questions – 'I should . . . be[come] a ghost & haunt the Brit[ish] Museum'; the second time as a native of a land without curse – 'I often think of the Garden at home as a Paradise . . . how I should enjoy to appear, like a Ghost amongst . . . [the] flowers.'[123] This spectral Darwin is, of course, a mere trick of Darwin's boat memory; he is nowhere really to be seen. But this same memory teaches the simple scientific lesson that we cannot always believe our eyes:

> when a savage sees a mark struck by a bullet, it may be some time before he is able . . . to understand how it is effected; for the fact of a body being invisible from its velocity would . . . be . . . inconceivable.[124]

There is always in Darwin the distinct possibility of a body being invisible. No wonder that in 1860 Asa Gray, the aptly titled Fisher Professor of Natural History, should write that 'several features of [Darwin's] . . . theory have an uncanny look.'[125] Gray goes on, in a book called *Natural Selection not inconsistent with Natural Theology,* to reassure his readers that this uncanny look disappears after patient examination, and that Darwin thus becomes consistent with Christian faith. For us, however, it is precisely the uncanny look which *aligns* Darwin with faith and which makes him look like the believer he was not.

chapter two

Marx and Angels

The Silly Lives of Saints and Communists

some have entertained angels unawares	the angel . . . last night took hold of my computer
(St Paul)	(Jacques Derrida)

Analogical

To find an analogy we must take flight into the misty realms of religion.
(Marx, *Capital*)[1]

The realm of religion is, for Marx, the realm of analogy; though religion is dead as a belief system it persists as a kind of poetry, a set of metaphors. As Matthew Arnold writes, 'the strongest part of our religion to-day is its unconscious poetry.'[2] The same might just be said of the *politics* of the day, for the strongest part of Marx's self-conscious raid on the metaphors of religion is the *un*conscious poetry of 'flight', a poetry that is itself religious; to 'take flight into the misty realms of religion' is, metaphorically, to become an angel. When, in 1845, Marx parodies the Book of Revelation, he mockingly declares 'I saw . . . a mighty angel . . . flying . . . across the heavens';[3] in *Capital*, twenty years later, Marx *is* that angel.

This vision of Marx is violently at odds with his insistence that, unlike idealist philosophy, 'communism [is] . . . no flight'; that, unlike utopian socialism, communism is no '*Voyage en Icarie*'; and that, unlike Louis Bonaparte's 1851 *coup d'état*, it is no '*vol de l'aigle*'.[4] Not for Marx the Hegelian owl of Minerva, the utopian Icarus, or Bonapartist eagle. And it is this more familiar, earthbound Marx who begins *Capital* by declaring that the only way to the 'luminous summits' of science is a 'steep path';[5] we must, he implies, walk rather than fly. This, of course, is advice he later ignores. However, in taking poetic flight and thus becoming 'the mighty angel' of his own parody, Marx is still in a sense being Marxian. For, following Feuerbach, Marx sees heaven as no more than a mirror: 'Man', he declares, 'has found only the reflection of himself in the fantastic reality of heaven'; if Revelation's 'mighty angel' turns out to be but a reflection of Marx-the-rhetorician it only proves, in a sense, the Feuerbachian point that 'theology is [in truth] anthropology'.[6]

This, though, is not the whole story; very few of Marx's angels answer to an anthropological or homogeneous idea of 'Man'. Indeed, since these angels are only ever accidents of rhetoric they represent or betray something profoundly heterogeneous, contingent and, therefore, historical. In Marx, angels take many and varied forms. In one sense they are the proletariat: the early Marx declares that 'the nobility of man shines forth upon us from their work-worn figures.'[7] In another sense they are Franziska and Guido Marx, the son and daughter who die in infancy and in so doing are mourned by their Victorian father as 'my poor little angel[s]'.[8] Yet they are also that *man* called 'Angels', the German for 'angels' being 'Engels', the co-author of much that is casually called 'Marx'. In reading Marx we often entertain Engels unawares. Jacques Derrida has remarked that 'Marx' is a plural name: 'there is', he writes, 'more than one of them';[9] what Derrida forgot to add is that the extra one is a man with the still more plural name of 'Angels'.

When Louis Bonaparte seizes power in France the Church's pragmatic alliance with the new regime is summed up, for Marx, by Cardinal Pierre d'Ailly's incredulous dismissal of his critics: 'The Catholic Church can only be saved . . . by the Devil . . . and [yet] you ask for angels.'[10] What we expect from Marx is something similar: namely, that the world can only be saved by the proletariat, so why ask for angels? Marx, however, *does* ask for angels. Writing in August 1852 Marx quotes, approvingly, a speech in which Ernest Jones asks for an angel in the wake of the failure of Chartism: '"I summon,"' declares Jones,

> 'the angel of retribution from the heart of every Englishman here present . . . Hark! you feel the fanning of his wings in the breath of this vast multitude!'[11]

This militant angel is, indeed, shadowed by others – not only the biblical angel of retribution, the child-killing Angel of Death, but two of that Angel's most recent victims: Marx's very own 'little angels', his children. Guido dies in November 1850 and Franziska in April 1852. In Victorian folk religion 'Angels is dead folk', and in the case of Guido they are also, like Jones' angel, militant: Marx called Guido 'Little Fawkes' 'in honour of the great conspirator' – Guy Fawkes.[12] Ernest Jones speaks, then, of more angels than he is aware; in asking for an angel Jones gets more than he bargains for.

So too does Marx in asking for Engels. In asking for his help as not only co-author but translator and editor, Marx employs a kind of ghostwriter, or guardian angel. As Willy Maley puts it, 'Engels is . . . Marx's ghostly double.'[13] To adapt Derrida, Marx allows Angels to take hold of his computer. Engels himself describes the partnership in domestic terms, as a kind of marriage in which his is 'the feminine intellect' – 'Marx', he writes, 'could very well have done without me'.[14] Engels thus plays the part of that familiar Victorian angel, the 'angel in the house'. As Terrell Carver argues, Engels's contribution to the partnership has often been underestimated; though Engels describes himself as 'second fiddle' the full quotation is 'I am *meant* to play second fiddle.'[15] Indeed, for Engels, the angel in the house might well be militant: 'within the family', he writes, 'the wife plays the part of the proletariat'. And, like the proletariat, Engels is quite able to take liberties: when, in 1847, the Communist League consulted local branches, or 'communities' over the 'Draft of a Communist Confession of Faith', Engels saw fit to covertly rewrite the text, as he confesses in a letter,

> I . . . draft[ed] . . . a new one which will be . . . sent to London *behind the backs of the communities*. Naturally, not a soul must know about this.[16]

Whether Engels ever wrote behind the back of Marx we may never know. In a sense, though, that is what Engels *has* to do when, following the death of Marx, he is left to supervise Samuel Moore's famous and influential 1888 translation of *The Communist Manifesto* – the final version of the 'Confession of Faith' that Engels had covertly rewritten.

When, in 1850, French law forbids anonymous newspaper articles Marx refers, as Mehlman has noted, to the State's fear of 'unheimliche Anonymitat';[17] and there *is* something *unheimliche* or uncanny about Engels's often anonymous, or underestimated role in the work of Marx. We should not be fooled by Engels' portrayal of himself as a 'feminine' and thus *heimliche*, or homely presence. As Marx observes, 'Engels arrived by another road';[18] and, in a sense, Engels is still on it when, in 1851, he successfully predicts that 'it would soon be time to attack Louis Blanc' – 'you [are]', jokes Marx, 'a *clairvoyant*, to say the least'.[19]

Engels may or may not have seen the future, but for Marx he *was* the future in the sense that, after his death in 1883, 'Engels made Marx *live on*, by constructing a narrative such that when Engels spoke, Marx seemed to speak.'[20] In *Capital* Marx claims that 'nobody . . . can live on the products of the future' and yet, fifteen years before, he writes that 'social revolution . . . can only create its poetry from the future'.[21] In his

1895 essay 'On the Early History of Christianity', Engels dares to create that poetry from the future of Christianity – the essay is concerned with the angel-filled biblical Book of Revelation. With Marx now dead Engels locates in Revelation several 'notable points of resemblance' between 'early Christianity [and] . . . the modern working-class movement'.[22] For Engels, of course, the future of Christianity is socialism; nevertheless, this particular flight of Engels once again draws Marx, albeit the spectre of Marx, into the misty realm of religion and angels.

Though for Marx this realm is purely analogical, for Engels it is part of the very real history of the future – and not only for Christians but also scientists. As Engels observes in 'Natural Science in the Spiritual World' (1874), it is none other than 'Isaac Newton [who] in his old age greatly busied himself with expounding . . . Revelation'.[23] Indeed, twenty years later, when the dying Engels ends up doing exactly the same he too finds in religion the trace of another scientific future – namely, mathematics: of Revelation's '666' he remarks that 'secret words . . . were . . . expressed in . . . [the] language of numbers' and 'the Chaldeans, who [first] pursued this [art] . . . were [later to be] called *mathematici*.'[24]

Engels goes on to remark that these mystical mathematicians would also be 'expelled from Rome . . . for "serious disorders"'; Engels's reading of Revelation thus chances upon a misrule or a radicalism that is at once scientific and political. This, however, is a combination that has no place in Marx; for only the most orderly of science is allowed into the 'Rome' or polis of Marxian metaphor. Though Marx espouses what he calls 'scientific socialism', when seeking a scientific metaphor for revolution what he comes up with is the orderly and non-revolutionary law of gravity. Speaking in 1856, he asks:

> Although the atmosphere in which we live weighs upon every one with a 20,000 lb force, do you feel it? No more than European society before 1848 felt the revolutionary atmosphere enveloping and pressing it from all sides.[25]

In *The German Ideology* Marx and Engels parody Hegelian idealism as the belief that 'men drowned because they were possessed with *the idea of gravity* [*Schwere*]';[26] Marx, though, does himself appear to be so possessed. Gravity just keeps on recurring as a metaphor or analogy – most conspicuously when in *Capital* he refers to

> the . . . way [that] the law of gravity [*Schwere*] asserts itself when a person's house collapses on top of him.[27]

Ironically, the house of gravity is itself about to collapse – just eleven years later Nietzsche declares we must 'kill the Spirit of gravity [*Schwere*]',[28] a declaration that is echoed by scientists for whom the law of gravity was becoming increasingly complicated by thermodynamics and, in particular, the idea of repulsion. Marx, though, will have none of this: he writes, again in *Capital*, that 'it is a contradiction to depict one body as constantly falling towards another and at the same time constantly flying away.'[29] Here Marx cannot reconcile gravity with repulsion; Engels, however, can do so – just a few years later, in his curious and neglected scientific treatise, *Dialectics of Nature*, he writes that

> from dialectics itself it can already be predicted that the true theory of matter must assign as important a place to repulsion as to attraction.[30]

As Engels goes on to explain, this natural dialectic is most obviously demonstrated in the misty, angelic realm of heavenly bodies: 'a solar system', he writes, 'is only formed by the gradual preponderance of attraction over the originally prevailing repulsion'. If there were only attraction or gravity the moon would fall to earth. So too would the angels; or at least that is the unwitting logic of Marx and Engels's description of meteors as 'fallen angels creeping shamefaced through the "infinite space" until they find a modest lodging'[31] – these angels, though fallen, creep rather than simply descend since their movement is governed not just by gravity but repulsion, not by one force but two.

'Double science' is, as Marx points out, the name that Aristotle gives to the study of wealth, but Marx's own 'science' is more double than he knows.[32] He boldly prophesies that 'the science of man will subsume natural science', that 'there will be *one* science';[33] this, though, never quite happens, Marx's science of man is too much influenced by Engels the keen amateur of the science of nature. And, indeed, in *Dialectics of Nature* this amateur clearly has problems in reconciling the two sciences; though Engels is ultimately arguing that nature, like man, is causal and law-governed he gives considerable attention to developments in contemporary science that suggest a very different nature.[34] Engels explores at length not only thermodynamics but kinetic theory, non-Euclidean mathematics and molecular theory – developments which, as Engels admits, threaten 'official physics' and point towards what he calls a 'centreless science'.[35] As the book's first editors point out, '*Dialectics of Nature* . . . anticipates [several] . . . twentieth-century discoveries.'[36] The editors are writing in 1934, by which time nuclear physics has verified Engels's claim that 'atoms . . . are [not] . . . the smallest known particles of matter', and Einstein's discovery of curved space has verified Engels's claim that 'a new, almost infinite field is opened up by the mathematics that *conceives curved as straight . . .* and *straight as curved.*'[37]

Though space for the later scientific Engels might just be curved, for the earlier political Engels it is as straight as a railway line: in 1859 Engels remarks that Marxian economics is 'as superior to the old . . . metaphysical method as the railway is to the . . . transport of the Middle Ages.'[38] This alignment with the railway is rehearsed in *The German Ideology*; here we read that 'production . . . is just as independent of the pure concept as the . . . use of railways [is] . . . independent of Hegelian philosophy.'[39] The *use* of railways may indeed be independent of Hegel but its linearity is not – witness Hegel's claim that 'Kant and Fichte were fond of flying off to the upper air . . . [but] I only try . . . to understand what is on the roadway.'[40] No wonder that Engels's remark about the straight as curved is followed by the ejaculation, 'O metaphysics!'[41] Within the increasingly 'centreless science' of his day Engels finds a rude violation of the metaphysics, or rationalism to which he still subscribes.

All the same, 'centreless science' is almost the correlative of what the young Engels celebrates as 'a free science of thinking'[42] – both sciences suggest a world of absolute or infinite interconnection. For the older, independent Engels this is an emergent empirical fact: in *Dialectics* 'the general interconnection of things' is an aspect of the 'coexistence of innumerable worlds in infinite space'.[43] By contrast, for Marx and Engels together, it is 'the bourgeoisie [that] . . . establishes connexions everywhere'.[44] Despite their hostility to capitalism, Marx and Engels welcome its new world of inter-connections as the moment in which 'the bourgeoisie . . . play[s . . . its] revolutionary part'. This world, indeed, is one in which Marx also plays a part, his often startling analogies do themselves establish connections everywhere, especially between economics and religion: 'to find an analogy', of course, we 'must take flight . . . into the . . . realms of religion'. In this sense religion is crucial to the world of infinite connection and, therefore, crucial to revolution. This, in some ways, was the conviction of utopian socialism; though largely secular, this particular brand of nineteenth-century socialism tacitly drew on religion to dream of revolution as a moment of total *human* interconnection, a moment in which:

> the instinct of the masses would be raised to an extraordinary power by common contact, by the prophetic feeling of great things to be achieved, by spontaneous, sudden, electric association in the street.[45]

For Marx, such centreless and unpredictable revolution could never be part of his own scientific socialism. But in this respect Marx is not the modern thinker he is sometimes said to be; instead he seems trapped in a mechanistic, Newtonian mind set that was increasingly being questioned.

Such questioning is reflected in Marx's own admission that history is not always causal: of Germany's 1848 revolution he remarks, 'Herr Campausen did not become Prime Minister *on account* of the March revolution but merely *after* [it].'[46] This, in a sense, anticpates Louis Althusser's 1960s Marxism which refutes any mechanistic reading of history and introduces the notion of 'absent cause'.[47] Althusser's thinking is post-structuralist, even post-Newtonian, yet something similar can be glimpsed within Engels's scientific speculations. Marvelling at Clerk Maxwell's discovery of the paradoxical existence of '*dark* light-rays', Engels remarks that 'the famous opposition between light and darkness disappears', the opposition which has 'always served as a rhetorical phrase for religion and philosophy from the time of the fourth Gospel to the *Lumières* of the eighteenth century.'[48] Writing ten years before Nietzsche's *Beyond Good and Evil*, Engels the amateur scientist glimpses the unravelling of binaristic, Enlightenment Christianity. This is almost Nietzsche without Nietzsche or, rather, Engels without Marx; for whilst Marx and Engels together declare that 'Christian ideas succumbed in the eighteenth century to rationalist ideas',[49] Engels on his own here glances momentarily in the direction of a paradoxical and unruly Christianity.

Though Marx himself may never glance in this direction, such Christianity does enter his writing through its many religious analogies; despite Marx's insistence that 'content [should] transcend . . . phrase'[50] or form, these analogies repeatedly upstage the economic point they are intended to illustrate. In 'The Eighteenth Brumaire' Marx rages against Louis Bonaparte's deployment of merely the *rhetoric* of republican Rome and never the politics: 'the ghosts of Rome' are raised but remain tame and dependent. In Marx, however, the ghosts raised by rhetoric have a life of their own. In this sense Marx is like the sorcerer to whom he compares the bourgeoisie, 'the sorcerer who is not able to control the powers of the nether world whom he has called up by his spells'.[51] The very fact that this simile can apply to Marx is itself evidence of how Marxian rhetoric raises ghosts which Marx cannot control. This is particularly true of the holy ghosts of *Christian* Rome, those powers of the higher world that Marx keeps calling up by his analogical spells. This is never more obvious than when, in *Capital*, Marx seeks to explain the value-relation between linen and the coat it is made into:

> its existence as value is manifested in its *equality* [*Gleichheit*] with the coat, just as the sheep-like nature of the Christian is shown in his resemblance [*Gleichheit*] to the Lamb of God.[52]

Here religious discourse so far exceeds the limits of analogy as to spill over into Marx's preliminary declaration that 'the linen recognises in [the coat] . . . a splendid kindred soul, the soul of value'. The unintended conceit or trick of this text is the formula 'equality of souls', precisely the doctrine that will later both excite and outrage Nietzsche, provoking him to declare: '"Equality of souls [*Gleichheit der Seelen*]," . . . this explosive concept which finally became revolution . . . is *Christian* dynamite.'[53]

For Marx, no such dynamite exists: 'Christians', he writes, 'are equal in heaven though unequal on earth.'[54] Unlike Engels, Marx never sees any revolutionary potential in Christianity; in so doing he produces a science of revolution that, to quote Marx himself, 'conceals the lack of a soul' or, to be more precise, *denies* it has a soul.[55] For the anarchist Mikhail Bakunin that was, in a sense, the problem with Marx – though Bakunin was no friend of religion he still feared that Marx would stifle what he called 'the *holy* instinct of revolt'.[56] Such stifling was often a conspicuous feature of mid-century political radicalism; writing in 1851, Ernest Jones declared that 'Revolution's soul is tame!'[57]

Confessional

In Marx the soul of revolution will not, though, be finally tamed; for Marx cannot write about revolution without lampooning religion, and in so doing he unwittingly lets religion loose. This is most obvious in *The Holy Family*; here Marx and Engels seek, through violent parody, to expose the Idealism of the New Hegelians, or 'Critical Critics', as 'nothing more than old transcendence distorted into a theological caricature':

> And Critical Criticism so loved the world that it sent its only begotten son, so that all who believe in him may not be lost, but have Critical life. Criticism was made mass and dwells amongst us . . . It does not regard it as a crime to be equal to God but alienates itself and takes the form of a master book-binder.[58]

In his determination to draw our attention to the unwitting theological caricature that is Idealism, Marx effectively caricatures that caricature. Indeed, he does this so often as to create within his writing a whole under-world of theological comedy; it is an underworld peopled by every possible opponent, not just neo-Hegelians but free-traders, bourgeois democrats and utopian socialists. Here we find 'superficial apostles', 'saintly epileptic[s]', 'comedy . . . saviours', 'Saint Max', 'Saint Bruno', a 'Jesus Christ-Kinkel' and a non-sensical 'Mr. Christ'. 'There is', writes Marx , 'no sense at all in Mr. Christ's arguments'.[59] To complete the divine comedy, there is even a Yahweh who shows his buttocks: at one point Marx declares that,

> to [the traditionalist], history shows nothing but its *a posteriori*, as did the God of Israel to his servant Moses.[60]

31

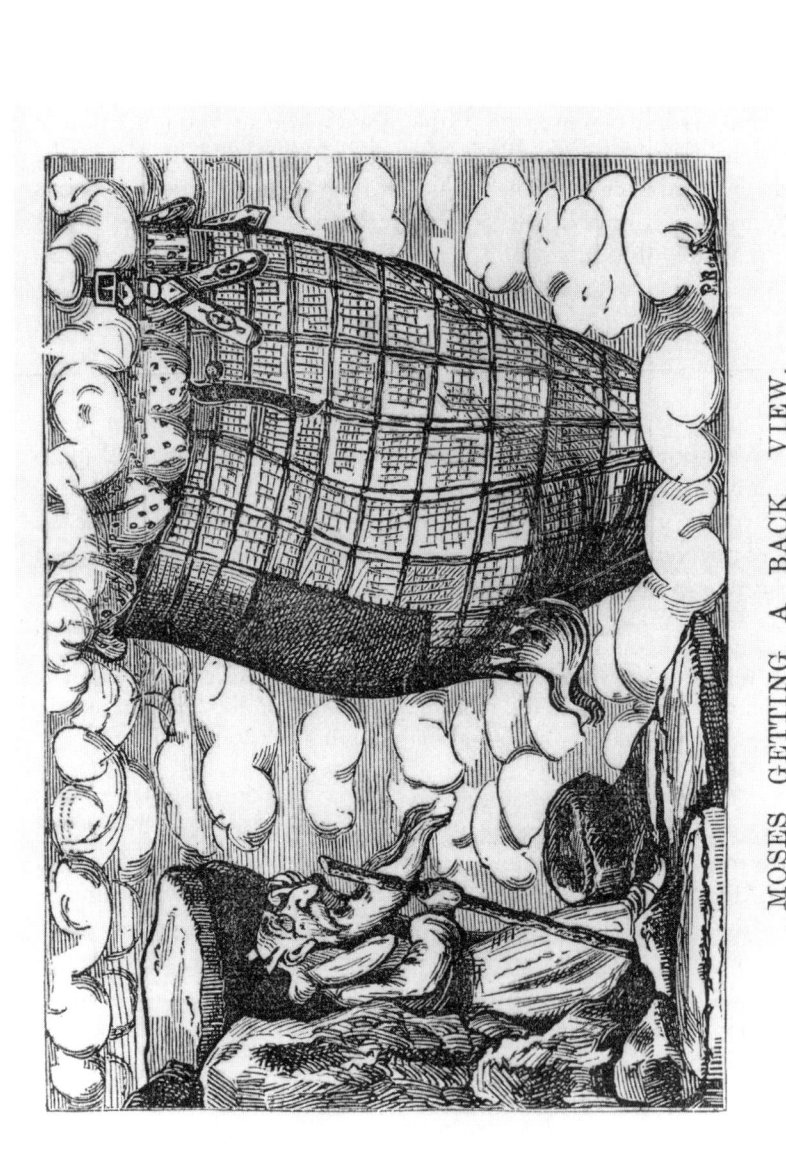

MOSES GETTING A BACK VIEW.

*And it shall come to pass that I will put thee in a clift of the rock, and I shall take away
my hand, and thou shalt see my back parts.*—EXODUS xxxiii., 23.

A NEW LIFE OF CHRIST.—Concluded.

17. He surpriseth his disciples.

18. He vanisheth.

Marx here glances at the biblical scene in which Yahweh tells Moses 'thou shalt see [only] my back parts' – precisely the scene which, in an 1882 issue of the secularist paper the *Freethinker*, inspired the notorious cartoon, 'Moses getting a Back View' (p. 32).

In this instance Marxian parody shades into a more general, Victorian counterculture.[61] Marx is writing just as widespread secularisation begins and, for almost the first time, Christianity is becoming the regular stuff of parody. We must appreciate that the Victorian death of God is not just a reputable story of loss and mourning; it is also a disreputable story of farce and laughter. It is not just about George Eliot supposedly crying even as she translates D. F. Strauss' demythologized *Life of Christ*; it is also about secularists laughing even as they read the *Freethinker's* 'New Life of Christ', a comic strip that appears in the Christmas number for 1882 (p. 33).[62] This is the laughter that can be heard in Marx. Here the laughter is also understood or even theorized: of Lucan's dialogues Marx observes that

> the Greek gods, who already died once . . . in Aeschylus's tragedy *Prometheus Bound*, were forced to die a second death – this time a comic one.[63]

Ten years later, Marx opens his 'Eighteenth Brumaire' with

> Hegel remarks somewhere that all the great events and characters of world history occur . . . twice. He forgot to add: the first time as tragedy, the second as farce.[64]

In Marx, it seems, the death of God is happening for the second time, as a kind of farce. Indeed, one senses that, for Marx, the farcical death of God is just an extension of the equally farcical *life* of God, that God and Christianity are always already farcical; for despite the official *Manifesto* claim that 'Christian ideas [had] succumbed . . . to rationalist ideas', the few believers that pass through Marx's pages are an *irr*ational crew of 'silly . . . Saints', 'hysterical pietists' and 'monosyllabic . . . Christian[s]', all high on the 'opium' of religion and reeling with '*drunk* religious feelings'.[65] Perhaps not all Christians had succumbed to rationalist ideas.

If so, Foucault would be right to speak of a nineteenth-century rediscovery of 'Christian unreason', a tradition of holy idiocy that celebrates

---

Illustrations on pp. 32, 33

'Moses Getting a Back View' from the *Freethinker*, © 1882.

'A New Life of Christ', from the *Freethinker*, © 1882.

Both illustrations by permission of the British Library.

what St Paul calls the 'foolishness of God'.[66] It is a tradition which Marx chances upon even as he seeks to ridicule both the New Hegelian and the New Testament. 'Criticism', he declares, 'was made mass . . . dwells amongst us and . . . humiliates itself to the extent of nonsense.[67] According to Søren Kierkegaard, 'Christianity cannot be introduced' but, in a sense, it cannot be parodied, or reduced to foolishness since it always already knows itself to be foolishness. Note how the laughter of Marx is pre-empted by Kierkegaard's 'pious jest[s]': 'I cannot', he writes, 'become serious . . . [for I am] smiling at myself.'[68] Again, note how Marx's theological caricatures are pre-empted by the devout Florence Nightingale: 'religious men', she insists, 'must be heretics now', and 'push [doctrines] . . . to the extreme'.[69] Yet again, Marx seeks to scoff at 'Saint Bruno the saintly epileptic' but in Dostoyevsky's *The Idiot* the nineteenth century has a 'holy fool' who is quite literally epileptic.[70]

Dostoyevsky's saintly fool is also a kind of rebel; this, though, would not impress Marx who insists that, as well as being secular, 'modern revolution [must be] . . . serious'.[71] Marx cannot or will not see the political point of Christian misrule. He does acknowledge that 'a Christian state . . . [would] dissolve itself,'[72] but Christianity's impossibilizing of the state is not so much socialism as a kind of anarchism. Most contemporary anarchists were, of course, defiantly secular, seeing God and state as correlatives.[73] Both Tolstoy and Nietzsche, however, would know better. George Woodcock sees Tolstoy as 'a *Christian* anarchist'; whilst Nietzsche declares that 'one may assert an absolute equivalence between *Christian* and *anarchist*' – 'Christ', he claims, was a 'holy anarchist who raised up the lowly . . . to oppose the ruling order.'[74]

Such holy anarchism, though never known as such, does have its moments in mid-century Britain. Witness, in particular, the activities of the many 'Chartist Churches' who, in the summer of 1839, adopted the practice of entering Parish churches *en masse* at the time of the Sunday service.[75] Most services proceeded without disruption, but one newspaper speaks of 'a tumultuous invasion of churches . . . by a revolutionary mob', whilst another includes reports of smoking, sleeping, drunkenness, stealing books and even 'using a pew drawer as a chamber pot'.[76] Marx does not arrive in Britain until 1848, but in 1855 he *does* witness, in Hyde Park, the huge Chartist-led protest against the Sunday Trading Bill. Of this protest Marx grandly declares: '*yesterday . . . the English revolution began*'. It is, though, a revolution that is neither secular nor serious for it took the form of workers ironically aping or parodying the religious zeal that had enforced the Bill; the aping was intended to expose the hypocrisy of the bourgeoisie who were spending Sunday in the Park rather than the church.[77] Indeed, even as Marx 'reports' on this revolution-by-parody, the degree of parody is redoubled to the point that the revolution almost turns into a wild and self-parodic church: the crowd's 'grunting . . . squawking . . . croaking, yelling, groaning [and] . . . shrieking' becomes, according to Marx,

> a babel . . . [or] concert . . . improvised [without] . . . instrumental accompaniment [where] the chorus had to make use of it own organs . . . [and in which] 'Go to church!' was the only recognisable sound [until] . . . 'He is a saint! He is psalm singing!' [was] . . . the ['ironic'] anti-strophe.

For Marx, the unaccompanied choral mob are themselves psalm-singing saints of a wild and ironic sort.

Elsewhere, Marx scoffs at 'silly . . . saints' and is wholly satirical when declaring of the anarchist Max Stirner, 'how deeply our saint has "penetrated" into the essence of communism'.[78] Here, though, in Hyde Park – or rather in Marx's essay – saints do appear to penetrate revolution; as well they might, since, as Engels observes, it was 'only the bourgeois period . . . [that] did away with the saints'.[79] Engels refers specifically to Catholic saints but it is precisely those saints whom Marx locates on the side of the Cologne revolution of 1848; this uprising of two thousand workers was dismissed by the conservative German press as 'a carnival jest [or] joke' but praised by Marx as the work of 'two thousand saints'.[80] These jesting, silly saints represent 'a droll revolution' that Marx cannot quite write; for though he would like 'to write . . . the biographies of these saints' it is more than he can do in 1848. 'Perhaps', he comments, 'there will be an opportunity one day to write an *Acta Sanctorum',* but that day never comes; the acts or lives of these particular saints are never written by Marx.

But then Marx *is* suspicious of such biographies; after all, it is specifically the *lives* of the saints that he dismisses as 'silly': 'the monks', he observes, 'wrote silly lives of Catholic Saints'. And what make these lives so silly is that 'the monks wrote [the] . . . lives . . . *over* the manuscripts on which . . . classical works . . . had been written'.[81] For Marx, this is an inverted metaphor for the still sillier way in which the neo-Hegelians were rewriting French economics or, as Marx puts it, 'wrote their philosophical nonsense *beneath* the French'. The irony is that in Marx's own writing it is *biographical* nonsense that, at times, shows through from beneath the economics. Recall, for instance, how in *The German Ideology* Marx and Engels suddenly depart from economics to write of

> fallen angels creeping shamefaced through . . . 'infinite space' until they find a modest lodging.

Our co-authors here happen to encode the story of their own exile – both are soon to be political refugees creeping across Europe until they find, in the case of Marx, a modest lodging in London. These particular angels are, in part, autobiographical angels.[82]

To slide from analysis to autobiography is the accusation that Marx and Engels make against Max Stirner, author of *The Ego and its Own*: 'Saint Max', they write, 'begins to speak not of *the man,* but of *himself*' – the silly lives of saints, it is implied, are still being written.[83] It is not, though, far from 'Saint Max' to 'Saint Marx', as Derrida has shown; and whilst the later Marx places increasing stress upon impersonal forces, he never quite abandons the ego and its own, nor his early assertion that 'the *man* is greater than the *citizen* and *human life* than *political life*'.[84] For Marx, the whole point of owning the products of our labour is that 'our productions would be as many mirrors from which our natures would shine forth'.[85] And this, it seems, is already the case with Marx's own productions – his texts; for there we *do,* at times, see his nature shining forth. Observe how, in *The German Ideology,* Marx describes a society without capitalism's division of labour:

> [such] a society makes it possible for me to . . . hunt in the morning, fish in the afternoon, rear cattle in the evening, [and] criticize after dinner, just as I have a mind.[86]

With the encroaching first person – 'me' then 'I' – Marx too seems to 'speak not of the man but of himself', or rather an idealized, orderly and almost saintly version of himself. A less flattering image of Marx is, though, offered by the *Economic and Philosophical Manuscripts*; this time it is an image encoded as the exact opposite of what Marx parodies as the capitalist's pseudo-religious life of self-denial:

> the less you eat, drink, buy books, go to the theatre, go dancing, go drinking, think, love, theorize, sing, paint, fence etc. the more you save and the greater will become that treasure which neither moths nor maggots can consume – your *capital.*[87]

Marx himself rarely showed restraint when it came to thinking, loving, theorizing and drinking (significantly, mentioned twice); indeed, one drinking bout ended with Marx and Engels breaking street lamps and being chased by the police – as Engels remarked at the time, 'nonsense is contagious'.[88] Just as hunting, fishing and criticizing describes the sensible life of a communist saint, so not-thinking, not-loving and not-drinking inverts the nonsensical life of the communist sinner. But both these 'lives of Marx' are *saints'* lives in the sense that both are palimpsest lives, lives that are written below other lives, other narratives, other texts.

For Marx, of course, *all* lives are othered or alienated: under capitalism '*my* life', he writes,

> belongs to *another* . . . my desire is the inaccessible possession of *another* . . . [and] my [every] activity is other than itself.[89]

Here, indeed, even the *voice* of Marx belongs to another, his words being strangely suggestive of a confessional discourse that is as old as St Paul's 'what I would, that do I not; but what I hate, that do I'. Curiously, it is a discourse that completely overtakes Marx when, in a letter to Ruge, he suddenly and almost absurdly declares:

> What is needed above all is a *confession*, and nothing more than that. To obtain forgiveness for its sins mankind needs only to declare them for what they are.[90]

Earlier in this same letter Marx declares that 'our task must be to latch onto [religion] . . . to *complete* [not abandon] the thought of the past.' Part of this religious past is, it seems, the strange thought of confession, the strange practice of asking forgiveness. According to Dostoyevsky's Idiot, 'being absurd . . . makes it easier to forgive one another';[91] in Marx's letter to Ruge, being absurd seems also to make it easier to *seek* forgiveness. And what *is* so absurd is that Marx gives us no idea as to *what* we are confessing or to *whom*. But then the whole absurd point of Original Sin is that we are always already guilty; and this is the absurdity which Marx chances upon when calling on us to confess an unnamed sin to an unnamed addressee. To adapt the words of Shakespeare's Antonio, 'I know not why I am so guilty' – the conundrum that most famously surfaces in Franz Kafka's *The Trial* (1925).[92] Marx usually *condemns* religion for being 'contentless [*inhaltslos*]', for being, if you will, a 'centreless science';[93] here, however, in this enigmatic call to confession, Marx seems for once to be positively *drawn* by the contentless or centreless character of religion.

The obvious, though unwitting, Marxian symbol for the centreless science of religion is, of course, the centreless halo; witness Marx's declaration that

> the criticism of religion is . . . in *embryo* [*im Keim*] the *criticism of that vale of tears* of which religion is but the *halo*.[94]

Religion is merely the outline or circumference of the suffering which is the true object of Marxian criticism; or rather, suffering *will become* the true object, for that criticism is still 'in embryo', still to-come. As long as Marx's writing is still distracted by religion it is itself at one remove from the dead centre of tears – it too is secondary, it too is suffering, or history happening for the second time and thus turning to farce. Raymond Williams famously argued that Marx's vision of history is tragic, George Steiner has argued that it is comic;[95] but both are right in the sense that the comic or parodic writer within Marx is, at times, struggling to be serious. This is most obviously the case in 'The Eighteenth Brumaire', where Marx finds Louis Bonaparte's *coup d'état* to be a pathetically comic repetition of his uncle Napoleon's accession to power. At such moments Marx is struggling to engage with a history that has not yet turned to farce, that has not yet happened twice. Indeed, since for Marx all history is in constant danger of happening twice the only authentic history is the history that has not yet even happened once. Such history is only to be found in the future; but the future *is*, in a sense, within Marx's range. 'The proletariat', writes Marx, 'holds the future in its hands', and this he does too, not only by invoking 'poetry from the future' but simply by being German: 'we Germans', he writes, 'have lived our future history in thought.'[96]

Marx refers to the democratic future of which Germany, in the 1840s, still can only think, or dream; however, in Marx's other essays at this time the German future that is being lived in thought is not democracy but totalitarianism – uncannily, the essays anticipate something of the anti-Semitism of the Nazi era. In 'On the Jewish Question' (1843), Marx identifies the capitalist class both with and as the Jewish nation, whilst in 'The Magyar Struggle' (1849), he proceeds to the astonishing prophecy that 'the next world war will not only cause reactionary classes to disappear . . . but also entire reactionary peoples.'[97] Insofar as Marx refers to Jews, he should have said 'the next world war but one'. According to Carver, 'Marx is 150 years ahead of his time', but in the 1840s he is almost exactly a hundred years ahead.[98] Indeed, in 1848 he numbers amongst 'the . . . seven deadly sins committed by Germany' the annexation of part of German-speaking Poland, an act of expansion and repatriation which culminated in

> many Poles . . . [being] given travelling facilities ['on the railways'] . . . branded with caustic, sent away with shorn heads and, if possible (as in Cracow), completely wiped out.[99]

Even as Marx describes one event he stumbles, with terrible precision, upon what we might call a repetition of that event. The Holocaust, though, is a repetition which refuses to be a repetition; as a uniquely appalling event it refuses to be something happening for the second time, refuses to become farce.[100] In that sense, the Holocaust is the 'pure' or purely tragic event for which the serious Marx is almost searching. It is not only an event that Marx chances upon in his description of the annexation of Poland; it is also an event that is actually made thinkable, perhaps even thought into existence, by the Marxian demand that history 'must be serious'. The Holocaust is the very 'vale of tears' which Marx acknowledges is *not yet* the object of his attention and, in that sense, is still to-come, still ahead of him.

Of course, if the Holocaust *is* somehow 'seen', or foreseen in Marx it must be from the perspective of not only 'we Germans' but also 'we Jews' – Marx is Jewish as well as German. There is also the perspective of 'we communists', for they too will be amongst those 'sent away with shorn heads'. The seriousness of Marx thus helps to make thinkable the future deaths *of his own*: his own race, his own party – deaths that are, in a sense, his own death. To do so suggests a kind of death-drive, even a kind of suicide.

Suicide is buried in Marx, and it keeps coming back: not only is Marx preoccupied with that most famous would-be suicide, Hamlet, but time and again he describes the bourgeoisie as, in effect, a suicidal class – a class that, in inventing capitalism, 'has . . . forged the weapons that bring death to itself'.[101] In 1844 Marx claims that '*suicide* is contrary to nature'; however if, as Marx later writes, 'everything seems pregnant with its contrary', then Engels is more Marxian than Marx in declaring that 'living means dying'. This, as Engels remarks, is 'the dialectical conception of life'.[102] It is also the Christian conception of life, dying-to-self being a familiar theme of the silly life of the saint, or Christian. And that is precisely Kierkegaard's contemporaneous conceit – Kierkegaard's leap of faith is 'a despairing leap', an abandonment or giving away of life.[103] For Marx, though, the despairing leap is no conceit; under capitalism it is a cruel fact of death – in 1851 he writes that 'in France . . . five million . . . totter on the precipice of non-existence', and in 1867 he observes that in Britain some had actually begun to leap:

> In many of the manufacturing districts [labourers] . . . were [not only] harassed to the brink of death . . . [but] . . . in some instances . . . driven to commit suicide.[104]

These labourers are in fact children, and by a terrible irony two of Marx's own children would one day commit suicide, in Eleanor's case as part of a suicide pact with Edward Aveling, the co-translator of *Capital*.[105] Suicide is, then, part of the future of both Marx and his writing; but his work is always already tied to suicide in the sense that social science, what Marx calls the 'science of man', famously begins its statistical analysis of human life with Emile Durkheim's 1897 study of suicides. In 1845 Marx himself writes about the suicide figures for Paris.[106]

As Dostoyevsky's Idiot is told, one attraction of suicide is that it is 'the only action I can start and finish by my own free will'; but the irony of suicide statistics is that they give rise to mathematical probabilities and frequencies which issue in the absurd notion that 'there is', as Florence Nightingale put it, 'a law which *compels* so many people to commit suicide in a[ny] twelve months'.[107] If so, it is not just my life that belongs to another but also my death – it too is alienated; indeed, it is alienated to the point that, according to the figures discussed by Marx, I am most likely to kill myself by jumping – to be specific, by either a 'voluntary heavy fall' or a 'voluntary plunge into water'.[108] Here Marx again encounters the despairing leap as a brutal fact of nineteenth-century death, as a leap that one does not survive. For the Christian, though, it is a leap that one might just survive; this is the almost absurdist conceit that surfaces in Christina Rossetti's 1848 poem, 'What Sappho would have said had her leap cured instead of killing her'.[109] The conceit surfaces again in the strange figure of Kierkegaard's leaping 'knight of faith': upon landing he is 'able . . . to transform the leap . . . to a gait, to express the sublime in the pedestrian'.[110] For Kierkegaard, the leap is of little value unless it is repeated in a transformed gait or walk. Whilst Marx laments the fact that tragedy is repeated as farce, Kierkegaard celebrates the possibility that the despairing leap is repeated as a farcical walk: 'the movement of faith', he writes, 'must be made contininully on the strength of the absurd'.[111] Had Marx read Kierkegaard he might have spoken of not only the silly *lives* of the saints but the silly walks; in fact, he almost does so in his parodic assaults on those silly saints the neo-Hegelians: witness how one 'saint . . . at best staggers rather than dances'; a second 'Saint . . . hurries in seven-league boots'; and another, 'Saint Bruno . . . wrestles with one of his own theses just as Jacob wrestled with God, with the only difference that God twisted Jacob's thigh, while our saintly epileptic twists all [his] limbs.'[112]

As a Jew, Marx is himself a descendent of Jacob, and though God, or his angel, twists only Jacob's thigh he is forever doomed to limp. Marx tries, in effect, to walk away from this inheritance, declaring 'I know nothing of a man if I merely know his name is Jacob.'[113] This, though, is particularly disingenuous given that Marx spent so much time writing, and thus wrestling, with a man called Angels. That, in a way, makes Marx a kind of Jacob, which is virtually how he twists, or styles himself when, to express the almost prosthetic effect of wealth that can buy a man 'six stallions', he declares – in a surreal flourish – 'I am *lame*, but money procures me twenty-four legs.'[114] The rich man may walk awkwardly with twenty-four legs, but still more awkward is the gait of those workers who are quite literally lame, those that have been crippled by the factory system, those whom Marx describes as 'crippled', or 'stunted monsters'.[115] The awkward, agonized gait of such workers may, at first glance, appear very different to the absurd, limping movements of the saints; however, the two could be mistaken for each other in the sense that the Marxian figure of the limping worker is marked, like the limping saint, with a promise or threat of transformation. Marx writes, strangely and metaphorically, of the proletariat's '*gigantic* children's shoes' but, contrasting these with the 'dwarf-like [and] worn-out . . . shoes of the . . . bourgeoisie', he predicts 'a vigorous future for this . . . Cinderella'. The proletariat may currently limp in shoes that are too big for it, but one day it will, like Cinderella, find shoes that fit, fit for revolution.[116]

Curiously, Marx omits to mention the shoeless Cinderella who famously loses a shoe in her flight from the ball. This omission is, though, symptomatic of Marx's more general, and eminently Victorian, failure to recognize the revolutionary potential of the ragged and undressed, those who do not wear shoes or at least not those made by 'shoemaker' Marx.[117] For Marx, the ragged and undressed includes that shadowy group the *lumpenproletariat* whom he dismisses as 'the scum . . . of all classes' and whose name literally means 'rags and tatters'. As Peter Stallybrass remarks, 'the name *lumpenproletariat* . . . suggests less the political emergence of a class than a sartorial category.'[118]

It is a category that might also apply to those who, to quote Marx, 'take off . . . [their] shoes . . . [believing they] are stand[ing] on hallowed ground'.[119] Marx is as dismissive of such shoeless saints as he is of the half-naked lumpen; but the saints have a revolutionary potential that is betrayed by their very shoelessness: the peasant's wooden clog, or *sabot*, is one of his most ready weapons – from 'sabot' comes 'sabotage'. No wonder the shoeless saint makes the bourgeois Kierkegaard anxious; writing in the late 1830s he cryptically declares, 'take off your shoes, you are standing on holy ground', but then adds, nervously, 'it won't help to be, as many are, unbreeched'.[120] Kierkegaard fears that the shoeless saint might also be breech-less or *sans-culotte*, as the French would say – 'a sansculotte' was a nineteenth-century nickname for any radical republican.

It takes the anarchist socialism of Bakunin to see the revolutionary potential in the ragged and breech-less lumpen;[121] it takes the neurotic theology of Kierkegaard to see a breech-less revolutionary in the shoeless saint. Nevertheless, breechless and radical saints *were* to be seen or, at least, imagined: witness that often neglected figure, 'Jésus sans-culotte', 'le "sans-culotte" de Nazareth' invoked by the revolutionary rhetoric of 1840s Paris. Witness too those thousands of Christian Chartists who in

1839 occupied churches where, of course, they were reported not only to smoke, drink, steal and sleep but also to urinate or, as the *Lancaster Gazette* delicately puts it, 'to x x x'.[122]

Oriental

> like an oriental figurine [that] . . . vanishes.
> (Marx, 1848)[123]

Set alongside Marx's idealized communist life of hunting, fishing, raising cattle and criticizing, the church-going Chartist's life of smoking, drinking, sleeping and urinating appears almost comically narrow, a life shrunken to the limits of the body. But then this *is* the bathetic way of religion, at least according to Marx; though he often dismisses religion as bodiless he also sneers that, 'Judaism . . . makes even the lavatory an object of divine law.'[124] This, for Marx, typifies the fact that 'the monotheism of the Jew is . . . in reality the polytheism of the many needs', a polytheism which places absolute value in the multiple or minute and which sees not God but gods. In this remarkable aside, Marx describes a Judaism that is subtly but significantly at odds with what he sees as the Christian-Hegelian claim that 'we encounter the human incarnation of God at every stage' – a claim which means, for Marx, that

> [although] the universal appears everywhere as a determinate particularity . . . the individual never achieves its true universality.[125]

The individual is, though, often overlooked by Marx himself, who in this respect still subscribes to the Hegelian universalism he so derides. Marx's commitment to the particular or small is most obviously belied by the way he continually employs the metaphor of smallness as an insult. Time and again he condemns as *little* or *shrunken* the post-revolutionary politics of 1848. Of France he writes, 'as the level of the revolution sank . . . the official celebrities . . . became . . . dwarf-like'; of Germany he remarks that 'the mountain moved and lo! – a mouse emerged'. 'The deluge', he adds, 'left behind no monsters . . . no revolutionary colossi . . . [only] thick-set bourgeois shapes'.[126]

Just three years before Matthew Arnold considers 'the Sea of Faith' withdrawing on Dover beach Marx considers the 'waves of . . . revolution'[127] withdrawing in Berlin. At the mid-point of the nineteenth century it is not only saints but communists who are beached, stranded. The difference, though, is that the communist is confident of another wave, or tide and so is not concerned with the peculiar little 'shapes' the sea has 'left behind'. By contrast, the Christian, with no hope of a returning sea, has nothing else with which to be concerned. As we know, Rossetti, who fears 'what will [happen] . . . in a world where there shall be no more sea', compares the 'Christian [to] . . . a sea anemone'.[128] Christians are beginning to shrink; they are not 'colossi' but anemones. In *The Idiot* even all-powerful God grows small: here we are shown a tarantula and assured that 'it was that same . . . all-powerful creature'.[129] For Marx, 'microscopes . . . are of [no] assistance' but they *are* increasingly needed by the Christian; as Kierkegaard cryptically remarks, 'the physicist uses the microscope . . . to see God'. As well he might, since, like Marx, one can now speak of 'the flea-jumps of . . . the New Testament'.[130]

If the God of the nineteenth century is becoming minute he is also and at the same time becoming multiple. 'Christ' is fast becoming another plural name. Florence Nightingale writes of 'many Christs', whilst Gerard Manley Hopkins declares that 'Christ plays in ten thousand places'.[131] For others, Christ does not so much *play* in many places as *work* and, therefore, grow militant: in France the revolutionary rhetoric of 1848 included 'le Christ des barricades'.[132] This threatening figure keeps returning; he is echoed in Oscar Wilde's talk of 'These Christs that die upon the barricades' and inflected in Barrett Browning's vision of 'every roadside Christ . . . [shaking] his nails in anger'.[133] At such moments, where Christ is not only plural but desperate, Christianity fits with remarkable precision Marx's account of Judaism – Christianity might also be a 'polytheism of the many needs'.

The many and needful Christs of Barrett Browning's vision appear in her poem *Aurora Leigh* (1857), where Marian is describing her hysterical flight through Catholic France; the 'roadside Christs' are, of course, crucifixes. And it is the wooden crucifix, particularly as imagined by Marian, that curiously haunts or disrupts Marx's account of thinking small, of reducing the material world to its simplest elements – namely, a stick:

> . . . even when the sensuous world is reduced to a minimum, to a stick . . .
> it [still] presupposes the action of producing the stick.[134]

To be specific, it presupposes the action of a carpenter; Marx insists there is no stick without the labour, or sweat of a carpenter – an insistence that is encrypted in the crucifix, since here is a stick to which is nailed the sweating figure of a carpenter. The nails which 'every roadside Christ' is shaking might, in this sense, be nails he himself has hammered in, nails that represent his alienated labour. This conceit is one that Christianity usually overlooks; it only becomes visible when the cross is re-read through the unwitting mediation of Marx. But that mediation becomes a little less unwitting when Marx jokingly declares, what could be more ominous and at the same time more absurd than to be nailed to the cross as a result of a trick . . . of 'the carpenter's.[135]

Thirty-eight years before Nietzsche explains 'How to Philosophise with a Hammer', Marx demonstrates how to *theologize* with a hammer, how to theologize in such a way as not simply to interpret the cross but change it, do violence to it.[136] Like Nietzsche, Marx instinctively seizes the hammer as a metaphor for transformative thought. Note that, for Marx, 'the Greek [sculptor] . . . broke . . . up [nature] with [an] Hephaestan hammer of art'; likewise, of 1789, Marx writes that 'the feudal structure . . . [was] smashed by the hammer of . . . Revolution'.[137] The hammer is not, though, the simple and unambiguous symbol that it would become when adopted, along with the sickle, as the very emblem of Soviet Marxism. This is because the actual Marxian hammer is caught up in the relative, multiple and automated world of modernity: at one point Marx cites Hegel's claim that 'he [who] acts as [a] hammer on what is under him . . . serves as anvil to what is above'; at another point Marx observes that 'in Birmingham alone 500 varieties of hammer are produced'; and at yet another he remarks that 'the [new] steam-hammer . . . [is] of such weight that even Thor himself could not wield it.'[138]

No easier to wield, or write, is 'the hammer of . . . Revolution'; it too is a giant hammer that dwarfs the individual, for Marx always insists on *world* revolution, on total rather than merely local transformation. Marxian revolution is, as it were, 'monotheistic' and proud of the fact. Nevertheless, what drives this totalization is the ever-increasing Westernization of the world in the mid-nineteenth century; as Marx himself observes in 1853, '[even] India . . . will [soon] . . . be . . . annexed to the Western world'. Soon, he implies, there will be no East.[139] For Marx, the East *must* disappear in that revolution can only come about once the whole world has passed through the era of industrialized capitalism. Make no mistake, the dialectical Marx belongs to the West. His materialism, however, sets him *apart* from the West, or at least the Hegelian West; in this respect, Marx is often looking East, as seen when, in 1848, he declares that 'an apostle of revolution is approaching from the East'.[140] Marx refers to the Tsar of Russia but this Eastern apostle, or oriental figurine, is also Marx himself – as a Jew he comes to Europe from the East, as a German he comes to England from the East.

Marx betrays something of this Eastern-ness when, again in 1848, he famously compares religion to oriental opium[141] – and in doing so unwittingly returns Western religion to its Eastern origins. After all, it is not just the apostles of revolution but the apostles of Christ that come from the East, a fact pointed up just a year later by another Victorian Jew, Benjamin

Disraeli: 'the Church', he writes, 'is a sacred corporation for the promulgation . . . in Europe of certain Asian principles.'[142] The Marxian apostle from the East is a necessarily religious figure, he has that status merely by being a figure of the other, or the stranger; this is simply the belief of many Eastern cultures. And it is to this belief that Derrida alludes when declaring that Marx himself is 'a glorious, sacred [and] accursed . . . immigrant' – for Derrida, Marx belongs to the Judeo-Christian tradition of the holy outsider, or sacred scapegoat.[143] This is a familiar tradition to Marx: heaping scorn upon the neo-Hegelian rejection of the body, or what Marx calls 'Love', he enigmatically and quite wonderfully declares that

> Love is 'the maid from a foreign land' who has no dialectical passport and is therefore expelled from the country by the Critical [or Idealist] police.[144]

This particular immigrant does *not*, however, belong to any religious tradition; despite bearing the Christian name of Love, she is 'an *un*christian materialist'. Though Marx himself is an immigrant whom Derrida can recover for religious tradition, the Marxian figure of Love refuses such recovery; she – and note that it *is* a 'she' – remains 'the something of this clumsy world' that has no Christian passport.[145] It is as if she is so absolutely an exile that she does not belong even to what Marx elsewhere calls 'the nation of . . . exiles' – she is an outcast even from the sacred and accursed condition of being an exile.[146]

This is the paradox of the 'unChristian' Christian name of Love – a name or figure that effectively represents all those unChristian Christians or radical saints who haunt both the fact and writing of Marxian revolution. Recall, if you will, the church-going Chartists, the Christs upon the barricades and the saintly anarchists. These together are the silly saints who confirm their identification with the expelled and immigrant Love by their complete unacceptability to the dialectical Marx; the Marx who is, despite himself, the Critical policeman insisting that 'modern revolution must be serious'.

The irony is that this philosophical Marx expels not only a host of silly saints but also a host of comical communists, including himself. To echo the fictional Nikolai Bakhtin from Terry Eagleton's *Saints and Scholars*: 'I fear for your revolution, my dear sir; I fear it will never succeed because you've not yet learnt to be frivolous.'[147] Bakhtin forgot to add that to learn to be frivolous you should look to saints rather than scholars.

chapter three

Stations

Freud's Christian Trains of Thought

My moods change like scenes a traveller sees from a train.
(Sigmund Freud, 1897)[1]

Station to station

At the time of writing *The Interpretation of Dreams* Freud had still not travelled to Rome; between 1895 and 1898 he had got as far as Italy on five occasions but each time something had prevented him reaching Rome.[2] This neurotic preoccupation with going or not going to Rome was expressed in a recurring 'set of dreams' in which Freud *sees* Rome but cannot enter; they are dreams that he believes are, in part, derived from what he calls 'facetious Jewish anecdotes'. Particularly important is the story of

> an impecunious Jew [who] had stowed himself away without a ticket in the fast train to Karlsbad. He was caught out, and each time tickets were inspected he was taken out of the train and treated more and more severely. At one of the stations on his *via dolorosa* [*Leidensstationen*] he met an acquaintance, who asked him where he was traveling to: 'To Karlsbad', was his reply.[3]

In the late-nineteenth century many an Eastern-European comic story began with a Jew on a train; it was a recurring source of black humour, or tragi-comedy. What distinguishes this Jew on the train, however, is that the rail journey is also a *via dolorosa*, the 'way of sorrow' that Christ follows to the cross. Moreover, in being asked where he is going, the Jew plays the part of the apocryphal Christ who, upon appearing to St Peter, is also famously asked *Quo Vadis?*, 'Where are you going?'[4] As Carl Schorske first observed, the poor Jew on the train to Karlsbad is a kind of Christ; this is a strange, almost absurd vision of Jesus on a train.[5] But then Christ *has* been seen on a train before, and by authors Freud knew well. In 1836 Kierkegaard writes of 'Christian understanding [as] . . . a steam engine going down a railway track'; in 1868 Dostoyevsky's *The Idiot* begins with its holy fool, the Christ-like Prince, in a third-class carriage on the Warsaw-to-Petersburg express.[6] Just one year later, Christ is actually driving the train: in Flaubert's *Sentimental Education* we read about a picture by the artist Pellerin that 'showed the Republic, or Progress, or Civilization, in the form of Christ driving a locomotive'.[7]

No such grand purpose ennobles Freud's shabby and Jewish Christ. Indeed, his *via dolorosa* may not even take him as far as Golgotha; for, whilst the Christ of legend answers the question *Quo Vadis?* with 'I am going to Rome to be crucified again', Freud's Jewish Christ replies 'To Karlsbad . . . *if* my constitution can stand it.'[8] There is also, of course, the problem that he has no ticket and is forever being made to get off the train. This Christ shares the suffering of the nineteenth-century Jew who, unwashed by Christian baptism, lacks what Heinrich Heine called 'the admission ticket to European civilization'; far from driving 'the locomotive of Civilization', the Jewish Christ is not even allowed to stay on board.[9] Whilst Flaubert's Pellerin sees Christ as at one with the time of the train, the time of modernity, Freud's Jewish Christ endures a tragicomic, on-off relationship with such time. This Christ is *in* time (he subjects himself to trains and their timetables), but it is painfully clear that he is not *on* time; if he ever makes it to Karlsbad-cum-Rome-cum-Golgotha he will be as absurdly late as Franz Kafka's belated Messiah, he who 'will come not on the day of the Last Judgment but the day after'.[10]

Freud, though, is *tragically* late when he himself is the untimely Christ-(not)-on-the-train. In 1920 Freud's daughter, who lives in Hamburg, falls gravely ill and Freud's desire to be with her is frustrated by the lack of trains: 'there were', he writes, 'no trains, not even a children's train'.[11] Freud had hoped to catch a 'children's train', a train that took children out of hungry, post-war Austria; indeed, Freud's hope is expressed in terms that identify him with Christ: 'Let us alter the saying', he writes: 'and say: Suffer *me* to come with the little children'. Freud, though, does *not* become this Jesus-on-the-children's-train. Freud the would-be Jesus is stuck in starving Vienna, and by the time he gets to Hamburg his daughter is dead.

Freud, it seems, is a would-be Jesus who is not *on* time precisely because he is so profoundly *in* time; the train that Freud-as-Jesus boards, or rather does *not* board, is an all too real train of history. Of the lack of trains in post-war Austria, Freud remarks: 'the undisguised brutality of our time weighs heavily on us' – even, it seems, on Christ.[12] That is the secret theological lesson of Freud's railway-Jesus, a lesson that is a secret even to Freud.

But then the Jew on the train has always been struck by not only 'the brutality of our time' but also the fragility of what we mean by 'time'. In 1843, Heine writes of the railways that 'even the elementary concepts of space and time have begun to vacillate'. In 1901, Freud records a dream in which, as 'a train was coming in [to the station] . . . the platform moved towards the train, while the train stopped still'.[13] By 1911 yet another famous Jew is writing on both the train and the space-time conundrum; his name is Albert Einstein, for whom the train demonstrates that time is relative: Einstein observes that events which may appear simultaneous to someone *inside* a moving railway carriage will *not* appear simultaneous to someone watching from the embankment.[14] *This* Jew on the train is struck not so much by the *brutality* of 'our time' but by the thought that there may be no such thing as '*our* time'; time as experienced and measured in one place may not be the same as it is in another.

The theory of relativity would be later taken up by others to produce quantum physics, which so violated Newtonian laws of cause-and-effect as to imply, according to Einstein, that 'God throws dice'.[15] For Einstein such an anarchic theology is quite unthinkable, just as it is for Freud: in 1933, he dismisses contemporary Anarchists as 'intellectual nihilists', adding that 'the relativity theory of modern physics seems to have gone to their head' with the result that

> science has been disposed of [and] the space vacated may be filled by some kind of mysticism or, indeed, by the old religious *Weltenschauung*.[16]

For Freud, what is alarming about the intellectual anarchism that surrounds relativity theory is not so much its political threat to social order but its religious threat to scientific order – he really does seem to fear a world run by a dice-playing, anarchic God. And well he might, for Freud's God does, at times, appear to play dice, or at least to play trains, which, in Freud's world, was almost the same thing. Whenever Freud and his children played the board game 'One Hundred Journeys through Europe', he literally played with both trains and dice; and in the late-nineteenth century, to travel on a train *was* to run considerable risk of an accident.[17] Indeed, the trauma resulting from railway accidents provided an early model for the understanding of hysteria. As many have observed, psychoanalysis begins on a train; more precisely, it begins with a train *accident*.[18]

It is an accident that psychoanalysis can never quite forget, and that is because one particular railway accident *keeps* happening to psychoanalysis: namely, the accident of meaning that so besets Freudian trains.

We must remember that, for Freud, trains are almost another name for those seeming accidents that are the very stuff of the 'talking cure': Freud famously compares 'free association' to the accidental juxtaposition of words that might come from a 'traveller sitting next to the window of a railway carriage and describing to someone inside the carriage the changing views which you see outside'.[19] The train analogy is extended when Freud adds that,

> in a line of associations, ambiguous words (or, as we might call them, 'switch-words'), act like points at a junction. If the points are switched across from the position in which they appear to lie in the dream, then we find ourselves on another set of rails; and along this second track run the thoughts which we are in search of but still lie concealed behind the dream.[20]

It is as if, for Freud, every line of thought is a *train* of thought; the phrase 'train of thought' appears time and again in James Strachey's English translation. Each time, though, the train is an accident of meaning, or translation – the play on words, the play with 'trains' is not present in the German original. What *is* there is the play that Derrida points up when he suggests that, in Freud, every *Wagen* ('wagon', or 'carriage'), is also a *Wagenis* ('wager', or 'risk'), – a wager that is, I suggest, a close relation of that most famous wager, Blaise Pascal's wager on the existence of God.[21] For whether or not God plays dice, Pascal's believer certainly does, and in Freud accidents of religious meaning have an uncanny habit of taking place in trains. This is never more obvious than when, as Gregory Zilboorg writes,

> Freud in *The Psychopathology of Everyday Life* [1901], reports how he remembers relating to a fellow train passenger his profound impression of the frescoes in the Duomo [Cathedral] of Orvieto. To his amazement, Freud was unable to tell at the moment . . . the name of the artist. By way of a series of free associations, he finally recalled the name of the master painter, Signorelli. By way of careful self-analysis, he concluded that he had repressed the name because of its first half, *Signor*, to which he had arrived via a number of associations, one of them being the German word *Herr*.
>
> It was a remarkable piece of self-analysis on the part of Freud. Yet what appears not less remarkable is that the piece of psychoanalysis done in 1898 . . . lacked the recognition of what now appears so obvious: *Signor* is the Italian equivalent of *Lord* in Church language, as is the German word *Herr*.[22]

Freud the train passenger, in analysing his own train of thought, somehow does not notice that the Christian God has stolen on board. He is ticket-less, of course. He is not supposed to be there.

A few pages later, as Freud recalls another railway conversation, the analysed train of thought again carries Christian passengers; for as Freud's travelling companion attempts to recall the Latin word *aliquis* ('someone'), what comes to his mind are, *inter alia*:

> '*Reliquien* [relics] . . . [St] *Simon of Trent* . . . *St Augustine* . . . [and an old gentleman on yet another train,] a real *original* [called] . . . Benedict'.[23]

This time, though, Freud spots the specifically Christian train of thought immediately: 'here', he declares,

> are a row of saints and Fathers of the Church: St *Simon*, St *Augustine*, St *Benedict* . . . [and] there was, I think, a Church Father called *Origen*.

Strangely, what is missing from Freud's analysis is his travelling companion's very contemporary reference to:

> the accusation of ritual blood-sacrifice which is being brought against the Jews again just now, and . . . Kleinpaul's book [1892] in which he regards all these supposed victims as incarnations, one might say new editions, of the Saviour.

Had Freud dwelt on this accusation he would have glimpsed a much darker 'Christian' train of thought: namely, the contemporary anti-Semitism that really did demonise Jews – the gentleman called Benedict, we should note, has 'the appearance of a huge bird of prey'. As we know, it is this darkest Christian train of thought that, within forty years, would connect with the trains that transported thousands and thousands of Jews to the Nazi death camps. Freud, of course, was not to know this at the turn of the century, but he might nevertheless have made a connection with contemporary trains, which were already entangled in the history of anti-Semitism. In Germany, when millions of East European Jews began to enter in the 1880s, irrational fears of infection were such that special railway stations were created at both Hamburg and Berlin in order to 'cleanse' and 'process' these Jews.[24] Again, in Austria, as early as 1884, the extreme pan-Germanist Georg von Schönerer, made the Rothschilds' Northern Railway into what Schorske calls the 'focus of his anti-Semitic nationalization crusade' – in the Reichsrat he launched several diatribes against what he termed 'Northern Railway Jews'.[25] For all the stories and jokes about the Jew on the train, any special identification the Jew enjoyed with the railway was always contested. The Austrian Jew, Theodor Herzl, spoke better than he knew when he asked, 'Who among us knows enough Hebrew to ask for a railway ticket in that language? The word doesn't exist.' In this sense, every Jew is doomed to be the ticketless Jew on the train to Karlsbad; there *is* no properly Jewish ticket, the Jew's place on the train is only provisional. This is clear not only in political fact but Freudian anecdote – witness, the story of

> a Galician Jew . . . travelling in a train [who] had made himself really comfortable . . . and put his feet up on the seat. Just then a gentleman in modern dress entered the compartment [and] the Jew promptly . . . took up a proper pose. The stranger . . . then suddenly asked . . . 'Excuse me, when is Yom Kippur (the Day of Atonement)?' 'Oho!', said the Jew, and put his feet up on the seat again.[26]

Freud experiences for himself how tenuous is the Jew's place on the train when, in December 1883 on the way to Leipzig, he opens a window only to be told to close it: 'There came a shout from the background: "He's a dirty Jew! . . . We Christians consider other people."'[27] For all its Jewishness, the train of Freudian anecdote keeps turning back into a Christian train that is, in a sense, going straight to the gates of the death camp.

Mindful of Freud's fascination with not only trains but Agatha Christie, Laura Marcus has coined the telling phrase 'The Oedipus Express'.[28] My point is that there is *murder* on the Oedipus Express, mass-murder. This is not, though, the single murder of the Christie 'whodunit' but something much closer to the total killing envisaged by that patient of Freud's who dreamt

> he was traveling in a railway-train. The train came to a stop in open country . . . He went through all the coaches in the train and killed everyone he met.[29]

Freud relates this dream in 1916, just one year before Edward Thomas writes about another train that makes an unplanned stop in open country:

> Yes. I remember Adlestrop –
> The name, because one afternoon
> Of heat the express-train drew up there
> Unwontedly. It was late June.
> The steam hissed. Someone cleared his throat.
> No one left and no one came
> On the bare platform. What I saw
> Was Adlestrop – only the name.[30]

If Freud's Oedipus Express is not, in the end, to be confused with Christie's Orient Express neither is it to be confused with Thomas's express; though both unwontedly halt in open country, Freud's train is nearer to Auschwitz than Adlestrop.

As Marcus points out, one of Freud's seminal childhood memories of rail-travel is his recollection of passing through Breslau railway-station where he saw gas lamps for the first time: 'they made him think of souls burning in hell!'[31] If Freud's first-hand experience of trains *begins* with souls burning in hell it nearly *ends* there too, for Freud's final journey, in 1938, was on one of the last trains out of Nazi-occupied Austria. Ironically, this train was the Orient Express, and on it Freud narrowly escapes the hell of the Holocaust:

> We didn't all leave at the same time. Dorothy was the first, Minna on May 5, Martin on the 14th, Mathilde and Robert on the 24th, ourselves incidentally not until the Saturday before Pentecost, June 3.[32]

As Paul Witz points out, the Breslau train-journey, some sixty years before, was also undertaken around the time of Pentecost; in that sense the train *to* hell and the train *from* hell both run (to quote Freud), at 'the same time'.[33] After Einstein, though, it is difficult to speak of 'the same time', an irony demonstrated not only by trains but also Pentecost which is, of course, a Christian holiday superimposed upon an older, Jewish festival. Freud often refers to the disagreement between the 'Jewish calendar'[34] and the Christian, and in this respect he is always doing double-time, time that is at once both Jewish *and* Christian. This is never more obvious than when Freud takes the train out of Austria, of which journey Freud writes:

> I sometimes compare myself with the old Jacob who, when a very old man, was taken by his children to Egypt . . . Let us hope it will not be followed by an exodus from Egypt.[35]

The train out of Austria may be a train *from* hell, but if it leads to Egypt, the place of Jewish slavery, then Freud is also on a train *to* hell. This is an ambiguity of which Freud is clearly aware. What he *does* seem to overlook is that the train is running not only to a Jewish timetable but a Christian one, for if Freud is imagining an escape to Egypt another obvious comparison is Christ who, when a child, is taken to Egypt to escape from the genocidal Herod.[36] On the train to England Freud is not only Jacob but Jesus, the *infant* Jesus; at last, Freud has caught a children's train out of Austria and, indeed, done so as a kind of a Christ, just as he once had hoped.

It is, though, a train that might trouble both the Freudian and the Christian, since for all the talk of relativity and a train that goes at once both to and from hell, we cannot avoid the simple, uncomfortable fact that the infant Jesus and the aged Freud each escape a massacre of the innocents that others are left to endure: in Christ's case, all male Jews under two; in Freud's case, six million Jews, including four of his five sisters.[37] In November 1938 Freud writes, from London, that 'the latest horrifying events in Germany aggravate the problem of what to do about the four old women between 75 and 80. To maintain them in England is beyond our powers.'[38] As a young man of twenty-nine Freud had written, 'I have often felt as though I had inherited all the passions with which our ancestors defended their temple and could gladly sacrifice my life for one great moment in history'; the fact is, however, that in 1938 the only way in which Freud could participate in a great, though terrible, moment of history *was* by sacrificing, or at least risking, his life.[39] Old, and dying of cancer, he chose not to. In this sense the departing Freud took a train out of history. The same may be said of the infant Christ; the only difference is that Jesus takes the train *back* to history, by returning to Jerusalem to be crucified. Indeed, Christ *keeps* taking the train back. Witness, of course, the *Quo Vadis* legend in which he is going to Rome to be crucified *again*; witness too Freud's fellow passenger with his talk of 'new editions, of the Saviour'.[40] According to this train of thought, the death-camp trains were packed full of new Christs.

Freud, though, does *not* follow this train of thought, he makes no remarks whatsoever upon these 'new editions of the Saviour'; the train of psycho-analysis cannot, it seems, bear such a heavy load. Freud knows that 'history weighs heavily', and is also well aware of the load or weight of the divine – referring to his collection of little Egyptian gods, Freud once remarked that 'my old and grubby gods . . . work as paperweights for my manuscripts'.[41] Divinity may weigh, literally, upon Freud's writing but Freud seems to sense that Christ might well be a quite impossible load to bear. In 1921 Freud cites the old conundrum:

> 'Christopher bore Christ; Christ bore the whole world; Say, where did Christopher then put his foot?'[42]

If Christ is an impossible load to carry then it is no wonder that Freud's Jewish Christ is continually made to get off the train to Karlsbad. Indeed, there is a sense in which the tragic, *via dolorosa* Christ is also continually being made to get off the psychoanalytic train, for this man of sorrows has no ticket to ride on a train that is invariably coupled to Jewish humour. As Adam Biro observes in his book *Two Jews on a Train,* this phrase alone provokes Jewish laughter.[43] Admittedly, Freud himself tends to think of psychoanalysis as 'my grave philosophy', and equally grave is, at least, his *vision* of the train: in 'A Case of Homosexuality in a Woman' (1920), Freud describes the analysis as a long and difficult 'train [journey] . . . into a distant country' where the analysand's 'resistance [to analysis] has in the same way withdrawn to a [still more distant] . . . boundary . . . beyond which it proves . . . unconquerable – Russian tactics, as they might be called.'[44] Here the train of analysis is deliberately imagined to repeat Napoleon's doomed incursion into the vast snow-bound interior of Russia; indeed, since Freud's patient once 'flung herself . . . on to the . . . railway line', Freud's Russian train has, as part of its Christian unconscious, not only Dostoyevsky's saintly Idiot arriving at the station in freezing Petersburg but Tolstoy's Anna Karenin – she who 'crossed herself' before famously flinging herself onto the Moscow railway line. [45] Freud, though, remains quite unaware of these quasi-Christs that steal aboard his train of analysis – in that respect, they too are no sooner on board than they are thrown off again. But that is because, despite himself, Freud's train is bound not so much for the tragic depth epitomized by Russia but rather the comic superficialities epitomised by England – in 1939 Graham Greene writes of 'Anglo-Saxon absurdity'.[46]

Freud does, of course, literally take the train to London in 1938, but as early as the 1860s he considers emigrating to England, a country that *is*, somehow, aligned with the theological absurdity of the dreams he seeks to rationalize. Note how, in 1916, Freud writes of a splendid dream in which, he is told, 'God wore a paper cocked-hat on his head'.[47] The very next dream-analysis involves an Englishman on 'a steamer between Dover and Calais' but, with this absurd vision of God in a hat, Freud himself could almost be on the steamer to Dover; for it is a vision which finds a distinct echo in that most famous English dream-train, the train in *Alice Through the Looking Glass*. Tenniel's illustration of the train features, in the same carriage as Alice, a caricature of Benjamin Disraeli wearing, of all things, a paper cocked-hat on his head (p. 56).[48] Not quite God with a silly hat on, but at least a Jewish Prime Minister. In England, it seems, even the most absurd religious dream might just find expression. When the Englishman on the steamer quotes the phrase,

'It is only a step from the sublime to the ridiculous',

a Frenchman replies,

'Yes . . . *le pas de Calais* – meaning that he thought France sublime and England ridiculous.'[49]

As well he might – observe that the Wolf Man's 'English governess . . . turn[s] . . . out to be an eccentric'; and that when Freud reaches England in 1938 he is positively beset by 'hordes of . . . cranks [and] lunatics . . . who send tracts . . . from the Gospels which promise salvation, attempt to convert the unbeliever, and shed light on the future of Israel'.[50]

This is not, by any means, the only occasion in which England is home

to what Freud calls 'the absurdities that religious doctrines put before us'.[51] At times, indeed, in England these absurdities are seen, or performed as something to be flaunted, even celebrated. Whilst Freud asks of religion, 'Am I to be obliged to believe *every* absurdity?', the Queen in Carroll's *Alice* has '"sometimes . . . believed as many as six impossible things before breakfast"';[52] again, whilst in Austria Freud diagnoses as paranoid a man called Schreber who believes that God communicates with him via a special 'ray-connection', in England at the same moment one William Coldbrook is able to publish a book on Revelation called *The Invention of the Telephone Predicted by Saint John* (1891);[53] and finally, whilst Schreber is treated for 'believ[ing] . . . he had a mission to redeem the world [once he is] first transformed into a woman', in England Florence Nightingale has already prophesied that 'the next Christ will . . . be female'.[54] Perhaps she should have said 'the next Christ will be *effeminate and, indeed, in England*', for Schreber gives 'the month of November 1895, as the date at which the connection was established between the emasculation fantasy and the Redeemer idea', and it was in November 1895 that Oscar Wilde famously stood for half an hour at Clapham Junction as both a convicted 'sodomite' and a Christ all mocked and ridiculed:

> On November 13th 1895 I was brought down here from London. From two o'clock till half-past two. . . . I had to stand on the centre platform of Clapham Junction in convict dress and handcuffed, for the world to look at. . . . Of all possible objects I was the most grotesque. . . . When people saw me they laughed. Each train as it came up swelled the audience. . . . For half an hour I stood there in the grey November rain surrounded by a jeering mob.[55]

Wilde, though, may just have known that such railway laughter was coming, for *The Importance of Being Earnest* is not only a comedy of English manners but a comedy of English trains:

> LADY BRACKNELL: In what locality did this Mr. James . . . come across this ordinary hand-bag?
> JACK: In the cloak-room at Victoria Station. It was given to him in mistake for his own.
> LADY BRACKNELL: The cloak-room at Victoria Station?
> JACK: Yes. The Brighton line.
> LADY BRACKNELL: The line is immaterial.[56]

Illustration on p. 56

'The man in white paper', by John Tenniel, from *Through the Looking Glass* (1871). By permission of the British Library.

In 1850 John Ruskin writes that 'the railroad is in all its relations a matter of earnest business'[57] and, though Wilde is concerned with *not* being earnest about trains, at Clapham Junction Wilde becomes a Christ for whom the comic potential of railway stations explodes into quite unbearable laughter. Here the author of *Being Earnest* endures, if you will, the unbearable lightness of being Christ, or at least of being at a station. For to stand at a station is, in a sense, not to *be* anywhere. As Martin Heidegger, the great philosopher of Being, remarks: 'railway stations . . . are not dwelling places', or not Being-places, one might say.[58]

For Heidegger, of course, the problem of Being is a universal problem; thus we get closer to Wilde – and, as we shall see, Freud – if we go via Derrida who writes, cryptically, of '*The Importance of (Not) Being Christian*'.[59] For Derrida, the general problem of Being is here strangely entangled with the particular problem of Being Christian; still more specifically, it is entangled with *Oscar Wilde's* problem with Being Christian. In this cryptic Derridean moment, Being seems to be, all at once, a Christian problem, a Wildean problem, an English problem, a comic problem and a train problem – and that, in a sense, is how Freud sees it as well. For when, in *The Psychopathology of Everyday Life* (1901), Freud jokingly says to one patient 'today we shall really be in Ernest [*Ernst*]', what he really means, *we* might jokingly say, is 'today we shall really be *in England*' since, after Wilde, whose notoriety spread across Europe, the Ernest joke is forever England.[60]

Just forty pages before, Wilde's name is one of a string of otherwise continental names cited by a woman who is trying to recall the name of Carl Jung; for this woman, at least, Wilde's English name has an uncanny place within the continental science of psychoanalysis.[61] But then, in a sense, Wilde is Freud's key English connection, since in England Freud *is* Ernest – not only Ernest Jones, his English friend and biographer, but Ernst, the son who had moved to England ahead of Freud.[62] The irony in all this is that, for Freud, at a conscious level, the Christian name that is forever England is the name of John; Freud has a 'cousin' called John who, after being a very close childhood friend, lives in England for the rest of his life.[63] John, of course, is a *really* earnest name, it being, as Freud himself points out, 'the favourite first name in European Christendom'.[64] This, though, does not prevent Freud's memory of cousin-John undergoing constant change; 'since childhood', writes Freud, 'John has had very many incarnations [*Inkarnationen*]'.[65] 'Incarnation', as we know, is itself a profoundly Christian word, or name, recalling *St* John's famous celebration of *the* Incarnation at the beginning of his Gospel; in this sense, one of cousin-John's incarnations is as God – elsewhere, Freud points out that the name 'John', or 'Jochanon' is 'compounded with an abbreviation of the Hebrew "Yahweh."'[66] Here again one of Freud's rare religious trains of thought chances upon Oscar Wilde. This time it is Wilde's absurdist declaration that 'anything may happen to a person called John' – not least, of course, to be called 'Jack' and then to be baptized as 'Ernest', thus exchanging *the* first name of Christendom for what, after Wilde, becomes (to use a telling phrase of Freud's), 'a name for someone *who could not keep his own*'.[67] To change from 'John' to 'Ernest' may seem like a fall from grace – but to change, it turns out, is in the very nature of grace, or God; for John-cum-Jochannon-cum-Yahweh is itself a name for someone who cannot keep his name. And that is one obvious lesson of *The Importance*, where John-cum-Jack Worthing finds out, in the play's final two denouements, that he *had* once been Ernest, it was simply that through being orphaned he had not succeeded in keeping his name. He had made the mistake of being left at Victoria Station.

Freud's *own* Ernest does manage to keep his name; indeed, it is passed safely on to his nephew, the boy whom Freud in 1920 recalls playing that *game* of keeping which Freud famously called *fort/da* – the game of repeatedly throwing a reel on a string into a curtained cot and then pulling it back.[68] As Derrida points out, the watching Freud asks himself why little Ernst 'never seemed to have the idea of pulling the spool behind him and playing at its being a [railway] carriage'.[69] Freud's Ernst will not play trains; instead, the child is stuck in a game of repetition in which Freud famously sees the terrible spectre of *Thanatos*, the death-drive that had just helped to propel eight million toward their deaths in the First World War. By contrast, Wilde's Ernest, who *is* exposed to the chances and changes of the railways from infancy, grows up to play the Christian game of change that is baptism. Wilde's train-wise Ernest knows nothing about the importance of Being but everything about the importance of becoming; and it is this Ernst that Freud is, unconsciously, looking for when he asks why Ernst does not play trains. Had Ernst done so there would have been no *fort/da*, no *Thanatos* – perhaps even no First World War. If only Ernst *had* played trains.

War to war

> It was on the . . . panic-stricken breath of war, that Freud's voice reached us.
> (Jacques Lacan)[70]

If the game of *fort/da* disturbs Freud then how much more the game of just *fort*!, the game of 'Gone!' that the boy starts to play once the First World War begins:

> A year later, the same boy . . . used to take a toy, if he was angry with it, and throw it on the floor exclaiming: 'Go to the fwont!' He had heard at that time that his absent father was 'at the front', and was far from regretting his absence.[71]

The game of 'Go to the fwont!' was, of course, played for real; indeed, it was a game at which Freud's own profession was particularly adept. With many soldiers leaving the front with shell-shock the army psychiatrists were turned, as Freud puts it, 'into something like machine guns behind the front'.[72] They too cried 'Go to the fwont!' No wonder one contemporary referred to Vienna's army psychiatrists as 'executioners'; the returning soldier was dead before he reached the front, killed before a shot was fired. It was, in a sense, an appalling realization of Freudian dreamtime:

> In dreams . . . what precedes an event usually comes after it . . . like a theatrical production by a third-rate touring company in which the hero falls down dead and the shot that killed him is not fired in the wing till afterwards.[73]

Simultaneity is a recurring problem in Freud. But then we might expect this, given that psychoanalysis is so entangled in the strange nature of time at the Front; writing in 1914, Freud remarks that the tortuous process of analysis

> is the same as when today an enemy army needs weeks and months to make its way across a stretch of country which in times of peace was traversed by an express train in a few hours and which only a short time before had been passed over by the defending army in a few days.[74]

Later on in the war, Freud compares psychoanalysis to 'air-reconnaissance'.[75] However, to see from the sky is to see all at once, to escape into a dimension in which simultaneity is not impossibilized by the partial perspectives of trench warfare; and it is this partial, disordered war-from-below that is uncannily evoked when Freud writes of the hero who falls before he is shot – note that he is writing in 1917. The trenches of Flanders are full of heroes who are effectively dead *before* they are shot: not only the shell-shocked returnees but the many who knew death was just a matter of time, and the still unluckier few who even bled before they were shot, those who literally sweated blood – as Wilfred Owen reports, 'Foreheads of men have bled where no wounds were.'[76]

Such men resemble Christ on the night before his crucifixion, the night when, according to Luke's Gospel, 'his sweat was, as it were, great drops of blood'.[77] Owen, faced by the untimely or anachronistic figure of the man who is dead before he is killed, thus chances upon the figure of Christ. And Freud does much the same thing at much the same time. Witness his wartime discussion of what he calls, after Nietzsche, the 'Pale Criminal', the back-to-front criminal in whom, absurdly, the 'pre-existence of the feeling of guilt [leads to] a [criminal] deed, [simply] in order to rationalize this feeling [of guilt]';[78] the 'Pale Criminal' whose guilt comes *before* his crime is, of course, a close relation of the 'Pale Galilean' – the Saviour who was killed for the crimes of generations not yet even born.[79] Freud himself does not seem to see the Pale Galilean as a Pale Criminal but then he leaves such investigations to us: 'let us leave it to future research to decide how many criminals are to be reckoned among these "pale" ones'.[80]

Since Freud is writing in 1917, we who are now doing that research are more concerned with just how criminal were the 'executioners' who cried 'go to the fwont!' Amongst these executioners we might even reckon Freud himself, if not as a psychiatrist then as a father. Freud was initially proud to see both his sons go to war: in 1915 he refers to Austria as 'that nation, in whose language we write, and for whose victory our dear ones are fighting'.[81] For Wilfred Owen, Freud's generation were, indeed, nothing but executioners: in 'The Parable of the Old Men and the Young' Owen famously relates the biblical story of Abraham and Isaac – this time, though, when God tells Abraham to kill a ram rather than Isaac

> . . . the old man would not so, but slew his son, –
> And half the seed of Europe, one by one.[82]

Owen's vision of a Eurocidal Abraham may seem a long way from Freud sending his sons to war but it is precisely how he imagines himself in this strange confession of 1900:

> How attractive to fantasize that you are . . . one of those mighty individuals who, by the power of their thoughts and their blazing eloquence alone, rule the city at the time when the heart of humanity is throbbing there; who out of conviction send thousands of human beings to their deaths as they pave the way for the transformation of Europe.[83]

If, in this peculiar moment, Freud is Owen's Eurocidal Abraham then, in the next moment, he is also Owen's *Isaac*; for Freud curiously adds that he is one of those executioners 'who . . . know that their own heads are not safe, and that one day they will lay them beneath the knife of the guillotine!' In somehow playing both killer *and* killed, Abraham *and* Isaac, Freud effectively revisits the drama that Kierkegaard had established, in a book Freud knew, as the primal scene of Christian selfhood.[84] This is, of course, that scene or moment of 'fear and trembling' in which the convicted sinner (Pale Criminal that he is) awaits, like Isaac, an imminent execution that is not, in the end, carried out – the Pale Galilean dies in his place. Indeed, in imagining the process of 'climbing the scaffold' to face the guillotine, Freud echoes that paradigmatic Christian self, Dostoyevsky's Idiot, for he too imagines what it must be like to 'put your head under the blade and . . . hear it sliding towards you'.[85]

Though Freud-the-victim may be a kind of Idiot, Freud-the-executioner – the figure who 'would send thousands to their death' – is someone else altogether, and it is in being, at once, both Isaac *and* Abraham, Christ *and* Pilate, that Freud chances upon that new scene of Christian selfhood, the trenches. For there, contrary to popular secularist narratives, Christ did not simply disappear but rather was re-imagined in the person of the soldier; and contrary to popular religious narratives, these soldier-Christs were not just passive victims but trained killers.[86] The 'Jesus in the trenches' may be nailed to a cross but he is still firing bullets. Admittedly he has, in a sense, been doing so for some while: in *The Idiot* one army general relates how in battle 'a bullet ricocheted off the cross on my chest and [went] straight through [another man's] . . . forehead'.[87] In Flanders, however, the cross fires not just one bullet but round after round, 'Golgotha' being a nick-name for No Man's Land, the site of fiercest battle.[88] In a bitter conceit, Owen writes of 'teaching Christ to lift his cross by numbers . . . stand . . . to attention . . . [and grow] familiar with the topography of Golgotha'.[89] The first Golgotha was, of course, a hill which in battle is a position of strength, or advantage; at the Front, then, a Christ familiar with Golgotha is a figure of strength as well as weakness, a killer as well as a casualty. And Christ is certainly a far from passive figure in 'Group Psychology' (1921), where Freud compares the Church to the Army; here, Christ is 'Commander-in-Chief',[90] the one who sends thousands into battle. Christ's capacity for doing so is only enhanced, of course, by the vantage point afforded by the hill of Golgotha, not to mention its tree, the cross: according to Freud, 'a person . . . on a tree can see everything that is going on below him [but] . . . cannot himself be seen'.[91] Indeed, once that person is nailed to the tree it too might just *become* a kind of weapon: when Freud visits one elderly hysteric she comes to the door 'armed [*bewaffnet*] with a small . . . crucifix concealed in her hand'.[92]

This Christian comes bearing arms; but then Freud is a Jew in anti-Semitic Vienna – for him, all Christians are, in a sense, armed. With the Nazi invasion of Austria, those whom Freud called 'Christian Aryan[s]' would come to the door quite literally armed, come to *your* door, that is.[93] Some Christians, however, did in effect *defend* the Jews; as Freud remarks, in 1935, 'only . . . Catholicism protects us against Naziism [sic]'.[94] Freud, it seems, lives at a time when Christ is not only armed but appears to fight on two sides at once. This was particularly clear in the *First* World War when, as Robert Graves observes, of the Battle of the Somme, 'Christ was being invoked alike by both the German and the Allies.'[95] However familiar Christ might be with the topography of No Man's Land he would still not know which way to shoot; in this respect the Christ of the First World War endured an appalling and absurd extension of Kierkegaard's 'armed neutrality'.[96] Christ's neutrality consisted not, it seems, in not shooting but in shooting *both* ways, at himself and . . . at himself. Well might Siegfried Sassoon ask, in 'Christ and the Soldier' (1916), 'be you for both sides?' As Wilfred Owen puts it, 'Christ is literally in no man's land.'[97] The topography of Golgotha had never been so difficult to map.

But if anyone could have done the mapping it was Freud, for the Golgotha of No Man's Land was very much *his* space. It is here his three sons are fighting. It is here that analysis takes place, in that 'stretch of country' which 'to-day an . . . army needs weeks and months to make its way across'.[98] And it is here that the psychoanalysts belong: Freud, fearful that psychoanalysis might be rejected by both the superstitious and the scientific, compares the position of analysts to that of war refugees who stand 'half-way between two hostile nations . . . and are treated as enemies' by both.[99] One obvious difficulty in mapping such a No Man's Land is that the war Freud has in mind erased so many landmarks, making a nowhere of somewhere; nevertheless, by 1921 Freud does, in a sense, map this nowhere for he adopts it, almost unwittingly, as a trope for that homeless, or nation-less, betwixt-and-between term, the ego:

> the repressed is foreign territory to the ego – *internal* foreign territory – just as reality . . . is *external* foreign territory.[100]

This is, of course, a rarefied and purely allegorical version of No Man's Land; though it may tell us much about the alienated ego, it tells us little about the pain and horror of the new Golgotha. But then Freud the allegorist, for whom 'everything is related to everything else', does tend to allegorize the pain of Golgotha; witness what happens when Freud is confronted with an hysteric who, under the pressure of Freud's hand on her eyes, sees, *inter alia*, 'a large black cross':

> I suspected an allegorical meaning and asked what the cross could be. 'It probably means pain', she replied. I objected that by 'cross' one usually meant moral burden. What lay concealed behind the pain?[101]

In so confidently declaring that the cross should have allegorical meaning, Freud appears untroubled by the possibility that the cross might just constitute that most terrible pain – pain *without* meaning. Here Freud seems to be a Jew who finds the cross all too easy to interpret, a Jew who is the exception to St Paul's rule that 'Christ crucified [is] unto the Jews a stumblingblock.'[102] This episode, however, dates from 1895, almost twenty years before the war, twenty years in which early Modernism would continuously lay liege to sense or meaning – a siege that climaxes with Nietzsche going so far as to announce 'the meaninglessness of suffering'; no wonder, then, that by 1914 Europe was ready to throw itself into a meaningless Golgotha.[103] This transition is clear in Freud's own writing, for by 1913 he *does* seem ready to read the cross as an affront to sense: 'the notion of a god dying', he writes, 'strikes us to-day as shockingly presumptuous'.[104]

Freud, it seems, is now ready to find the cross to be a stumbling-block, he is ready to stumble, as it were; but to stumble is, perchance, to limp which is, of course, another sign of being Jewish, of having wrestled, like Jacob, with an angel. And indeed, Freud certainly talks about limping from the beginning of the century. In a letter composed in May 1900, alluding to an unspecified bout of depression, Freud declares:

> when breath threatened to fail me in the struggle I prayed the angel to desist, and that is what he has done . . . since then I have been noticeably limping. Well, I really am forty-four now, a rather shabby old Jew.[105]

Twenty years later, after a whole world war spent stumbling over the disputed 'stretch of country' that is analysis, Freud's limping is profoundly symbolic; for come the end of his post-war meditation, *Beyond the Pleasure Principle*(1920), Freud declares, or rather quotes: 'What we cannot reach flying we must reach limping . . . The Book tells us it is no sin to limp.'[106] We should note the 'us'; Freud here identifies his work with 'the slow advances of . . . scientific knowledge' – it is not just the shabby old Jew who limps but also that gleaming new giant, modern science. Twentieth-century science may well believe it strides ahead of religion, and often Freud echoes this conviction; however, at the end of *Beyond*, he senses that wherever secular science goes, there the limping figure of the Jew will be. This is quite literally the case, in that the most exciting area of inter-war science, quantum physics, was not only inspired by Einstein but so dominated by Jews that it was known as 'Jewish physics'.[107] It is also metaphorically the case in that, for Freud, the various inventions of modern science mean that 'Man has, as it were, become, a kind of Prosthetic God . . . [whose] auxiliary organs . . . have not [yet] grown on to him and . . . [so] still give him much trouble'; scientific man may be a God but he is only a Prosthetic God, a God with limbs that do not yet work properly – he still limps, as it were, just like the Jew.[108]

It is in 1929 that Freud writes of the 'Prosthetic God', by which time

Freud himself has a prosthetic jaw; it had been fitted in 1924 to replace the parts of his jaw that had become cancerous. By 1929, then, Freud's chief difficulty is not in walking but in speaking.[109] He thereby lives out, with uncanny precision, the curious psychosomatic fate of the woman called Mathilda who, as Freud records, '"accidentally ran a nail through her foot [and] . . . a few days afterwards . . . died of lockjaw" – as a result of this displaced antisepsis'.[110] For 'Matilda' read 'Freud' – or, to quote Freud from elsewhere, read 'this Mathilda for that Mathilda', since Freud too dies because of his jaw;[111] and, indeed, it is almost as if the infirmity comes to the jaw from the foot, for thirty-eight years after describing himself as 'a shabby old Jew' with a limp, the dying Freud begins his very last book, *Moses and Monotheism*, with a striking vision of sublimely strong feet: 'To my critical sense', he declares, 'this book . . . appears like a dancer balancing on the tip of one toe.'[112]

In the same prefatory note Freud remarks that, since he arrived in England, many well-meaning strangers 'have pointed out to me the way of Christ'; and, certainly, by dreaming of balancing on one toe Freud has, in a sense, left the way of the Jew. For, in the nineteenth century, Jacob's mythical limp increasingly led to insistent, pseudo-scientific claims that Jews had flat feet.[113] By contrast, the nineteenth-century Christian might be said to have the pointed feet of the ballet dancer – or at least, as Freud would have known, that is how Kierkegaard sees it; *à propos* 'the movement of faith', Kierkegaard observes:

> the [Christian] dancer's hardest task is to [land] . . . in . . . a definite position, so that not for a second does he have to catch at the position but stands there in it in the leap itself.[114]

Landing as he does on such little ground, this Christian dancer could be mistaken for Saint Christopher, whose impossible task of bearing Christ prompts Freud to ask, of course, 'where did Christopher . . . put his foot?' Christopher, it seems, could also stand on one toe. And if to do so is to stand like a surrealist Kierkegaardian saint then Freud is still more saintly when declaring, 'I hover, so to speak, in the air.'[115] Freud might, then, be speaking better than he knows when, again in 1938, he complains that 'surrealists have apparently chosen me for their . . . saint'.[116] Of course, for Kierkegaard, every saint is a surrealist saint of a sort, and Freud – whose original name, 'Sigismund', is a saint's name – is certainly surrealist when balancing on one toe within a year of his death. Freud has one foot in the grave, but it is pointed and poised like a ballet dancer.

Freud, though, was not buried but cremated; so, to be precise, he has one foot not in the grave but in the ashes. And this he knows, in that, just five years before, his books had been burned in Berlin and, as his hero

Heine once wrote, 'Where men burn books / They will burn people also in the end' – *Jewish* people, of course; as Freud reminds Jung: 'one way or other, the Jew will be burned'.[117] Freud's balletic toe recalls, then, an earlier Freudian foot, the one that leaves 'an imprint . . . in ashes', the ashes of Pompeii.[118] This is the foot of the eponymous heroine of Wilhelm Jensen's novel, *Gradiva*. The name 'Gradiva' – literally, 'the girl who steps along' – is given to a girl in a Roman bas-relief, a girl who is imagined to have been in Pompeii when Vesuvius erupted; as Freud observes:

> [she had] one foot rested squarely on the ground; the other, lifted from the ground in the act of following after, touched it only with the tips of the toes, while the sole and heel rose almost perpendicularly.[119]

Poised on the toe of one foot, the aged Freud may cut the figure of a Kierkegaardian saint, the figure of one who defies both gravity and the grave; but he is also and at the same time haunted by the spectre of an incinerated 'Jew', one who is utterly defeated by the deadly gravity of falling ash. In short, the balletic Freud is a figure both of Christian levity and Jewish gravitas.

This gravitas is also to be felt in Freud's 1914 analysis of Michelangelo's statue of Moses; this Moses is seated whilst clasping the Tablets of the Law and 'has', observes Freud, 'his right foot rest[ing] . . . on the ground and his left leg . . . raised so that only the toes touch the ground'.[120] Though raised, this left foot speaks of enormous Jewish gravity for the simple and terrible reason that it is raised only in order that Moses can 'spring to his feet . . . [and] dash the Tables to the earth'.

Bridge out into

What, though, should be made of the *joking* Jew, he who so *cheats* gravity that, like the hovering Freud, he has not just one foot off the ground but two? The Gentile may never really know. For in the joke about the 'Jew . . . in a train [who] . . . put his feet up on the seat', as soon as the 'gentleman in modern dress entered the compartment . . . the Jew promptly . . . took up a proper pose' – this Jew puts his feet down as soon as he thinks a Gentile may be looking; he only defies gravity when the Gentile is not looking.[121] Nevertheless, what the reader here sees, or over-sees, is a Jew who, with his outstretched legs, makes a sort of human bridge. And that is what we also just occasionally glimpse in Freud's own writing; for, time and again, Freud is surreptitiously building bridges. In Breuer and Freud's *Studies in Hysteria,* Breuer confesses to all 'the gaping lacunas' that their 'hypotheses have [only] . . . concealed rather than bridged!';

Freud, though, is less confident of this neat distinction. In 1934 he writes in a letter that 'where there is an unbridgeable gap [*Lücke*] in history and biography, the writer can step in and try and guess how it all happened'.[122] Freud's work is full, he implies, of hypothetical bridges; and, indeed, often these bridges are weak. Commenting on not just dreams but dream interpretations, Freud observes that 'No connection [is] . . . too loose, no joke too bad, to serve as a bridge [*Brücke*] from one thought to another.'[123]

As if to underline the point, when interpreting one of his own dreams, through a chain of punning associations, Freud confesses that it is 'as if nothing were sacred to my urge to create . . . word-bridges [*Wortbrücke*]'.[124] In his *New Introductory Lectures* (1933)Freud insists on the scientist's 'assured knowledge of the external world' and declares that, without this knowledge, 'we might build bridges just as well out of cardboard as out of stone'.[125] But if Freud builds bridges out of loose connections and jokes then he too builds absurd, improbable bridges; and indeed, in coming up with a cardboard bridge, Freud unwittingly builds a bridge worthy of the very Surrealists whom he is so keen to disown. However, *before* there were any Surrealists around to appropriate him, Freud was quite prepared to be seen building absurd buildings; in *The Interpretation*, he boldly declares that 'we have been obliged to build our way out into the dark'.[126] Freud, it seems, is building a bridge that may lead nowhere, a bridge out into darkness. It is a conceit that is not just surreal but quasi-religious; if, earlier in *The Interpretation*, 'nothing were sacred' against Freud's urge to build word-bridges now it is clear that these absurd bridges themselves might just be sacred, *darkly* sacred. And none is more absurdly sacred, or religious than the almost self-parodic word-bridge that Freud has just been building: namely,

> *Pélagie—plagiarism—plagiastomes* [large fish . . .]—fish's bladder . . . [and finally] . . . overcoats, which obviously signify a piece of sexual equipment.[127]

Pélagie, or Pelagia is, as Freud explains, a character in *Hypatia*, Charles Kingsley's novel about the early Church – and, indeed, though Freud does not see it, we might read in(to) this bizarre chain of associations a surreal Christian comedy. It is a comedy in which early Christians actually *become* the fish they adopt as their secret identities, fish which in turn provide the bladders, which in turn become the overcoats, which in turn 'obviously signify [that] . . . piece of sexual equipment' known as a condom.[128] In short, for Christians read condoms. If this is comedy, it is undermined by the fact that Kingsley's *Hypatia* is primarily about the early Christians raping and murdering the eponymous female philosopher. On this particular word-bridge stand not only Christians who are absurd but Christians who are killers; even this comic bridge is being built out into the dark.

A year later, in the *Psychopathology of Everyday Life* (1901), the figure of another Christian appears on another dark, Freudian bridge. Freud is telling the story of a man on a train who, on a 'pitch-dark night', is crossing the frontier between France and Spain over the Bidassoa Bridge and, in doing so, recalls a poem that declares 'the soul is already free'; quite why this line comes into his head the man cannot fathom until he later discovers that, over the page in the book in which the poem appears, is another poem that opens with 'On Bidassoa Bridge there stands a saint grey with age'.[129] Grey as he is, this saint stands on a bridge that builds out into the dark that is death; indeed, the saintly, Christian claim that 'the soul is free' is far from convincing – if only because this freedom is not shared by the Jew: forty years later Walter Benjamin also stands on the French-Spanish border as he attempts to flee Nazi-occupied France – upon being told that an exit visa is required, Benjamin commits suicide.

Like frontiers, bridges have been used to control the movement of Jews.[130] Hence the relief with which Freud, in describing his flight from Austria, writes 'Over the Rhine bridge and we were free!'[131] The Rhine bridge had only recently fallen into Nazi hands, but in Catholic Europe bridges have always been alien to the Jew, have always been Christian in the sense that, as Immanuel Velikovsky notes, 'the Pope as 'Pontiff' is named after *pons*, the Latin for 'bridge.''[132] The Jew, it seems, might have especial reason to suspect a bridge; and there is evidence that he does: in 1901 the Jewish thinker Georg Simmel aphoristically delares that, 'one cannot live on a bridge'; whilst in *Daniel Deronda* (1876), a novel Freud knew well, the Jew Mordecai declares that 'the generations are crowding on my narrow life as a bridge . . . and the bridge is breaking'.[133]

In 1916 Freud laughs at 'the foolish saying: "Life is a suspension bridge',," but, since this follows a dream about a 'bridge [that] suddenly broke', the laughter is somewhat nervous.[134] As Simmel implies, one can only *die* on a bridge, a conceit that, with the First World War, relates to Christian as well as Jew. In 1918, after months in the trenches 'walk[ing] the unchristian ways of Christendom', Wilfred Owen is killed trying 'to bridge the [Sambre] Canal . . . with duckboards'; 'Owen . . . was . . . helping to fix them', writes Edmund Blunden, 'when he was hit and killed.'[135] And Owen is not the only Christian soldier for whom the bridge represents death. As Wyndham Lewis declares, 'a little group . . . [are] crossing a bridge. The bridge is . . . the *war*'; again, in Eliot's *The Waste Land* (1922), the crowd on London Bridge famously shades into soldiers at the Front:

> Unreal City,
> Under the brown fog of a winter dawn,
> A crowd flowed over London Bridge, so many,
> I had not thought death had undone so many.
> Sighs, short and infrequent, were exhaled . . .[136]

With the War, every bridge, even London Bridge, is a bridge of 'sighs'; something has changed, bridges will never be quite the same – not even for Christians.

Or at least that is how it seems in Freud for whom, with the onset of war, the Christian on the bridge is no longer the secure figure of the saint grey with age. Witness the dream that Freud records in 1916, the dream of a man who imagines he is a medieval Crusader-King who famously sailed through storms to reach the Holy Land:

> *He was walking, with two people whose names he knew but had forgotten when he woke up, across a very high, steep iron bridge. Suddenly they had both gone, and he saw a ghost-like man in a cap and linen-clothes. He asked him if he was the telegraph-boy. No. Was he the driver? No. Then he walked on further . . .* While he was still dreaming he felt acute anxiety, and after he had woken up he continued the dream with a phantasy that the iron bridge suddenly broke and he fell into the abyss. . . . The driver made him think of Uhland's poem about King Charles's Voyage, and reminded him of a dangerous sea-voyage with two companions during which he had played the part of the King in the poem.[137]

This Wartime Crusader on the bridge may *never*, alas, grow grey with age; for he walks across a bridge that can suddenly collapse, exposing an 'abyss' below. It is as if the War has reminded this dreamer of a medieval and intensely Christian world characterized not only by the Crusades but also by the fear of the abyss of hell; after all, the Christian soldiers of Flanders inhabit a world full of trenches, shell-craters and mass-graves.

Though it is conventional to speak of the First World War as destroying Christian belief, in Freud we sense that the War reanimates at least the Christian belief in hell. This irony is clear in *Thoughts for the Times on War and Death* (1915), where Freud talks of 'the war in which we had refused to believe'; here, albeit for only a moment, it is as if the War has proved so appalling as to shatter the *un*belief of modern humanism. We had refused to believe in our own inhumanity and have now been proved wrong.

It is usual to think that Freud is one who analyses the psychical forces behind belief; but occasionally he also seeks to dissect *un*belief, to ask why we do *not* believe. This is precisely what Freud is doing in the late text, 'A Disturbance of Memory on the Acropolis'(1936). Here Freud asks the simple question, 'Why should incredulity arise in something which promises to bring . . . pleasure?'[138] The question is prompted by Freud's recollection of a holiday trip to Greece some thirty-two years before when Freud stands on the Acropolis and is surprised to find himself thinking: '"So all this really *does* exist, just as we learnt at school!"'[139] Freud is, quite simply, surprised by his own doubt: he 'had been quite unaware that the real existence of Athens, the Acropolis, and the landscape around it had ever been objects of doubt'. But if Freud is surprised by doubt, *we* are surprised by the analogy he draws to express his surprise:

> If I may make a slight exaggeration, it was as if someone, walking beside Loch Ness, suddenly caught sight of the famous Monster, stranded upon the shore and found himself driven to the admission: 'So it really *does* exist – the sea-serpent we've never believed in!'

Some eighteen years after 'the war in which we had refused to believe [*glauben*]' Freud now imagines himself confronted by a '*sea-serpent* we've never believed in [*geglaubt*]'.[140] The phrasing has not changed, but the location has; this time it is not in Vienna that Freud is driven to belief but on the shore of Loch Ness. If it feels odd to think of one of our greatest European atheists as a kind of believer, it is still more odd to think of him doing his believing beside a cold Scottish Loch. It is almost as if the 'Sea of Faith' that first famously withdrew on Dover beach in 1867 has now made a bizarre return on the shore of Loch Ness and, indeed, thrown up an over-sized fish for good measure.

Freud, of course, *has* encountered the sea of faith, or what he calls, after his Christian friend Oskar Pfister, the 'oceanic feeling'. 'It is', writes Freud,

> a feeling which [Pfister] . . . would like to call a sensation of 'eternity', a feeling as of something limitless, unbounded – as it were, 'oceanic' . . . One may . . . rightly call oneself religious on the ground of this oceanic feeling alone.[141]

Freud adds, however, that 'I cannot discover this "oceanic" feeling in myself'. Freud, it seems, feels he lives inland, far from any sea of faith; and so he does, in the sense that the 'young science' of psychoanalysis occupies

> a stretch of new country, which has been reclaimed [*abgewonnen*] from popular beliefs and mysticism. . . . It is a work of culture – not unlike the draining of the Zuider Zee.[142]

The sea, though, is not so easily drained from the reclaimed land of psychoanalysis; even when the sea is gone it still leaves its traces, above all its fish. As Freud remarks in *The Interpretation,* his 'first scientific task . . . concerned [a study of] the nervous system of . . . fish' and, in a sense, he never stops studying nervous fish.[143] For, as Freud reminds us, we are all fish of a kind: 'not only are all . . . man's ancestors descended from aquatic creatures . . . but every . . . human being spent the first phase of its existence in water . . . as an embryo in its mother's uterus'.[144] If we are not, though, born aquatic then we might just become aquatic upon entering the clinic: psychoanalysis is 'open', writes Freud, 'to the suspicion of being an . . . esoteric doctrine eager to . . . fish in troubled waters'.[145] In a letter to Fliess, Freud once wrote, 'I believe I am in a cocoon, and God knows what sort of beast will crawl out'; this, perhaps, remains a mystery but Freud's patients do, at times, emerge as fish: in another letter to Fliess, written less than two years later, Freud makes the cryptic remark that 'a patient with whom I have been negotiating, a "goldfish," has just announced herself'.[146] A week later Freud adds, 'the goldfish . . . has been caught'. Again, Freud is dealing with a fish out of water; this time, though, Freud is surprised not by doubt but stupidity, for in a further letter to Fliess, written in 1901 whilst on holiday at the seaside, Freud remarks that 'keeping company with . . . fish has already made me thoroughly stupid [*verdummt*]'.[147]

And when fish make Freud stupid they also make him pious, as *The Interpretation* reveals just a year before, in 1900; here Freud dreams a displaced version of an experience he once had on an English beach – the dream throws up a quite stupid piety. First, Freud the beach-comber:

> I was . . . occupied with a starfish . . . when a charming little girl came up to me and said: 'Is it a starfish? Is it alive?' 'Yes', I replied, '*he* is alive', and, at once, embarrassed at my mistake, [I] repeated the sentence correctly ['*It is alive*'].[148]

Next, Freud the dreamer, dreaming a displaced version of this mistake:

> I said [in my dream], referring to one of Schiller's works: 'It is *from* [Schiller] . . . ' but, noticing the mistake, I corrected myself, 'It is *by* [Schiller] . . . '.

Finally, Freud the interpreter:

> The dream replaced the . . . ['*he*'/'*it*'] error . . . by another into which a German is equally liable to fall. '*Das buch ist von Schiller*' should be translated not with a 'from' but with a 'by . . . '. The dream-work effected this replacement because of the magnificent piece of condensation that was made possible by the [similar] . . . sound of the English 'from' and the German adjective '*fromm*'.

The German word 'fromm' means pious; Freud thus gets from starfish to piety by way of a linguistic mistake and a dreamed displacement of that mistake. Freud's accidental piety is both stupid and fishy.

If this rare and fleeting moment of stupid piety comes through keeping company with fish, then there is a bizarre, dreamy logic in the fact that Freud is never more splendidly stupid than when he dreams of pious sea-voyages. For though Freud claims that he has no 'oceanic feelings', and insists that he belongs to the reclaimed land of psychoanalysis, his letters keep betraying a strangely heroic, sea-going Freud. As late as 1936 Freud declares, 'when one first catches sight of the sea [and] crosses the ocean . . . one feels oneself like a hero'; as early as 1879, Freud declares that 'there are still strange ebbs and flows; at times they carry me to the crest of certainty, and then everything flows away again and I am back on dry land. I do believe, however, that the sea is gaining'.[149] This sea in which 'I do believe' is indeed gaining; ten years later it has grown as large, or as oceanic, as the Atlantic: writing to Pfister, Freud observes, 'I [have] acquire[d] a notable similarity to Columbus. Like him, I long for – land.'[150] Freud may long for land but he is doomed to yet more sea, yet more oceanic feeling; in 1897 he writes, to Fliess, 'we shall not be ship-wrecked. Instead of the channel [*Durchfart*] we are seeking, we may find oceans [*Meere*]'.[151]

This is, of course, the fate of all those who are drawn to the sea by the oceanic feeling, the feeling of an infinitely receding horizon; Freud, though, rages against this fate, telling Fliess that 'if we do not . . . cap-size, if our constitutions [*Konstitutionen*] can stand it, we shall arrive. *Nous y arriverons*'. Freud refers, of course, to the psychoanalytic cause, but his words have a political unconscious. For whilst Freud and Fliess have, as ambitious physicians, the *physical* constitutions to guarantee arrival at a metaphoric Promised Land, as Jews they have no *political* constitution to guarantee the actual Promised Land of Israel.[152] Freud was by no means a Zionist but there is a sense in which his 'I long for – land [*Land*]' is also longing for *a* land; the German word '*Land*' can mean 'country' or 'homeland', and in 1897 the Jew does not have one. As Freud writes two years later, 'my children . . . [have no] . . . father-land of their own'.[153] By the 1930s, of course, with the rise of the Nazis, Freud's longing for a land is redoubled. As early as 1934 Freud writes to Pfister, 'events in Germany [mean that] . . . three members of my fam-ily, two sons and a son-in-law, are looking for a new country and have not yet found one'.[154] Freud adds, since Pfister is Swiss, that 'Switzerland is not one of the hospitable countries' – 'its constitution', he might have said, 'cannot stand it', cannot stand more Jews. The same may be said of all those countries to whom Jews, on overcrowded boats, sought entry – many were literally floating from country to country.[155] When, in 1936, Freud remarks of himself and his brother on holiday in the Aegean that 'we assumed . . . that we should be not allowed to land in Greece' he chances upon a terrible future.[156]

It is all too apt that Freud's 'we shall arrive' is premised by the possibility of being *dead* on arrival: 'the more detailed exploration [of the oceans] . . . will be left', Freud tells Fliess, 'to those who come after us'.[157] For Freud, death haunts not only the sea but the beach, even the pleasure beach: in 1897 he writes of the 'wish . . . that I might find, as Goethe once did, a skull on the Lido'.[158] This skull is surely the queerest fish (n)ever washed up on the Freudian shore; and indeed, it is all the more queer, or peculiar insofar as it is a Jewish skull. Freud's world, of course, was one in which racial 'science' led increasing numbers to echo Johann Friedrich Blumenbach's belief that 'even a layman could identify [a] . . . Jew's skull'.[159] What might make the skull on the Lido a Jew's skull is that Freud's world is also one in which the Jew has a problem with water. Witness Freud's repeated reference to anti-Semitic jokes about the Jew who never takes a bath and, of course, the story of the Jew on the train who will never make it to Karlsbad (literally, 'Karl's-bath'), the spa-town that many critics interpret as representing Christian baptism.[160] Even if the Jew-on-the-train does get baptized the water might well send him mad, or at least that is the satiric 'wisdom' of Freud's Viennese contemporary Fritz Löhner, who was convinced that converted Jews bore all 'the signs of baptismal hydrocephaly!'[161] The *fin-de-siècle* Jew is, though, not just *mad* in the water but *dead*; or at least that is the terrible gist of Nietzsche's remark that 'the ship of Christianity threw overboard a good part of the Jewish ballast'.[162] In the twentieth century, come the Holocaust, the Jews themselves would prove to be the ballast; there are, in a sense, six million skulls on the Lido.

In early 1900 Freud wrote to Fliess, 'I have just acquired Nietzsche, in whom I hope to find words for much that remains mute in me.'[163] What remains mute in Freud is precisely Nietzsche's conceit of the casting adrift or beaching of Israel. It is, though, a conceit that Freud is just beginning to articulate or, rather, weep over; for in *The Interpretation* Freud dreams he is 'sitting [in Sienna] on the edge of a fountain . . . greatly depressed and almost in tears'.[164] It is a grief he relates to the biblical vision of exiled Israel as a beached and stranded nation: Freud quotes the line, 'By the waters of Babylon we sat down and wept.' Freud, it seems, is learning the ancient Jewish lesson that the water-side is a place to weep, a lesson underlined by that curious 'skull on the Lido'.

If, though, the skull has a racial, or religious identity, it is as much

Christian as Jewish, for the dead centre of Christianity is Golgotha, which literally means 'the place of the skull'.[165] Of course, a lido or pleasure beach is an improbable location for Golgotha, but then, for Freud, or rather the Wolf Man, God may well be found dead on the beach:

> when [the Wolf Man] . . . heard that Christ had once cast out some evil spirits into a herd of swine which then rushed down a precipice, he thought of how his sister in the earliest years of her childhood, before he could remember, had rolled down on to the beach from the cliff-path above the harbour. She too was an evil spirit and a swine. It was a short road from here to 'God-swine'.[166]

If, for the Wolf Man, God is identical with the swine then God too has fallen down a precipice and landed dead on what has become the beach onto which the Wolf Man's sister had fallen. The skull on the Lido might be God's.

Could Freud himself ever entertain such a thought? Could he ever conceive of the beach as a place to replay the Christian drama of Easter?[167] Perhaps; when the girl on the English beach asks of the starfish Freud has just picked up, 'Is it alive?' Freud replies '*He is alive.*' This, of course, is the central affirmation of the Easter liturgy, a liturgy that Freud would have known well, if only from his childhood church-going.[168] 'He is alive' is not just a linguistic error, it is also a Christian error, or rather, *the* Christian error, since dead men do not come back to life – the skull is a stubborn reminder of that. There on the English beach Freud is not only being stupid but stupidly Christian. That, though, is what comes from keeping company with fish.[16]

Part II

Four Fish and an Umbrella

We are not 'Christians' or 'non-Christians'.
(Derrida, *Le Toucher*, 2000)

So radical a defence of Christianity that to many it may
seem like an attack.
(Kierkegaard, *The Point of View*, 1859)

The absurd: that is where Christianity begins.
(Kierkegaard, *The Sickness Unto Death*, 1849)

I should believe only in a god who understood how to dance.
(Nietzsche, *Thus Spoke Zarathustra*, 1892)

chapter four

Subterranean Soul

Dickens' Cryptic Church

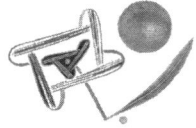

Now ye are the body of Christ. (St Paul)	What is a crypt? . . . All is cryptic. (Jacques Derrida)[1]

Undermining the city

In *Pictures from Italy* (1846), Dickens records a visit to the Cathedral in Parma that is followed by a descent to what he calls a 'subterranean church'. The 'roof', we read, was

> supported by marble pillars, behind each of which there seemed to be at least one beggar in ambush . . . From every one of these lurking-places, such crowds of phantom-looking men and women, leading other men and women with twisted limbs, or chattering jaws, or paralytic gestures, or idiotic heads, or some other sad infirmity, came hobbling out to beg, that if the ruined frescoes in the cathedral above, had been suddenly animated, and had retired to this lower church, they could hardly have made a greater confusion, or exhibited a more confounding display of arms and legs.[2]

Beneath one church lies another, a lower or subterranean church which – to echo Derrida – is not only a crypt but cryptic, a confounding 'confusion . . . of arms and legs'. To '*de*crypt' the crypt, we might, in the first place, read this confused church, this foreign body of Christ, as a displaced version of that mid-century Church of England which Dickens himself termed a 'quarrelling body'.[3] Victorian Anglicanism was riven by movements from both within and without: 'here more Popery, there more Methodism', wrote Dickens. For all their obvious differences, Victorian Catholicism and Dissent were – like the 'cathedral above' and the 'lower church' – mirror-images of each other in the sense that both were beyond what Mrs Trollope called 'the sacred pale of [the] established church', both were the object of fear and suspicion.[4]

Parma's Cathedral crypt is not, though, limited to reflecting the religious topography of England; this crypt may also be read as asylum, clinic, prison, slum, hell or night. Indeed, the crypt's capacity to be almost anything other than a crypt makes it very much a part of what Dickens calls 'my dream of churches', a strange 'vision of great churches which comes rolling past me like a sea'.[5] Dreamy and in motion, these Italian churches differ radically from Dennis Walder's account of Dickens's 'churches [as] stable . . . features of the landscape'.[6] But it is not simply that, in *Pictures*, Dickens is anatomizing the foreign, cryptic body of Roman Catholicism, for the church that Dickens writes is always, in some sense, cryptic – always, as it were, written from below. In *Great Expectations*, when Pip is turned upside down by Magwitch, 'the church . . . [is] made to go head over heels'; likewise, in *Our Mutual Friend*, the Church of St John 'with [its] four towers at the four corners . . . resembl[es], some . . . monster . . . on its back'; no less upturned is Coketown's 'New Church', the steeple of which terminates 'in four short pinnacles like florid wooden legs'.[7] Whilst the early Church was renowned for 'turn[ing] the world upside down', Dickens's churches – as if subject to the inversion of some unmentioned carnival – are *themselves* often the wrong way up.[8] In *Great Expectations*, once Pip is upon his feet again, he confidently recalls that 'the church [finally] came to itself'; however, given that Joe happily holds the 'Prayer-Book upside down', Pip's confidence might be misplaced.[9] Though Mr Wopsle still looks forward to the time when 'the Church [is] . . . "thrown open," ' that time, it seems, has already come, in the sense that the church no longer occupies a fixed or discrete cultural space. At the conclusion of Magwitch's trial, 'the audience got up (putting their dresses right, as they might at church *or elsewhere*)'; here church shades into courtroom, theatre and, indeed, 'elsewhere'.[10]

The name for that 'elsewhere', according to Thomas Carlyle, is writing: 'Pamphlets, Poems, Books', he declares in 1840, 'these are the real working effective Church of a modern country'.[11] For Carlyle, the Church, as traditionally conceived, belongs to the now superannuated world of the voice: 'While there was no . . . Printing', he declares, 'the preaching of the voice was the natural sole method [of guiding souls]'. There is, then, an especial significance in Dickens' remark in *Pictures* that '[although] many churches have crypts and subterranean chapels . . . I do not *speak* of them'. If, as Derrida suggests, 'to crypt is to cipher', or to write in code, then these crypted churches are always already a kind of writing.[12] But then so too is that ancient, underground church of the catacombs which so interests Dickens on his visit to Rome – for this is the church which exists, in the New Testament, primarily as a collection of letters: St Paul's 'Letter to the Romans', and so forth.[13] To be more precise, though, these letters are purloined letters, since we read what is not addressed to us. For the Derridean, they are postcards in the sense of being at once both private and public.[14] Indeed, it is to these New Testament postcards that *Pictures* effectively returns us, for here too the church is written in letters that are not, in the first instance, addressed to us; instead, 'the greater part of the descriptions were . . . sent home, from time to time, in private letters'.[15]

To speak, though, of Dickens's 'Postcards from Italy' – the original name for the travelogue was 'Travelling Letters' – is to distinguish Dickens sharply from Carlyle.[16] For Carlyle, the church vanishes into a writing that is still invested with all the ontology and indeed Englishness of the Book: 'He that can write a true BOOK . . . is he not the Archbishop of . . . All England?'; by contrast, in Dickens's 'Postcards from Italy' the church issues in a writing that is, quite literally, homeless and open-ended.[17] To draw again on Derrida, the 'grand and dreamy structure[s]' of Italy's churches cannot suppress their own 'structurality' – the un-structure or anti-structure that is, for Derrida, in the very nature of structure.[18] Certainly, St Peter's Church in Rome 'is an . . . edifice with no one point for the mind to rest upon', its archi*text*ure affords no centre.[19] Here (and there), church shades into writing, *ecclesia* into *écriture* – we should not forget that *écriture* can be translated as 'scripture'.

In *A Tale of Two Cities* the Dickensian church again gives us writing, or at least a parable of what Derrida calls the 'adestination' of writing, its tendency to go astray; although the 'destination' for Roger Cly's funeral procession was the 'old church of St Pancras', *the body never arrives* since, unknown to the procession, Cly is still alive.[20] With Cly as a kind of dead letter, the church here takes part in a macabre anticipation of Derrida's famous dictum that '"a letter can always *not* arrive"'.[21] The dead and the dead letter become indistinguishable in the case of the 'solitary coffin' which, in *Pictures,* Dickens encounters at the great 'Pits' outside Rome; the coffin enacts, twice over, a failure to arrive: firstly, in the sense that its final destination is not 'the church' but rather this 'blank, open, dreary space'; and secondly, in the sense that Dickens recalls how, seeing 'two initial letters scrawled upon the top . . . [I] *turned away*'.[22] These wild, Italian parables of adestination were soon, though, to become a fact of *English* death as, in response to overflowing church graveyards, the Cemetery Acts of 1852–3 decreed that the dead would no longer be interred in churchyards, would no longer get to church. Instead, they were now to be taken out of town to suburban burial grounds.[23]

To suggest that Dickens's cryptic church should be read solely in terms of writing and its detours would, though, be to follow Carlyle too closely;

unlike his mentor, Dickens also sees the church as part of an *enduring* oral-cum-aural economy. Substituting the 'labyrinth' of the crypt for that of the ear, Dickens's churches (like Manette's Soho corner), are very often an 'Ear of a place' – a place for *sound*, whether that be the 'grand tones' of the organ, the resounding of the 'clergy-man's voice', or simply 'echoes of the roof'.[24] Indeed, in *The Old Curiosity Shop* once Little Nell is outside the church she stops 'to fancy how the noise [of the children] would sound inside'.[25] For Nell, this church is not just a place in which she listens but, more particularly, a place in which she might listen to *herself* – she is, inevitably, a part of the noise outside. Derrida suggests that the idea or ideal of hearing-oneself-speak (*s'entendre parler*), is a vital part of the phonocentric dream of speech; and if we listen to the 'knell' in 'Nell' we might well declare that the church is never more phonocentric than when the bell tolls.[26] In vibrating, the bell not only rings but acts like an eardrum; it thus epitomizes the seemingly unmediated self-presence of *s'entendre parler*. In *Little Dorrit* the bells of Ludgate Hill, after initially ringing out 'Come to church', proceed to hammer out, 'They *won't* come' – in so doing they appear to hear themselves speaking.[27]

The church bell's implication in an oral-cum-aural economy may well mean the bell will always toll, nostalgically, for presence; however, the bell in Dickens also belongs to an oral-cum-aural *sub*culture which in relation to the period's newly dominant literate culture is a subversive, or subterranean force. As if anticipating 'the madness of bells' in Derrida's *Glas,* the church bells in Coketown are 'barbarous', whilst those in Genoa and London are, indeed, 'maddening'.[28] When we read, or hear of 'discordant bells', 'conflicting bells', 'confusion of bells', and 'bells of all degrees of dissonance', the church bell becomes, via a cryptic slippage, a kind of *Babel(l)*.[29] Note that, in *Hard Times*, one particular sentence begins with 'bell' and ends with 'babel'.[30] And what makes this Babel of bells so subversive is its violation of the conventions of signification, a violation most obviously pictured in *Little Dorrit* where, at the close of the Sparklers' wedding celebrations, 'the thousand churches [of Rome] rang their bells *without any reference to it*'.[31] If the church bells of Rome thus affect a Babelian anarchy, those of pre-Revolutionary France threaten nothing less than full-blooded insurrection: in *A Tale of Two Cities* we are warned that 'the church bells [now] . . . ringing pleasantly in many an airy steeple over France, should [soon] be melted into thundering cannon.'[32]

Maddening and barbarous bells are, though, always-already a kind of thundering cannon, or rebellious noise; for this reason alone, the churches in Dickens are part of that oral or rhetorical energy which so often troubles the silences of the Dickensian page. This becomes obvious in

Little Dorrit when Mr Meagles explains how, when the Fifth Commandment is read out on Sundays, he is always inclined, for the sake of the orphan Tattycoram, "'to call out, Church [meaning 'shame!']'"; however, he never actually does so.[33] Here, the liturgical, literate church is contested by 'Church!' as an oppositional cry; this latter church, the 'Church!' that Meagles *would* but does *not* call out, being both enigmatic and suppressed, is doubly cryptic. Since Greek for 'church' is *ecclesia,* meaning 'called out', this vocal church is also cryptic in the sense that it punningly recalls an ancient and deep-buried sense of church. It is, though, a sense of church that here remains under the erasure, if not censorship, of the literate institution.

This censoring, literate church is never more conspicuous than in *Bleak House*, where the illiterate Jo is mystified to 'see the good company going to the churches on Sundays, with their books in their hands'.[34] These readerly churches are, indeed, an extension of literate London: 'the town awakes [and] . . . all that . . . reading and writing . . . recommences'; if then, through Jo, the novel opens up a space outside or below the literate church – Jo sweeps 'the churchyard step' – the novel is also involved in a subversion of London itself. Jo, as a 'dweller in the tents of Tom-all-Alone's and a mover-on upon the surface of the earth', recalls the New Testament declaration that 'here we have no continuing city'.[35] Now that Dickens's urban churches are no longer burial-sites, no longer the literal dead-centre of the Victorian metropolis, those churches disrupt any fixed or centred sense of the city. And this is mirrored in *Pictures*, where the Cathedral of Modena houses 'people . . . kneeling in all directions', where 'St Peter's . . . tires . . . itself with wandering round and round', and where Rome is 'a vast wilderness of consecrated buildings'.[36] A wilderness is where one gets lost – if 'the crypt', as Derrida remarks, 'leads astray' then Rome's crypted churches lead *the city* astray; the conventional understanding that the nineteenth-century city subverts the church is turned on its head.[37] As Dickens observes, 'it is an awful thing to think of the enormous caverns that are entered from some Roman churches, and *undermine the city.*'[38]

What makes these caverns so 'awful . . . to think' is not just that they house 'graves, graves, graves' but that, as 'ghastly passages . . . with cold damp stealing down the walls, drip-drop, drip-drop', they return Dickens to the damp passages that were increasingly and *literally* undermining Victorian cities – namely, the sewers. It is no accident that Victor Hugo, writing eighteen years later, talks of sewers as 'excremental crypts'; echoing the intensely moral tone of Victorian sanitary reform, Ruskin goes even further toward churching the sewer: 'a good sewer', he writes, '[is a] far holier thing . . . than the most admired Madonna ever printed.'[39]

The sewer–church analogy undergoes a tacit but radical reversal with Nietzsche who, in 1889, declares that 'the Christian movement has been from the very first a . . . movement of outcast and refuse elements of every kind'.[40] For all its shock-value, Nietzsche's declaration only rehearses a conceit already inscribed in the refuse dump that was Golgotha (Christ was killed on Jerusalem's rubbish tip). The conceit is echoed, and indeed celebrated, by the young and Catholic Terry Eagleton: 'the Church', he writes, 'is [not just] a city on a hill [but] . . . the dung of the earth.'[41] Whether Dickens is closer to Nietzsche or Eagleton is impossible to determine, but the conceit they share is certainly anticipated by the 'pestiferous and obscene' churchyard in which Mr Krook is buried; there are also the churchyards surrounding Todgers', all of which are 'overgrown with such straggling vegetation as springs up . . . from damps . . . and rubbish'.[42] The sewer and the church come even closer in *Pictures*; for, given the Victorian habit of considering the poor to be 'moral sewerage', Parma's dark crypt of beggars, idiots and the infirm *is* a sewer-church.[43]

If, for Dickens, Italy's crypts are a displaced version of all that undermines the Victorian city then the 'chattering jaws . . . paralytic gestures [and] . . . idiotic heads' of Parma's subterranean church become an inflection of all the disease and infirmity which characterized or caricatured Britain's urban underworld.[44] The church, of course, was literally connected with disease by dint of its overflowing and miasmic graveyards.[45] There is, though, in Dickens an apprehension that the church is itself a kind of disease. This is clear in *Little Dorrit* where the description of London on a Sunday, when nothing stirs save church bells, culminates in the remark that 'up almost every alley . . . some doleful bell was . . . tolling, as if the Plague were in the city'.[46] Here again Dickens anticipates Nietzsche, who was to write that '*making* sick is the true hidden objective of the church'.[47] Dickens writes better than he knows when declaring, in a letter, that 'as to the Church, I am sick of it'.[48]

Amongst the churches of Italy Dickens is sick, it seems, in the sense that they disrupt his very ability to think; he finds that St Peter's allows 'no one point for the mind to rest upon', dreams of a Cathedral which is 'inconceivable throughout', and compares 'sitting in any of the churches [in Genoa]' to taking 'a mild dose of opium'.[49] Admittedly, this capacity to disorder the mind is more obviously a feature of Italy's Catholic churches, a feature of Dickens's notorious anti-Catholicism; but disordered and deranged minds are also to be found in Dickens's English churches – and not just the 'lunatic' revivalists. Mrs Snagsby's 'becoming cataleptic' whilst listening to Chadband getting his evangelical 'steam up' is perilously close to David Copperfield on his wedding-day when 'the church', he observes, 'might be a steam-power loom in full action, for any sedative effect it has on me'.[50] Again, in being carried upstairs 'like a grand piano', Mrs Snagsby is not far from Mrs Miff the Anglican pew-opener who is herself 'such a pew of a Woman'.[51] Just as Mrs Snagsby loses not only consciousness but identity (thus becoming a grand piano), so both David and Mrs Miff also come close to such loss of self; all three are like that 'score of people' in *Dombey and Son* who 'lost themselves every Sunday . . . among the high-backed pews'.[52] Pip's 'vague sensation' that 'it was Sunday, and somebody was dead' is, perhaps, not so vague.[53] Of Parma's cryptic church we might even say 'it was Sunday and somebody was in-bits-and-pieces'; for like Lacan's pre-Oedipal infant this church is a 'fragmented body', a *corps morcelé*:

> If the ruined frescoes in the cathedral above [with its 'heaps of foreshort-ened limbs'] . . . had retired to this lower church, they could hardly have made a greater confusion . . . of arms and legs.[54]

In their very various ways, Dickens's churches make light, it seems, of not just being human but *being*. This is hardly surprising in the sense that Dickens is, on the whole, writing from within a Church of England that as well as being (or not being), a 'quarrelling body' is, according to J. H. Newman, 'the veriest of nonentities'.[55] In Catholic Italy, indeed, Dickens is writing about churches whose belief in 'the Real Presence' of the body and blood of Christ makes *un*real the presence or being of both bread and wine. In this sense, a strangely emblematic figure within Dickens's cryptic Church is the unregenerate Quilp seated in Bethel chapel and 'chuckling inwardly over *the joke of his being there*'.[56]

Of course, if *to be* is *to be seen* then being is also made light of amongst the dark and *un*seen interiors of the churches in Marseilles; in *Little Dorrit* these shadowy churches almost embody or make literal what theologians call the 'Church Invisible': they are 'the freest' from the 'universal stare'.[57] According to Foucault, the universal stare is a primarily medical stare: 'Western man', he writes, 'constitutes himself in his own eyes as an object of [medical] science'; in Dickens, however, the church might just escape or even confound this clinical gaze.[58] Of the 'heaps of foreshortened limbs' painted upon the cupola of Parma's Cathedral we read that 'no operative surgeon, gone mad, could imagine [them] in his wildest delirium'; insofar as the Cathedral is subjected to a clinical gaze, that gaze is blinded by the madness against which it defines itself.[59] As we know, for Foucault, 'men [had] . . . to wait . . . until Dostoyevsky and Nietzsche' before regaining the 'madness . . . which belonged . . . to the Christian experience of the Renaissance'; Dickens's account of Parma's insane Renaissance frescoes comes close to bringing that wait to an end.[60]

'Not my father's house'

Beneath this same Cathedral Dickens envisages a church that threatens not only reason but property: 'behind each of [the] marble pillars there seems to be at least one beggar in ambush'.[61] When, in *A Tale of Two Cities,* we read of 'churches that are not my father's house but dens of thieves' we might well return to Parma's subterranean church.[62] We might also return to the old crypt into which Little Nell is taken where, 'in the time of the monks . . . amid . . . gold and silver . . . and precious stuffs and jewels, . . . hooded figures . . . told their rosaries of beads'.[63] Here the church again shades into a quasi-criminal underworld, just as it does in *Oliver Twist* where a reference to the Quakers is encrypted in the ironic chapter-heading that reads: 'How Oliver passed his Time in the improving Society of his reputable Friends' – for Fagin's den of thieves read the Society of Friends.[64] Victorian fears of both Catholicism and Nonconformity play a part at such moments, but if the church that Dickens writes is shrouded in criminality it is closer to Kierkegaard's contemporaneous declaration that 'the world of crime forms a little society . . . on the outside of human society . . . [much like] the society of Christians.'[65] This is echoed in one of Nietzsche's many dark thoughts on the church: 'here public openness is . . . lacking; the hole-and-corner, the dark chamber is Christian'.[66] The hole-and-corner is where the church *began* – under Roman rule, it was initially outlawed, secretive. We are reminded of this by Dickens's visit to both the Roman catacombs and St Peter's 'dungeon', places that help make sense of *Great Expectations'* intriguing presentation of the jailbird Magwitch as a kind of St Paul.[67] When Magwitch declares, '"I've been put out of this town and put out of that town . . . stuck in the stocks, and whipped and worried and drove"' he echoes St Paul's 'five times received I forty stripes save one. Thrice was I beaten with rods, [and] once was I stoned.'[68]

In Dickens, the church does not, though, simply occupy a romantic space on the 'wrong' side of the law; after all, a den of thieves by another name might just turn out to be a prison. Foucault argued that 'for the church . . . confinement represents . . . a police whose order will be entirely transparent to . . . religion', and Dickens certainly describes London's Sabbatarian churches as a 'stringent policeman'.[69] Indeed, in *Pictures,* he writes of priests who carry 'candles . . . like truncheons'; no surprise, then, that the 'innumerable churches [of Florence] . . . *arrest* our lingering steps'.[70] Elsewhere in Dickens's crowded cities, church and prison at times appear almost cheek-by-jowl: Marshalsea Prison stands only 'a few doors short of the church of Saint George'; 'the great black dome of Saint Paul's bulg[es] . . . at [Pip] . . . from behind . . . Newgate Prison'; and in Rome the dungeon of St Peter so presses on the oratory above that the 'gloom of the . . . old prison . . . [is] on it'.[71]

To read, then, 'prison' for 'den of thieves' – thus 'the churches are not my father's house but a prison' – clearly makes a dark kind of sense; indeed, this reformulation also makes illuminating non-sense in that, for Dickens, the church is a prison precisely insofar as it *is* 'my father's house'. Crucial to this equation is the time when Dickens's own father was in Marshalsea for debt, a time of which Dickens himself remarks that 'Sundays . . . I passed in . . . prison'.[72] For the young Dickens, church-going shades into prison-going; prison, like church, is 'my father's house'. The adult Dickens is thus telling his own story when he observes that, following one particular ceremony involving figures representing Mary, Joseph and the Infant Saviour, the presiding monk 'locked up the whole concern (Holy Family and all)'.[73] By incarcerating the model family ('model' in both senses of the word), the Dickensian church also tells *its* story, since it *does*, in a sense, serve to discipline or police the family. In this light the priest's candle is not just a 'truncheon' but a phallus, whilst the sacrament of marriage is an elaborate policing of desire; hence Wemmick and Miss Skiff, 'ranged in order at those fatal rails'.[74] Likewise, David Copperfield, recalling his wedding, describes 'the pew-opener arranging us, like a drill-sergeant, before the altar'.[75] To marry is to enter, it seems, not just a church but the quasi-military regime characteristic of the nineteenth-century prison.[76] Indeed, merely to begin to desire outside marriage could incur the penal system's ultimate sanction; or, at least, that is the lesson of Stephen Blackpool's nightmare in which he who is already married finds his marriage to another turning into a burial service following his own execution: 'in an instant what he stood on fell below him, and he was gone'.[77]

Though Stephen begins his nightmare alongside his bride, he ends it alone 'before a crowd so vast, that . . . all the people in the world . . . could not have looked . . . more numerous'. In becoming a site of execution the church subjects Stephen to an appalling isolation and thereby mimics something of the 'solitary' prison system so vigorously attacked by Dickens in the 1840s.[78] This system, in which solitude was expected to cause 'the prisoner . . . to turn inward . . . and repent', drew heavily on various institutional practices of the church, in particular meditative prayer and the confessional. Dickens knew this well, as is clear from the way the inspectors of Mr Creakle's solitary system prison, upon encountering the dazzling piety of Uriah Heep, 'shad[e] . . . their eyes . . . as if they had just come into a church'.[79] If the churches in Dickens *do* constitute a species of prison it is one run on the solitary system; after all, as Christ remarks, 'in my father's house are many rooms'.[80] In his 1860 essay, 'City of London Churches', Dickens recalls how 'I open[ed] the door of a family pew, and shut myself in.'[81] Foucault argued that the Catholic 'confession [is] . . . inscribed at the heart of [Western] . . . procedures of individualization';[82] if so, for the Protestant Dickens, the family pew is a displacement of not just the solitary cell but the confessional box. Shutting himself in is an act of individuation as well as incarceration.

But what distinguishes Dickens's pew from Foucault's confessional is that the pew entails visibility: 'the clerk', records Dickens, 'glances at me knowingly'. Though cryptic, Dickens's churches – like the pews – are never a site of absolute invisibility; indeed, what invisibility there is tends, paradoxically, to enhance visibility, the visibility of others. The principle is that of Jeremy Bentham's Panopticon design of prison, 'in the central tower [of which] one sees everything without ever being seen'.[83] See how Oliver Twist spends hours at Fagin's garret-window, looking out but never being seen: it is 'as if he . . . lived inside the ball of St Paul's Cathedral'.[84] The same Panopticon principle is at work in that 'mouldy old church' in *Dombey and Son*, where the very hiddenness of the worshippers increases their powers of surveillance: 'Miss Nipper [felt] that the eyes of [the congregation,] which lost itself weekly among the high-backed pews, were upon her.'[85] Could it be that the churches of Marseilles are 'the freest' from 'the universal stare' simply because, on the Panopticon principle, the *un*seen is the one who *sees*? After all, for both Dickens and his contemporaries, the church, in the form of St Paul's Cathedral, frequently functioned (literally as well as symbolically), as a surveillance tower. Witness how Lucy Snowe, in *Villette* (1853), 'mount[s] to the dome' of St Paul's to look out over London; how Henry Mayhew, in 1850, records that to gain 'a bird's-eye view of the port, I went up to the [Cathedral's] Golden Gallery'; and how James Grant, another mid-century social investigator, begins his 1837 study of *The Great Metropolis* by imagining precisely the same.[86] Indeed, in 1849, the *Examiner* reports that '"crow's nests"' were erected 'above the cross of St Paul's for the purposes of [a] sanitary survey'.[87] It should not surprise us, then, that in *Martin Chuzzlewit* 'the cross . . . of St Paul's . . . tak[es] . . . note of what[ever the murderer Jonas] . . . did'; that in *Great Expectations* the 'great black dome' of St Paul's is 'bulging at' Pip; and that, in *Little Dorrit*, the talk following the death of the murderous Merdle 'swell[s] . . . into such a roar . . . that a solitary watcher . . . [on the gallery] above the Dome . . . would have perceived the air to be laden with [the rogue's] . . . name'.[88]

For all its implication in Panopticism, the dome of St Paul's does not, though, simply reproduce Bentham's 'hierarchical organisation . . . of power' – it also lays bare the *ambiguities* of surveillance.[89] If the watcher above the dome is 'solitary' then his fate resembles not just the guardian in the central tower but the prisoner in the cell; likewise, since Oliver Twist is not free to leave Fagin's house, 'living inside the ball of St Paul' describes both a view *and* an incarceration. Refigured in terms of St Paul's dome, Bentham's watchtower no longer implies a position of pure power. Indeed, as part of Dickens's intuitive reworking of the politics of surveillance, St Paul's dome serves to feminize, or *dome*sticate the gaze ('dome' has at its root *domus*, Latin for 'home'). Through St Paul's, then, Dickens turns the phallic tower into a mammary dome – Peggotty's work-box displays a 'pink-dome[d]' St Paul's. Dickens thus complicates the gaze of surveillance with the gaze of the mother.[90] For 'dome' read 'dame', as in *A Tale of Two Cities* where the whole of Paris is overlooked by 'the watching towers of Notre Dame'.[91] Church, mother and gaze again coincide in *Bleak House*: in the chapel at Chesney Wold, immediately after the vicar declares '"O Lord . . . in thy sight"' Esther suddenly, and for the first time, encounters her mother's 'handsome proud eyes': 'shall I ever forget the . . . beating at my heart, occasioned by [that] . . . look?'[92] By rivaling the '*Lord's* sight', the maternal gaze here works at the expense of the Father's; if Notre Dame is the 'Cathedral of Our Lady' then this is the church of '*my* Lady', Lady Dedlock.[93]

That the gaze of Dickens's Church should play between dome and dame may not surprise, a Victorian woman's place being in the dome, or *domus* (home); but what does surprise is that 'my Lady' does not leave the house of God as she finds it. For her gaze is set in opposition to the gaze of not only a *heavenly* Father but also an earthly one: this meeting of eyes between mother and daughter reflects something of Lacan's mirror-stage, that 'moment' in a child's development which *precedes* the entry of the father – 'her face [was] . . . like a broken glass to me . . . I . . . seemed to arise before my own eyes'.[94] In excluding the father, 'my Lady' is also like a glass or mirror to 'Our Lady', our lady of the Virgin Birth – she too functions as a mother without a father.[95]

By violating conventional marital codes, 'Our Lady' and 'my Lady' together suggest not only that 'churches . . . are not *my father's* house' but also that the house of God is not a home, or at least not a family home. For all its disciplining of the family, the church that Dickens writes is never, it seems, a purely domestic space; it is only ever home *from* home. The beggars and idiots in Parma's crypt are not so much a family as a community or crowd; the dark and hooded monks who once lived in Little Nell's crypt are all male; and in *Little Dorrit* the tourists who 'prowled about the churches' were there through a 'general unfitness for getting on at home'.[96] There is, indeed, a sense in which the church is always to some extent unhomely in precisely the sense of *unheimlich,* that term of Freud's which translates as 'uncanny'. The dark, unnerving and even Gothic aspects of Dickens's churches have been felt before, and none of these churches are more Gothic than those of Marseilles, which are not only peopled with shadows but dotted with 'winking lamps', lamps that seem to be communicating some secret.[97] If Freud is right, if 'the uncanny' *is* 'the name for everything that ought to have remained hidden . . . but has come to light' then these Marseilles churches are profoundly uncanny.[98] Indeed, when, later in the novel, Little Dorrit seeks temporary refuge in St George's Church only to be greeted by the Registrar, a specifically sexual secret threatens to come to light; at first, he recommends that she just wait by his fire, but 'his surveying her with an admiring gaze [soon] suggest[s] . . . something else to him':

> 'Stay a bit. I'll get some cushions . . . and you and your friend shall lie down before the fire. Don't be afraid of not going in [to the prison] to join your father when the gate opens. *I'll* call you.'[99]

If the registrar's homely way suggests an *un*homely motivation, then his 'gaze' becomes an uncanny wink in our direction. This church that is 'not my father's house' ('"don't be afraid of not . . . join[ing] your father"'), corresponds to Freud's *'unheimlich* house', the unhomely home that translates, according to Freud, as the 'haunted house'.[100] In this case the haunted house is the house of God, and what haunts it is sexuality.

Foucault claims that Victorian sexuality functioned, paradoxically, as an open secret; and, indeed, as here, it is in bringing sexuality to light that Dickens's churches are most uncanny.[101] For Freud, the uncanny is exemplified by disclosure of the *'Heimlich* parts of the human body, [the] pudenda', and, to quote St Paul, it is precisely 'those members of the body [of Christ] which we think to be less honourable' that are, as it were, exposed to view when Dickens, rehearsing the ritual inversion of the carnivalized body, turns his churches 'head over heels'.[102] An inverted body reveals what it should not, what is not honourable. The 'less honourable' body parts are almost literally exposed in Parma's subterranean church, such was the notorious reputation of Italian crypts: writing in 1820, one British travel-writer remarks, of St Peter's 'subterranean chapel', that it was no longer open to both sexes since 'the sanctity of the place had not saved it from being converted into the scene of those licentious intrigues which its obscurity seemed calculated to favour'.[103] When Dickens describes a crypt occupied by both men and women as an animated version of the 'arms and legs . . . entangled . . . together' in the Cathedral frescoes we cannot but infer some dark and licentious secret.

Dark or not, all secrets stage or enact the question of 'Truth', and so do Dickens's secretive and riddling churches. This is most conspicuous in *A Tale of Two Cities* where, within a page of reading that 'Notre Dame

[is] almost equidistant' from the two extremes of poverty and wealth, we learn that 'Man had got out of the Centre of Truth.'[104] If equidistance implies a kind of centrality, then the eccentric exception to this rule of eccentricity (the rule that 'Man had got out of the Centre'), is Notre Dame; though, of course, she is only *almost* an exception since she is only 'almost equidistant'. The connection is itself eccentric; Notre Dame renders the relationship between church and truth as a riddle, or cryptic. In so doing, Notre Dame takes us a long way from *official* mid-Victorian thought, according to which truth, as made in the image of contemporary Anglicanism, is national, established and male. With Notre Dame we may be closer to that *un*official account of truth articulated in 1843 by Cardinal Newman: 'in certain cases a lie is the . . . [best] approach to truth.'[105] We may, though, be even closer to Nietzsche's later and anarchic invitation to 'suppos[e] . . . truth a woman'; in *A Tale of Two* Cities Dickens supposes truth (via), the woman that is a church called 'Our Lady'.[106] Clearly, we are a long way from the towering phallocentrism of the early Ruskin's declaration that one of

> the moral habits to which [Protestant] England in this age owes . . . [its] greatness [is] . . . a sincere upright searching into religious truth [which is] . . . only traceable in the [church] tower, sent like an 'unperplexed question up to Heaven'.[107]

It is no accident that, with regard to the question of truth, Dickens should, by contrast, focus on Notre Dame, a church that is neither male, Protestant nor English. Indeed, just as Dickens's churches are always in some sense cryptic, so his English churches are often, to some extent, foreign: in *Little Dorrit* a 'congregationless Church . . . [in Cheapside] seem[s] . . . to be waiting for some adventurous Belzoni [the Egyptian explorer] to dig it out and discover its history'; in 'City of London Churches' Dickens explores structures 'unknown to far greater numbers . . . than the ancient edifices of the Eternal City'; and in *Dombey and Son* the London congregation that lost themselves among high-backed pews constitute an 'integral portion of Europe'.[108]

If the foreignness or elsewhere-ness of Dickens's churches entails some account of truth or knowledge, it is most obviously inscribed in that description of St Peter's as an edifice 'with no one point for the mind to rest upon . . . and [which] tires itself with wandering round and round'.[109] For Dickens, St Peter's perpetual refusal of intellectual stasis is 'not religiously impressive', but for Ruskin, writing just seven years later, exactly the same experience is celebrated as the very spirit of the Gothic church: 'The vital principle', he writes, 'is not the love of *Knowledge,* but the love of *Change* . . . that restlessness of the dreaming mind, that wanders hither and thither among the niches . . . pinnacles . . . wall and roof.'[110] Both men write a church which entails a mind that changes rather than knows; but where Ruskin sees a vital principle, a principle of life, Dickens sees repetition and exhaustion, the 'wandering round and round' of the death instinct. However unfollowable it may be, the church that Dickens depicts never erases the 'crypt' in cryptic. The perpetual displacement implicit in Dickens's cryptic church is not so much a case of 'always-already else-where' – as in Ruskin's Gothic church – but rather of always-already below.

Just as Dickens leaves Parma's Cathedral only to enter a subterranean church so, at the very end of *Little Dorrit,* having 'walked out of the church', the newly-wed couple 'went down. Went down . . . Went down . . . Went down . . . went quietly down into the roaring streets, insepa-rable and blessed.' If we misread the *streets* as 'blessed', albeit for a split-second, it is as if here too Dickens chances upon a 'lower church'. Moreover, just as Parma's beggars-in-ambush momentarily threaten an inversion of the economic order, so here, through the 'up' of the 'uproar' that is the novel's final word, the roaring and blessed streets effect a coded inversion of the 'down, down, down, down, down' of the couple's descent. In each case, in writing the church from below, from *socially* below, Dickens uncovers a shadowy, cryptic community which threatens change that is not only intellectual but economic and political. To quote from the very end of Barrett Browning's *Aurora Leigh,* published in the same year as *Little Dorrit:* 'new churches, new oeconomies . . . '.[111]

Postscript, or the left umbrella

In 1858, a year after Little Dorrit was published, Dickens writes an essay called 'Please to Leave Your Umbrella', a wonderfully mad meditation upon how

> I have gone into churches where I have been required to leave my Umbrella [outside] in a sham medieval porch, with hundreds of eventful years of History squeezed in among its ribs. I have gone into public assemblages of great pretensions – even into assemblages gathered together under the most sacred of names – and my Umbrella, filled to the handle with my sense of Christian fairness and moderation, has been taken from me at the door.[112]

What must be left outside the main body of the church is Dickens's umbrella; however, since it is 'filled to the handle with . . . Christian fair-ness', the umbrella constitutes, defiantly and absurdly, a church outside the church, a Christianity outside Christianity. In much the same way, my *discussion* of the umbrella must be left outside the main body of this chapter, in a postscript. For all its 'sense of Christian fairness' Dickens's dripping umbrella is too absurd, too trivial and too wet to be housed within this dry and churchy chapter. A Christian umbrella cannot, though, be completely forgotten for it recalls the dripping figure of the Victorian believer stranded on Dover beach, the 'Sea of Faith' all withdrawn. But *un*like Arnold's melancholic believer, Dickens's Christian umbrella has a comic and even surreal energy – an energy that, just a few years later, comes into full view with Comte de Lautréamont's astonishing and conceitful definition of artistic beauty as 'the fortuitous meeting, on a dissection table, of a sewing machine and an umbrella'.[113] This conceit would one day be adopted and celebrated by the Surrealists. In this sense, Dickens's absurd Christian umbrella has a future within Surrealism. To put it another way: through Dickens's umbrella, Christianity is written into the pre-history of Surrealism, or at least what we might call Surrealism's umbrella strand (or should that be 'stand'?).

We here come close to Kurt Schwitter's 1924 declaration that Surrealism is 'the spirit of Christianity in the realm of art'.[114] But though close, this is not *quite* the same, for in Dickens's umbrella we see not so much the *spirit* of Christianity as the *materiality* of Christianity, its entanglement in things, objects, even clutter. In Dickens's case it is a church-going umbrella but there are hundreds of other *Christian things:* candlestick, lectern, pew, organ, thurible, chasuble; above all, there is, or was, that paradigmatic Christian thing: the relic. The relic is a stray, displaced, redundant and, as it were, accidental thing. In that sense, every relic connects Christianity with the surrealist object; every relic thus does the work, the almost idle work, of Dickens's umbrella.

That work, indeed, extends to connecting Christianity with Surrealism's close but rarely acknowledged neighbour: deconstruction. In Derrida's *Spurs* the Surrealist's umbrella makes a reappearance when Derrida, with almost exaggerated seriousness, offers a profound philosophic meditation upon the words, '"I forgot my umbrella"' – words found, 'isolated in quotation marks', among Nietzsche's unpublished manuscripts.[115] Derrida, alluding to Lautréamont's umbrella along the way, ends by declaring that Nietzsche's forgotten umbrella represents the tendency to forget which 'belongs to the [very] nature of Being'. However, if anyone could remember Dickens's *Christian* umbrella they might dare to suggest that *Christianity* is the umbrella which Nietzsche forgot – that Christianity is the oft-forgotten umbrella of the Nietzschean-cum-Surrealist-cum-Derridean 'tradition' of unreason.

This umbrella is not forgotten by Edmond Gosse – though he does, admittedly, mistake it for a parasol when, in *Father and Son* (1907), he writes of the evangelical Sarah Flood who, upon visiting the Great Exhibition of 1851, was so outraged by the nudity of the classical sculptures that she simply 'ran amok', 'smash[ing] the nude figures with the handle of her parasol'.[116] Never has the Christian umbrella been more spectacularly unreasonable. In 1900, however, it does have another memorable moment when Oscar Wilde, within a year of his death-bed conversion to Catholicism, considers going to the Vatican:

> This time I really must become a Catholic, though I fear that if I went before the Holy Father with a blossoming rod it would turn at once into an umbrella.[117]

For Wilde, the moment of conversion, the moment of meeting the Pope, is also the moment of the surreal umbrella; whilst Dickens takes an umbrella to the church-door, Wilde dreams of taking one inside. For Wilde, though, it is only an imagined umbrella; there is still no *actual* churching of Lautréamont's surreal umbrella. This event 'takes place' on the night of October 26, 1859 in the village of Llanallgo on the island of Anglesea when, following a shipwreck in which hundreds were drowned, the local fishermen laid out many of the beached corpses in the local church. As Dickens writes:

> The pulpit was gone, and other things usually belonging to the church were gone, owing to its living congregation having deserted it . . . and yielded it up to the dead. The very Commandments had been shouldered out of their places, in the bringing in of the dead; the black wooden tables on which they were painted, were askew, and on the stone pavement below them . . . were the marks and stains where the drowned had been laid down. The eye, with little or no aid from the imagination, could yet see how the bodies had been turned, and where the head had been and where the feet. [118]

Viewing the church after the event, Dickens offers an account that is at its most moving and yet most surreal when he describes the sheer miscellany of objects left behind:

> [a] frying-pan . . . was still there. . . . [and] hard by the Communion Table, were some boots that had been taken off the drowned . . . soaked and sandy . . .[119]

A frying-pan, a pair of soaking boots, and a Communion Table (a table for dissecting the body of Christ), – not quite Lautréamont's fortuitous meeting but close; maybe as close as real life or death will ever get. Indeed, it is as close as we may ever *want* it to be, since a dissection table is a place for a corpse and, as Dickens reminds us here, it is around a corpse that objects often *become* unrelated and thus 'meet'. In this real, historical instance it is true that the meeting is, in a sense, fortuitous – the scene does have a kind of beauty; but it is also tragic, even appalling. Here in this lonely Anglesey church, with the dripping boots as a terrible substitute for Lautréamont's umbrella, the paradigmatic Surrealist dream turns into a nightmare upon impact with history. Lautréamont's umbrella is no sooner churched than it is historicized, and no sooner historicized than it is traumatized.

This, though, should not be surprise us, for Dickens's church-going umbrella has 'hundreds of eventful years of History squeezed among its ribs'. And the same is true of the now-stranded Christianity for which the umbrella stands. Squeezed or hidden within Christianity is not only the pre-history of Surrealism but also that traumatic history of death otherwise known as the history of religious intolerance and extremism; we should not forget that what must be left at the church door, along with the umbrella, is a sense of 'fairness and moderation'.

Any history encoded within Dickens's church-going umbrella will be far from regular, or easy to decipher, for the umbrella 'drips[s] . . . with the sound of an irregular clock'.[120] But once Christianity is stranded or beached, it is also like an irregular clock, far from the tide of official Western history – the very history that Christianity (with its BC and AD), had previously defined. If though, by the second-half of the nineteenth century, Christianity has become an irregular clock, it is also an *unpredictable* clock, one that may go off when you least expect it; as Nietzsche puts it, 'Christianity is still possible at any time'.[121] This is both a warning and a promise.

chapter five

The Love that Dare Not Speak its Christian Name

Oscar Wilde's Perversion

Behind

Prodigious efforts are being made by the Ritualists
to enlist converts, or rather I should say perverts.
(*Ritualism, the Highway to Rome*, 1867)[1]

In mid-Victorian England any conversion of which one disapproved was
termed a perversion; as Austin Farrer reminded the readers of his life of
Saint Paul, even this most famous Christian convert was, to his fellow
Jews, an 'audacious pervert'.[2] By the *end* of the Victorian period, any
sexual act of which one disapproved was also termed a perversion; as
Havelock Ellis writes in 1897, 'a pervert . . . told me that he has made
advances to upwards of one hundred men.' In the case of Oscar Wilde
we have a 'pervert' in both the old and the new senses of the word.
Indeed, the Catholicism with which he flirted throughout his life and to
which he finally converted at his death was, for many, inextricable from
the scandal of his sexuality.[3] The Victorian dread of the Catholic was
very often shadowed by the emergent spectre of the homosexual: writing in 1867 the evangelical William Hogan declares, 'I know no other
reptile in all animal nature so filthy . . . as a Roman Catholic priest.'[4]
For Hogan's contemporaries, the missing link between the Catholic and
the homosexual was the conspicuous figure of the dandy or Decadent
who in many cases infamously combined both 'perversions'. As Ellis
Hanson demonstrates in *Decadence and Catholicism*, it was increasingly
difficult to distinguish one from the other. To echo Dorian Gray, 'one
hardly [knows] . . . whether one [is] . . . reading the spiritual ecstasies of

94

some medieval saint or the morbid confessions of a modern sinner'.[5] This confusion or conflation is echoed in Wilde's 1890 remark that 'the Saint and the . . . Hedonist certainly meet – [indeed] touch in many points'.[6] Ten years later they also kiss as Wilde, now exiled in Italy and within months of his conversion, writes of his passion for 'a young Seminarist' from the Cathedral of Palermo – 'I gave him', writes Wilde, 'a book of devotion . . . and every day I kissed him behind the high altar.'[7] Here Wilde and seminarist, sinner and saint, pervert and convert turn both *to* each other and *into* each other.

But the convert is, by definition, one who turns into *someone else*, one who changes so radically that the change does not, in a sense, happen to *him* at all. As Derrida writes, 'conversion ought to be the surprise of an event happening to "myself," who am therefore no longer myself'. For Derrida, conversion is a name for the radical discontinuities that beset identity or being; it names, if you will, 'The Importance of Being Someone Else', or rather the inevitability.[8] And that is precisely what happens in *The Importance of Being Ernest*, where Jack's baptism as 'Ernest' is eclipsed by the discovery that he is the long-lost son of Miss Prism – that he is already, as Gwendolen says, 'someone else'.[9] For Jack, baptism or conversion does not so much effect change as merely name or mark it.

In the face of this change the only question for Jack is Gwendolen's: 'What', she asks, 'is your Christian name, now that you have become someone else?' The answer turns out to be 'Ernest', but for a giddy, farcical moment Jack appears to exist without a Christian name, to have become someone else at a speed that defeats the very act of Christian *naming*, i.e. the act of baptism that has given him the seemingly redundant name of Ernest. For a brief moment Wildean farce reminds us that the Christian naming or explaining of the world is fast losing its authority, that the late-Victorian world of Darwin *et al.,* increasingly defies traditional Christian categories.

This is a moment that threatens to repeat upon the world of Wildean comedy, a world in which, to echo Lady Markby, 'as a rule, everybody turns out be someone else' – *Christian names notwithstanding*.[10] When Mrs Erlynne points out to Lady Windermere that 'we have the same Christian name', Lady Windermere is no nearer realizing that Mrs Erlynne is her long-lost mother.[11] The Christian name, it seems, guarantees nothing. As Wilde enigmatically remarks, 'anything may happen to a person called John' – even the famously Christian name of 'John' cannot check the contingency of human being.[12] For Wilde, a person called John might turn out to be someone else; indeed, he may even turn out to be the proto-homosexual, imprisoned prophet and tragic clown that is *Oscar Wilde*. Wilde reminds us that 'John' is 'the disciple whom [Jesus] . . . loved', that 'John' in Hebrew is 'Jokanaan' the imprisoned prophet of *Salome*, and that 'John' in Italian is 'Giovanni' from which derives 'zany', or clown – Wilde's fellow inmates at Reading Gaol are 'the zanies of sorrow'.[13] In *The Importance* we read that 'Jack is a notorious domesticity for John',[14] but elsewhere in Wilde we sense that 'John' is itself a domesticity, or code, for the notorious Wilde. In being more than one kind of 'John', Wilde floats free of the self-identity that the Christian name had been supposed to guarantee. Commenting on the fact that he was christened as 'Oscar Finegal O'Flahertie Wills Wilde', Wilde once remarked:

> When one is unknown, a number of Christian names are useful, perhaps needful. As one becomes famous, [however,] one sheds some of them, just as a balloonist, when rising higher, sheds unneccesary ballast . . . Soon I shall . . . be known simply as 'The Wilde'.[15]

By the time this happens Wilde is not just famous but infamous. Unburdened by Christian names, the infamous Wilde almost *becomes* the name for what his lover, Alfred Douglas, memorably called 'the love that dare not speak it'.[16]

The irony, however, is that Wilde gives that love a Christian name, a Christian character that is not simply or narrowly Catholic.[17] Dreaming as he does of 'rechristening everything', Wilde intuitively makes a link between being queer and being Christian. The link, in the late-nineteenth century, is the common capacity to shock or scandalize, for with the onset of secularization there is an emergent sense that Christianity is odd, eccentric and even offensive – thus recovering what St Paul called 'the offence of the Cross'.[18] As Foucault argues, it is only in the age of 'Dostoyevsky and Nietzsche [that] . . . scandal . . . recover[s] its power as revelation'; Nietzsche himself declares, 'it is indecent to be a Christian today'.[19] Wilde, it seems, lives out this cultural logic – there is a sense in which his pursuit of scandal or indecency is a means towards the end of revelation, or faith. In 'The Ballad of Reading Gaol', Wilde recalls the disciple who 'does it with a kiss', the kiss of another man; for Wilde, though, this disciple is not just Judas but also John, 'the disciple whom [Jesus] . . . loved'.[20] The Wildean disciple may not only betray with a kiss but love: 'I still behold', writes Wilde-the-poet, 'The . . . face of . . . Christ . . . / Whose smitten lips my lips so oft have kissed.'[21] Wilde the would-be convert also kisses, of course, the young seminarist in Palermo – and these are kisses by which conversion itself undergoes conversion; for in kissing him 'behind the high altar' Wilde provokes in his reader, the queer and almost unthinkable thought that Wilde-the-convert comes to God from behind, that – with respect to the Church – Wilde, to quote one of his queerest stage directions, 'enters from behind'.[22]

This difficult, awkward thought finds a forbidding echo in T.S. Eliot's remark, *à propos* Baudelaire, that 'Satanism . . . was an attempt to get into Christianity by the back door'.[23] Given the long association between Satanism and sodomy, Eliot's assertion is, as Hanson observes, 'fraught with all the sexual meanings of . . . anal penetration'; and certainly the Decadent movement was eager to explore such meanings. Central to this is J. K. Huysmans, whose work Wilde knew well; in his novel *Là-Bas* (1891), Huysmans describes a black mass in which:

> 'The . . . priests, in their baseness, often go so far as to celebrate the mass with great hosts that they then cut through the middle and afterward glue to a parchment, arranged in the same manner, and use abominably to satisfy their passions.'
> 'Divine sodomy, in other words?'[24]

For Huysmans, the answer is 'yes'; and indeed, in Wilde too there are moments which threaten to translate into something like Huysmans's black, sodomitical mass. Observe, if you will, how, in *Salomé*, Jokanaan cries 'Get thee behind me!' – 'Get thee behind me, *Satan*', as it were – to one he has just called the 'daughter of Sodom'.[25] This potent mix of divinity, homoeroticism and occultism recurs in 'The Sphinx':

> He strode across the waters, mailed in beauty . . .
> You kissed his mouth with mouths of flame: you made the horned god your
> own:
> You stood behind him on his throne: you called him by his secret name.
> You whispered monstrous oracles into . . . his ears.[26]

Divine sodomy in veiled words? Perhaps, but the very veiledness of this esoteric coming-from-behind opens Wilde to the charge of posing as not just a sodomite but an occultist. In daring to come to a god from behind Wilde cannot help but go, or at least appear to go, the still more daring way of the occult. This is a world to which Wilde was introduced not only by Huysmans but also Freemasonry, a society described in 1884 by Pope Leo XIII as 'the Kingdom of Satan'; Wilde was a life-long Mason and belonged to a chapter that is said to have had a particular interest in the occult.[27] We know very little about Wilde's necessarily secret Masonic life, but its influence may yet prove to have been a dark one; to quote the resonant words that come at very end of Act One of *An Ideal Husband*: 'Put out the lights, Mason, put out the lights.'[28]

The light, though, does not go out; for to see God from behind is, in one sense, simply to see God as Moses famously did:

97

And the Lord said . . . it shall come to pass, while my glory passeth by, that
I will put thee in a cleft of the rock, and I will cover thee with my hand while
I pass by: And I will take away mine hand, and thou shalt see my back parts.
(Exodus 33.21–23)

As Joss Marsh points out, this curious scene took a strong grip of the
late-Victorian imagination; it provides the text for an infamous cartoon
in an 1882 issue of the *Freethinker* (see p. 32), and prompts in Freud's
'Wolf Man' the question of 'whether Christ had a behind'.[29] The question of whether angels have a behind also makes a late-Victorian
appearance in Edward Carpenter's curious essay 'Angels' Wings' (1898);
here too the question is charged with infantile anality as Carpenter, by
now a well-known 'Uranian', recalls a childhood trip to the National
Gallery:

> [There was] Archangel Michael, so strong and handsome . . . And as we
> marvelled at the god-like figure clad in mail, we saw its huge dark wings
> spread behind it; and wondered again how they fitted . . . But the painter
> kept the front of the figure only towards us, and round to the back of the
> picture there was no means of coming.[30]

Christian art, it seems, does not allow angels to turn their back on us; after
all, in Genesis it was angels whom the men of Sodom desired.[31] By
contrast, in Jewish scripture, it is *only* the back parts of God that Moses
can see: 'no man [shall] see me and live', says the Lord. Here Moses is a
world away from St Paul's conviction that 'now we see through a glass,
darkly; but then face to face'.[32] The world that separates Moses and Paul
is the Hellenic world of Platonism, with its confident movement away
from mere shadows and reflections, a movement that in Plato's 'Simile of
the Cave' entails the cave-dweller turning away from the wall to *face* the
light.[33] This privileging of face recurs and persists throughout Western
philosophy. Even Emmanuel Levinas, for all his mistrust of traditional
metaphysics, still speaks of the 'face of the Other'; whilst back in 1795
Tom Paine's *The Age of Reason* insists that 'through [science] . . . man
can see God . . . face to face'. This convention is most obviously inscribed
in the struggle for 'recognition' at the centre of Hegel's master-slave
dialectic, the influence of which is such that even the anti-philosopher
Nietzsche declares, 'Let us look one another in the face.'[34]

Wilde, though, will not accept philosophy's invitation to go face to face:
as Guido declares, 'I cannot any more / Stand face to face with beauty.'[35]
Wilde seeks a different encounter. As a dandy he positively hopes that
people will talk behind his back – it is a recurring Wildean joke. Lord
Dartington, for example, declares:

Why, there are lots of people who say I have never really done anything wrong in the whole course of my life. Of course they only say it behind my back. [36]

Behind Wilde's back people not only talk but draw: in 1895 Toulouse-Lautrec depicts the 'disgraced' Wilde from behind, as a passing figure (p. 100). This is the back behind which everyone has been talking, the back of one who really *has* done something 'wrong'; but it is also (or almost), the back of God in the sense that the pose mirrors Wilde's recurring intuition that God hides *His* face. Wilde-the-poet speaks not only of 'God's veil' but of 'him who now doth hide his face', whilst in *Salome* we learn that 'Elias . . . is the last man who saw God face to face.'[37] *If* Wilde comes to God from behind it is, in part, because he has learnt the Mosaic or Jewish lesson of negative theology that one cannot see God directly. In *Dorian Gray*, the young actress Sybil Vane, who is called both 'sacred' and 'divine', is appearing at a theatre run by a Jew who invites Dorian to come and meet her after the performance: 'The old Jew', remarks Dorian, 'seemed determined to take me behind, so I consented.' Here, to encounter the 'sacred', to meet the 'divine', one must go the way of the old Jew; to adapt Lord Henry's response, '"What a way to find one's divinity!"'[38]

We usually think of Wilde as Hellenizing religion, insisting as he does that Christ spoke not Aramaic but Greek; we usually think too that, for Wilde, to homoeroticize is also to Hellenize: hence Wilde's talk of 'the Greek passions of Christ'.[39] But to homoeroticize Christ is to dream of encountering the divine from behind which is, of course, to Hebraize, to go the way of Moses – the way, of the 'old Jew'. There is then a queer, paradoxical sense in which the Greek way to God necessarily becomes the Jewish way.

This, for Wilde, is not simply a lesson in negative theology; it is also simultaneously a lesson in history – in particular, the back-side of history. For what Wilde offers us is an almost anal, or excremental vision of the sheer squalor and pain of lived history. The theatre which Dorian sees from behind is a 'wretched hole' and, indeed, in the 'pit' of that hole, the 'dreadful orchestra . . . pit', is a 'young Hebrew at a cracked piano'.[40] 'The Jew wanted', says Dorian, 'to tell me [*Sibyl's*] . . . history'; however, between them, the old Jew and the young Hebrew unwittingly tell something of their own history, the history of the Jews. As we know, this is a

---

Illustration on p. 100

Drawing of Oscar Wilde by Toulouse-Lautrec (1895), from *La Revue Blanche* (1895). By kind permission of the Bibliothèque nationale de France.

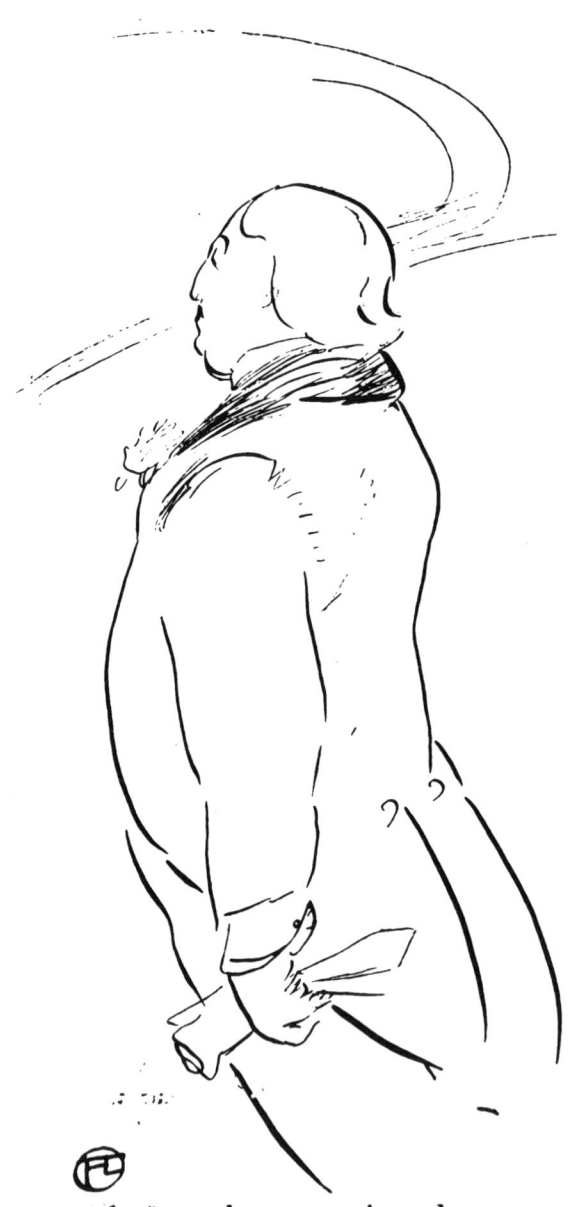

montré la force de ces passions de camp.

hideous and dreadful history of holes and pits otherwise known as ghettos and mass graves. We cannot escape the uncanny fact that the haunting figure of 'the Jew at the cracked piano' has become one lasting image of the Holocaust: witness, *The Pianist*, Wladyslaw Szpilman's account of how, as a Jew in Nazi-occupied Poland, he survived by playing an out-of-tune piano.[41] In the old Jew's theatre, history goes wild: 'in [my] . . . box', says Dorian, 'I forgot that I was in . . . the nineteenth century'; it is as if 'he had lived centuries of pain . . . and torture' – centuries of Jewish pain and torture.[42]

To see history from behind, through an odd or homoerotic hole in the text, is to go the way of the queer theorist, Leo Bersani. In a reading of Jean Genet, Bersani interprets anal intercourse as a 'seismic shift [away from] the [traditional] injunction to find [only] . . . each other in the [face-to-face embrace]', an embrace in which 'you are content to allow others to make history'.[43] By contrast, anal intercourse offers the possibility of 'coming not [to] . . . each other but . . . *to the world*'; here there are not two faces turned toward each other but, in Genet's words, 'four eyes staring in front of them' – all 'look[ing] . . . into the future'. For Bersani, anal intercourse is uniquely set towards a vision of history and the world; in coming from behind one's vision is projected towards the history ahead. The words, 'the Jew took me behind, I consented' might then be a thinly-veiled homoerotic code, an echo of the contemporary, continental preoccupation with the figure of the homosexual Jew.[44] Bersani might argue that Dorian sees so far into the terrible future of Jewish history because, in some sense, the old Jew took him *from* behind.

If Bersani is right, then to see God from behind is to see God projected into history and the world. And that is precisely what happens in Wilde, who reminds us that God was once a 'Galilean peasant' and declares that 'that which is purely human, that is God-like, that is God'.[45] For Wilde, the face of God is unseeable not because of its blinding glory, but rather its sheer humanity. God-as-Christ is always-already vanishing into the crowd of human history. Witness 'E Tenebris' which opens with the prayer, 'Come down, O Christ' and ends with: 'peace, I shall behold . . . /The wounded hands, the weary human face.' It is in 'Rome Unvisited', a contemporaneous poem, that Wilde speaks of 'Him who now doth hide His face'; God, it seems, hides His face behind the 'weary *human* face'.[46] That human face becomes Wilde's own when, in another early poem, the unendurable face of Christ is also the weary face of the late and tragic Wilde:

> why must I still behold
> The wan white face of that deserted Christ,
> . . .

> [Who] . . . now in mute and marble misery
> Sits in his lone dishonoured House and weeps. . . .[47]

Wan, white, deserted, dishonoured and house-bound, the first-century face of Christ anticipates the late-Victorian face of Wilde. This is history as one damned face after another, with Christ as yet another face. Indeed, in 'Sonnet to Liberty' Christ is *every* other face; for here, glancing at the history of revolution, Wilde speaks of 'These Christs that die upon the barricades'. Christ thus falls, quite literally, into line with history – the barricade line is a line of Christs. In *Dorian Gray* we read that, 'passion makes one think in a circle', but *Christ's* passion, it seems, makes Wilde think in a line.[48]

Lines

> 'You must certainly read between the lines.'
> (*An Ideal Husband*)[49]

Passion again makes Wilde think in a line when, the morning after abandoning Sybil, Dorian visits Covent Garden market; amongst the many curious details, is this:

> A long line of boys carrying crates of striped tulips . . . defiled in front of him, threading their way through the huge . . . piles of vegetables.[50]

Here the primary, intended, meaning of 'defiled' is to march; the word has strong military associations. The secondary, purely connotative, meaning is to be sexually violated. On both counts the line of boys is entangled with 'the lines of cruelty . . . [and] lines of suffering' that feature on the next page – these are the lines which have just appeared on the face of the portrait, and which Dorian interprets as 'the burden of his passions and his sins'. Dorian's interpretation echoes the discourse of Atonement, and thus the defiled line of boys is entangled with not just passion but *the* Passion, Christ's bloody Passion. Indeed, in '*threading* their way' the boys anticipate those 'scarlet threads of life' by which Dorian later seeks 'to find his way through the sanguine [blood-red] labyrinth of passion'.[51]

Thread, however, is thin: 'Threads snap', we read, 'you [can] . . . lose your way in the labyrinth'; and so we do in the sense that Dorian's thread of boys somehow leads us to the bloody passion or suffering of the young male soldier. For if to 'defile' is to march, then, even as the thread of boys becomes the later '*scarlet* thread' so those boys evoke the 'thin red line' of the British army, or what Wilde elsewhere calls 'the red ways of war'.[52]

Dorian's blood-red labyrinth names, for Wilde, not just sexual passion but military history. Lady Bracknell famously protests that 'the line is immaterial', but in this case the line is all too material, all too historical. For Wilde, far too many boys have been marching to war, and his early poetry is marked by a surprising determination to witness their death. To quote 'The Burden of Itys': 'I the dying boy will see.'[53] And so he does. Sometimes the boys are dying on generalised, unnamed battlefields: Wilde writes of 'the air [that] is horrid with men's groans' and 'the iron hail and screaming shell'; at other times, the boys are dying on the specific battle-fields of Victorian Britain's colonial wars: in 'Ave Imperatrix', 'the dead boy lies . . . not in quiet English fields' but in 'Kandahar . . . Cabool . . . [and] Delhi'.[54] Within some thirty years this catalogue would include the fields of Flanders and Ypres and it is, in a sense, to these fields that Dorian's line of boys defiled, or marched – it is a simple fact of history that many who were boys in 1891 would die as young men in the blood-red labyrinth of the trenches. One such boy was Wilde's elder son, Cyril, who was six years old at the publication of *Dorian Gray* and died at Neuve-Chapelle in 1915. 'I the dying boy will see' has an almost prophetic force.

In the 1890s many *were* beginning to fear the end of the so-called 'Victorian peace', a fear comically replayed in Wilde's theatrical drawing room:

> SIR ROBERT CHILTREN: You are not going to plunge us into a European
> war, I hope?
> MRS CHEVELEY: There is no danger, at present![55]

For Wilde, though, danger is always present in the sense that suffering stretches our experience of the present. In prison, Wilde writes that 'suffering is one long moment', so long indeed that 'a young Galilean peasant [once] imagin[ed] . . . he could bear . . . the burden of . . . [not only] all that had already been . . . suffered, [but] all that was *yet to be . . . suffered.*' This is, of course, the (il)logic of the Atonement in which Christ, to echo T. S. Eliot, 'foresuffered all'.[56] Wilde's young Galilean peasant belongs, it seems, to the line of boys who march straight to the future of suffering. Witness the poem 'Humanitad', which appears to envisage a whole generation of boys defiled, or influenced, by Decadence and bound for a new scene of agony; the poem speaks of a 'brotherhood' who are concerned with how 'Grecian boys die smiling', who pursue 'the last, perfect creed', 'feed on wild unrest' and 'pass / With weary feet to the *new Calvary.*'[57] And that is precisely what happens; for, as Philip Hoare argues in *Wilde's Last Stand: Decadence, Conspiracy and the First World War*, many of the educated 'elite' of 1914 were propelled to the new

103

Calvary of Flanders by an obsession with death inherited directly from the Decadents:

> Where the Decadents of the 1890s had celebrated romantic death, their modern inheritors faced the reality. The mauve opium poppy of Chelsea became the blood-red corn poppy of Flanders.[58]

In Wilde, though, the opium poppy is already the poppy that remembers the dead: his Duchess of Padua declares, 'I took the scarlet poppies from the corn, / And made a little wreath.'[59]

If Wilde's own wreath, or sense of the dead, anticipates Flanders, then it is a wreath for the dead on *both* sides, for British propaganda frequently constructed Germany as the centre of Decadence. The pre-war reputation of Berlin, along with the work of the German-speaking 'homosexualists' and newspaper reports of 'the German [soldiers'] . . . sexual perversion', convinced many that the war against Germany was a war against Decadence.[60] This conviction culminated in Noel Pemberton Billing's infamous newspaper claim that the private performance of *Salome* in February 1918 was part of a German-inspired homosexual conspiracy to corrupt the moral fibre of the British.[61]

Wilde, we might say, had a peculiar war; his 'sons' appear to be fighting on *both* sides, a paradox that Wilde himself explores, again in 'Humanitad' and again through the figure of Christ: here he declares that 'we' the 'brotherhood' are at once both

> The spear that pierces and the side that bleeds,
> The lips betraying and the life betrayed.[62]

As both side *and* spear, the man who is kissed *and* the man who kisses, Wilde's Christ endures a double and self-reflexive death. This particular death took place, according to Wilfred Owen, in 1917; writing a letter in May of that year, Owen delares

> Christ is literally in no man's land . . . Greater love hath no man than this, that a man lay down his life – for a friend . . . Thus you see how pure Christianity will not fit in with pure patriotism.[63]

Such talk of a man-loving, non-patriotic Christ – a Christ who is to be found, or 'read' between the lines – is dangerous talk from a soldier at the front. It is, however, profoundly biblical talk, recalling, as it does, the prosecuted Christ of Luke's Gospel, the Christ of whom his accusers say: 'We found this fellow perverting the nation.'[64] In February 1918, Billing makes exactly the same accusation against Wilde; 'the cult of Wilde', he claims, was altering what it meant to be British. What Billing neglects is that Wilde was also altering what it meant to be Christian. Owen, writing from the trenches, quotes this from *De Profundis*:

> 'There were many Christians before Christ; the astonishing thing is: there have been none since.'[65]

Owen sees not only Christ disappearing into No Man's Land but Christians too, and to articulate this he finds it necessary to quote the imprisoned Wilde. This begs a question: might the twentieth-century disappearance of the Christian have something to do with the late-Victorian scandal of the homosexual?

The answer, I suggest, is 'yes' – that there *is*, at the end of the nineteenth century, a complex relationship between the new visibility of the homosexual and the new *in*visibility of the Christian. In one sense, it is simply that the emergence of secularization coincides with the emergence of sexology: in 1888 Nietzsche declares 'there have been no Christians at all'; in 1891 Krafft-Ebing announces the existence of the homosexual.[66] It is a simple fact of historical coincidence that just as the homosexual begins to become visible so the Christian begins to disappear from view. This, though, is only a part of the story, for the disappearing of the Christian in the nineteenth century is also a paradoxical trick of the fact that often *everyone* was still supposed to be a Christian. As Kierkegaard writes,

> In the beginning there was no Christian at all.
> Then everyone became a Christian – and that's why once again there is no Christian.
> That was the end. Now we are at the beginning again.[67]

For the riddling Kierkegaard, now that not everyone is a Christian, once again there *are* Christians; now that the Christian is defined *against* the unbeliever, the Christian becomes newly visible. What is more, he becomes visible at precisely the same time as the homosexual; both come into view together: the homosexual emerges from the closet, the Christian from the crowd.

They then both walk straight into the clinic. For, just like the homosexual, the Christian is now exposed to the gaze of medical science: Nietzsche's talk of 'the Christian infection' and 'religious neurosis' may seem conceitful, but for many late-Victorian psychologists the Christian really is a clinical case. This development is not lost on Wilde who, in his *Oxford Notebooks*, writes that 'the terrible war against religion of our own day has come . . . from . . . the laboratory'. This is the cultural (il)logic at work in *The Importance* when Jack announces that he has in his possession 'certificates of Miss Cardew's birth, baptism, whooping cough, registration, vaccination, confirmation and the measles; both the German and English variety.'[68]

Cecily's *religious* biography – baptism and confirmation – here shades into her medical history, and *both* pass into the regulatory operations of the State. Cecily thus anticipates the figure of Wilde in court, for he will stand there not only as an 'invert' of 'diseased mind' (Queensberry's own words) but, in a curious and conceitful sense, as a *Christian*. Douglas, writing of Wilde's trials, declares, 'certain it is that persecution will no more kill this instinct in a man . . . than it killed the faith of Christian martyrs'.[69] Douglas intends only an analogy but he chances upon something more, for the ironic fact of history is that Wilde's legal opponents are not so much the old, Christian establishment but rather the emergent, secular order. The law to which Wilde finally falls prey is not the ancient, church-inspired law against sodomy but rather the new statute of 1885 which is pushed through by the atheist MP, Henry Labouchère.[70] When Wilde takes Queensberry to court he takes on not only a fierce opponent of Decadence but also an aggressive Secularist. Queensberry had requested in his will that 'I be buried as a Secularist' and supported the *Freethinker* when it was accused of blasphemy in the 1880s, what Marsh calls 'the "heroic" decade' of Secularism.[71] And it is precisely as an heroic Secularist that Queensberry is styled when confronting Wilde in court: *Reynolds Newspaper*, in its description of the first trial, lionizes Queensberry as the 'Agnostic [who had been] intrigued out of his Seat'.[72] Though Queensberry accuses Wilde of 'posing as a Sodomite' not as a Christian, Queensberry comes from a 'militant Secularist' tradition that, in its more extreme moments, often conflated the two 'crimes'. In 1847 the *Oracle of Reason* declared, in capital type, that 'THE GOD OF THE CHRISTIANS IS A LEWD, IMPURE, GROSS, AND OBSCENE PERSON.' In 1841 the same Secularist paper condemns the Bible as

> a history of lust, sodomies . . . and horrible depravity . . . [whose] heroes . . . [sh]ould be strung up to the first lamp-post.[73]

Being strung up, in fact, is exactly what *could* happen to 'sodomites' until the law condemning them to death was changed in 1861; and, indeed, in 1886 the ultimate Bible hero, Christ, is almost strung up *with* the sodomite when the Secularist G. W. Foote dismisses the crucified Christ as 'the effeminate figure on the cross'.[74]

Just nine years later that crucified effeminate figure is Wilde. He is strung up not at the first post, but the first stop – the first stop on his rail journey from Wandsworth to Reading Gaol:

> On November 13th 1895 I was brought down here from London. From two
> o'clock till half-past two . . . I had to stand on the centre platform of
> Clapham Junction in convict dress and handcuffed, for the world to look
> at . . . Of all possible objects I was the most grotesque . . . When people saw
> me they laughed. Each train as it came up swelled the audience. . . . For half
> an hour I stood there in the grey November rain surrounded by a jeering
> mob.[75]

Acutely aware of his intense, even theatrical, visibility (he is on a 'platform', before an 'audience'), the convicted Wilde is here staged as the
newly visible homosexual. However, he is at the same time staged as the
crucified Christ, mocked and scorned. Indeed, standing at Clapham in the
rain before a jeering audience, Wilde is yet another figure – namely, that
'uncouth Christian' who, in *Dorian Gray*, is also seen standing theatri-
cally in London rain:

> [in] the Park last Sunday . . . close by the Marble Arch there stood a little
> crowd of shabby-looking people listening to some vulgar street-preacher
> . . . yelling . . . to his audience. It struck me as being rather dramatic . . . A
> wet Sunday, an uncouth Christian in a mackintosh . . . [76]

For perhaps the first time in the history of the English novel the Christian
emerges from the crowd as truly other, truly marginal; so marginal, in
fact, that he is utterly extraneous to the plot of the novel – the 'uncouth
Christian' is never mentioned again. We could not be further from that
first novel, *Pilgrim's Progress* (1678), where, of course, the character
Christian is at the very centre of the narrative. After two centuries of the
English novel in which Christian gradually vanishes into the bourgeois
Everyman of the *Bildungsroman*, he finally re-emerges as a man in a
mackintosh who has nothing whatsoever to do with the novel's narrative
logic or direction but everything to do with its *il*logic, or indirection. The
Christian in the mackintosh is not only an illogical figure but the very
figure *of* illogic.

This strange, wet, extrinsic figure will not go away; rather, he persists
through the literature of both modernism and postmodernism, reap-
pearing in several guises, first in James Joyce's *Ulysses* (1922), as that
sublimely extraneous figure 'the man in the macintosh', of whom we
know almost nothing except that he is a 'dog of a christian!'[77] Four years
later, in Virginia Woolf's *Mrs. Dalloway*, 'our man' is a woman: namely,
Miss Kilman, the evangelical tutor who combines her liminal role in the
novel with wearing a mackintosh:

> outside the door was Miss Kilman . . . in her mackintosh, listening to what-

107

ever they said . . . Yes, Miss Kilman stood on the landing, and wore a mack-intosh.[78]

Sixty years later, the Christian in the mackintosh is, still more absurdly, that keen Joycean, Jacques Derrida; in 'Circumfession', the word-processing Derrida is the man *at* the 'Macintosh' on yet another rainy Sunday:

> today . . . rainy Easter Sunday . . . I began to 'initialize', as Macintosh says.[79]

Derrida is 'initializing' commands to tidy up his computer screen, to delete stray or 'arbitrary' files; these commands are intended 'to fish out the aleatory', but try as he might he cannot fish, or delete that supremely aleatory fish, the man in the macintosh. For he can turn up anywhere – as Leopold Bloom exclaims, 'Where the deuce did he pop out of ? He wasn't in the chapel I swear!' We might now suspect that he *was* in the chapel, particularly after reading *Mrs. Dalloway*, where people who just 'turn up' go by the crypto-Christian name of 'queer fish':

> . . . odd unexpected people turned up; an artist sometimes; sometimes a writer; queer fish in that atmosphere.

The fishy Miss Kilman – fishy, of course, in her wet, Christian world of 'mackintosh an[d] . . . umbrella'[80] – is also queer; she is not only odd but in love with Elizabeth Dalloway. Similarly queer is Joyce's man in the mackintosh for he is, as Frank Kermode argues, prefigured by the poten-tially homosexual figure of the biblical 'Boy in the Shirt', the young man who plays a minute and mystifying part in Mark's Gospel. As Kermode puts it,

> At the moment of Jesus' arrest, says Mark – and Matthew agrees – all the disciples forsook . . . [Jesus] and fled. And both agree further that his captors then led him to the high priest. But between these two events Mark alone inserts another: 'And a young man followed him with nothing but a linen cloth about his body; and they seized him, but he left the linen cloth and ran away naked.' And that is all Mark has to say about this young man. The difficulty is to explain where the deuce he popped up from.[81]

One strategy for Kermode is to do what some theologians have done and argue that this incident is the remnant of a longer episode from a secret, Alexandrian Gospel in which the young man is naked under his linen cloth because he is on his way to be baptized under cover of night; the other disciples then fall asleep and Jesus is surprised with the youth. The poten-tially sexual import of this encounter was clear to Clement of Alexandria, who sought to condemn the Carpocrations, a libertine sect who emphasized precisely that import. In their version of the secret gospel it is not only the young catechumen who is naked, but Jesus.[82]

Wilde, like many other Decadents, certainly knew well the esoteric and Gnostic work of Clement, and it is quite possible that he was also aware of his Secret Gospel, or indeed the Carpocrations' version.[83] There is, then, a sense in which the odd, queer figure of St Mark's naked young man is emblematic of the alternative, or 'Fifth Gospel' which, as Dollimore stresses, the later Wilde often dreamt of writing.[84] The Decadent decade produced many alternative Gospels – Wilde's *Salome*, for instance, inspired Enrico Gomez Carillo's *The Gospel of Love*; but what distinguishes Wilde's unwritten gospel is that it is *not* esoteric or gnostic.[85] When Wilde speaks of 'the secret of Christ' he is referring to a modern sense of self:

> 'Know thyself' was written over the portal of the antique world. Over the portal of the new world, 'Be thyself' shall be written . . . That is the secret of Christ [86]

This quasi-existential secret contains within it, though, another secret: namely, the secret of writing, the secret of who writes Christ's secret message, 'Be thyself', over the portals of the new world. In *De Profundis* we sense that it might be no-one; in prison Wilde reads a gospel put together by *no-one*: 'every morning . . . I read a little of the Gospels, a dozen verses taken by chance anywhere'.[87] The conceit of an accidental, unauthorized gospel repeats upon *De Profundis* as, just a few pages later, Wilde refers us to John's Gospel and how, when the people

> brought [to Jesus] . . . one taken in the very act of sin and showed him her sentence written in the law . . . he wrote with his finger on the ground.

Why Christ writes, or what Christ writes (if anything), the Gospel does not record; in that sense it is a kind of doodling, writing-for-writing's sake. It is, moreover, a writing that haunts Wilde's own since he is himself 'one taken in the very act of sin'.

So too is Miss Prism in *The Importance*, when it is discovered that she has a child whilst still unmarried: 'Unmarried!' cries Jack, ' I do not deny that is a serious blow. But . . . who has the right to cast a stone?'[88] Jack alludes, of course, to what Christ says when writing in the dust; for a moment Christ himself, the writing-Christ, is almost on stage, though not quite. But then British theatre censorship clearly prohibited the portrayal of *any* biblical character, let alone Christ; in this sense the Victorian Christ was forever offstage, confined to the page. And it is precisely this censoring of the Bible which was invoked to prevent the British staging of

Salome;[89] indeed, as an unstageable play about someone taken in adultery
– namely, Herod – the text might almost *be* the writing of Christ, his
writing for the sake of writing. For Wilde, the true 'secret of Christ' is the
secret of *writing*, the secret that Christ *can* write and, indeed, that he has
written *Salome*. 'Christ's place', claims Wilde, 'is with the poets'; we
should not, then, be surprised that the voice of Christ can be overheard
when, for no obvious dramatic reason, Herod suddenly breaks off from
a long speech to cry 'I thirst!' and in so doing ventriloquises the final cry
of the crucified Christ, a cry that is itself a piece of Jewish scripture: Christ
is quoting Psalm 69 which reads, 'my throat is dried . . . [but] in my thirst
they gave me vinegar to drink'.[90] This is a text that the young Wilde knows
well but, strangely, chooses to reject: when, in 'Humanitad', he rewrites
the Passion so that it is '*we* [who] are . . . crucified', Wilde declares, 'no
need have we of hyssop-laden rod'.[91] The later Wilde is, however, himself
a man 'taken in sin' and Christ, therefore, *has* begun to write, or ghost-
write, Wilde's text; not only in *Salome* but also in 'Pen, Pencil, and
Poison', where Wilde quotes Thomas Wainwright's account of
Rembrandt's *The Crucifixion*:

> The moment rapidly approaches when, nearly torn asunder by His own
> weight, fainting with loss of blood . . . and His black tongue parched with
> the fiery death-fever, Jesus cries, 'I thirst.' The deadly vinegar is elevated to
> him.[92]

With his tongue blackened, Christ's 'I thirst' quotation is an almost
black scripture; indeed, there is a sense in which Wilde's gospel *is* black.
A few months before his conversion Wilde announces the colour of his
incipient faith: 'my position is curious: I am not a Catholic: I am simply
a violent Papist. No one could be more "black" than I am.'[93] Wilde is
here referring to the emblematic black of the Jesuits; his faith, though, is
also marked by the emblematic black of the violent Anarchist. Just two
years before, Wilde declares that Prince Kropotkin has 'the soul of that
beautiful white Christ that seems coming out of Russia', but since
Kropotkin was an Anarchist this white Christ is set against a black background.[94]

In 'The Soul of Man', Wilde declares that 'a Nihilist who rejects all
authority . . . is a real Christian', but the Anarcho-Christian is also, for
Wilde, a real 'black', for the gospel at work in Wilde is black with the
black of an anarchy that is heavily influenced by North Africa, in particular Egypt.[95] This anarchy is what George Gissing called the 'sexual
anarchy' of the *fin de siècle*, an anarchy centered on the Orient, a 'place'
which, as Edward Said points out, offered a whole range of 'sexual experience not available in Europe'.[96] For Wilde, it also offered a whole new

range of *religious* experience; in Wilde, Oriental anarchy is not just sexual but theological – witness, in *Salome* the 'dangerous doctrine . . . that cometh from Alexandria', the doctrine that 'God is in what is evil'.[97] Such a dangerous and anarchic doctrine is evident in the way that Wilde rethinks Christianity through the Egyptian mythology of Alexandria. Clement's second-century *Gospel of the Egyptians* was a popular Decadent text, or subtext, and what we have in Wilde is the trace of his very own Gospel of the Egyptians. In *De Profundis* Christ's body is said to have been 'swathed in Egyptian linen', whilst in 'The Sphinx' we are reminded of how the 'Holy Child' escaped to Egypt.[98] Addressing the Egyptian Sphinx herself, Wilde cries, 'Sing to me of the Jewish maid who wandered with the Holy Child, / And how you led them through the wild.' Though we never hear this song, the rest of the poem leads Christ 'through the wild' excesses of Egyptian myth for, though never again the explicit subject of the poem, Christ returns in exotic, oriental disguise: first as 'he [who] strode across the waters . . . [to] touch . . . [the] black breasts [of the Sphinx]', and then as a kind of Osiris, 'the god [who] is scattered here and there'.

Badly cast

'The world is a stage, but the play is badly cast.'
('Lord Arthur Savile's Crime')[99]

For Wilde, Egypt has the capacity not only to scatter but also to disturb and even shake: as poet, Wilde cries: 'come, great Egypt, shake / Our stage.'[100] Wilde is here calling on the actress Ellen Terry to play the part of Shakespeare's Cleopatra and thus shake the British theatre. Though Terry never plays the part, the god-scattering gospel of Egypt does shake the stage of Oscar Wilde. Indeed, in *An Ideal Husband* this shaking is almost literal:

(A chair falls in the drawing room)
SIR ROBERT CHILTERN: What is that!
LORD GORING: Nothing. . . . there is no one there
SIR ROBERT CHILTERN: I heard a chair fall in the next room. . . . Some one has been listening. . . .
LORD GORING: No, no; there is no one there.
SIR ROBERT CHILTERN: There is some one. . . . Someone has been listening to every secret of my life. . . .
LORD GORING: . . . you are excited, unnerved. I tell you there is no one in that room.[101]

A chair falls and yet no one is there – it is as if the stage has been shaken. We soon learn that someone *is* there but for a few moments we witness a stage shaken by no one, a God-like no one who knows 'every secret of my life'. This, in a sense, is the shaken Theatre of the Absurd: 'What is that!', There is no one there' – the philosophical resonance is clear. Just before, Sir Robert Chiltern, remarking on his childless marriage, declares that 'God has given us a lonely house' and for Wilde's late-Victorian audiences, used to an almost wholly secular drama, the house of the theatre is indeed lonely; quite simply, God is *not* in the house, the Bible and its characters can*not* be staged.[102] When, therefore, the chair falls in what is thought to be an empty room, the stage shakes with the uncanny possibility that God *is* in the house – that God might, like 'The Sphinx Without a Secret', be sitting in an empty room. The woman, or Sphinx, in this short story of Wilde's, pretends she has some romantic secret and so makes regular visits to a strange house, but when the landlady at the house is asked if the woman 'met someone [t]here?' the landlady replies:

> '[No,] she simply sat in the drawing room . . . she always came alone, and saw no one.'[103]

If there is a *religious* significance to this drawing room, it answers well to an age that espoused what George Eliot called 'genteel Christianity', an age that *could*, as Samuel Butler pointed out, 'conceive of . . . our Lord Himself drinking a cup of tea'. The Victorians were never far from imagining God sat alone on a chair – their Poet Laureate, Tennyson writes: 'I sit as God . . . contemplating.'[104] For Tennyson, of course, it is not only God who sits on His own but us, and it is the same for Wilde. For just as the secret-less Sphinx '*saw* no one' so, when a chair falls on its own, we *hear* no one, *really* hear no one – or at least that is the fiction until the culprit is discovered. Like the Sphinx, we have proved alarmingly adept at conjuring up someone who is no one, a wholly invisible and imaginary figure.

Equally adapt is Algernon who, in *The Importance*, conjures up his imaginary friend Bunbury, and Bunbury too is finally 'exploded'. But then that is precisely the fate of the Victorians' imaginary friend, God; this is the point of the play, a point that expands with Lady Bracknell's response:

> 'Exploded! Was he the victim of a revolutionary outrage? I was not aware that Mr. Bunbury was interested in social legislation.'

For Nietzsche's Zarathustra, God is, quite simply, 'dead' and the same goes for Hardy who solemnly attends what he calls 'God's Funeral'; for the splendid Wilde, however, God is exploded by an anarcho-socialist

bomb.[105] Indeed, to make things still more splendid, it is quite possible –
on reflection – that Mr Bunbury was on the *side* of the bombers. Consider
Lady Bracknell's inference that Bunbury is 'interested in social legislation',
is himself a socialist; if she is right Bunbury would be the tragi-comic
victim of his own revolutionary outrage, exploded by his own bomb – a
suicide bomber, as it were. And this, in a sense, is how Nietzsche sees God,
not only declaring that 'God is dead' but also describing the doctrine of
'equality of souls' as 'Christian dynamite';[106] for Nietzsche, the egalitarian
God might also be interested in social legislation. Like Mr Bunbury,
Nietzsche's God is not just exploded but explosive.

When Wilde once described himself as 'something of an Anarchist', he
also declared that Anarchism's 'dynamite policy is very absurd'.[107] And
for Wilde, *Christian* dynamite is not just equality but also absurdity; when
Christian explosives go off in Wilde it is their absurdity that is explosive.
Witness Miss Prism's handbag: 'Here', she says, 'is the stain on the lining
caused by the explosion of a temperance beverage, an incident that
occurred at Leamington.'[108] Akin to the Temperance Movement's
exploding beverage is the Dean of Chichester's exploding clock; in 'Lord
Arthur Savile's Crime', the Dean is given a clock that features a figurine
of 'Liberty' and has, unbeknown to the Cathedral Dean, been designed by
an 'Anarchist', and intended to kill. However, it rather splendidly does
nothing of the kind:

> When we examined it, we found it was a sort of alarm clock, and that, if
> you . . . put some gunpowder . . . under a little hammer, it went off when-
> ever you wanted [and every time 'the goddess of Liberty fell off']. Papa said
> it must not remain in the library, as it made a noise . . . and does nothing
> but have small explosions all day long. . . . I suppose they are quite fash-
> ionable in London. Papa says they do a great deal of good, as they show
> that [the secular goddess of] Liberty can't last, but must fall down.[109]

The Dean is right: anti-secular, Christian 'dynamite' *is* alive and well in
late-Victorian London; throughout the East End the Salvation Army was
renting and buying theatres in order to put on its 'music-hall' evangelism,
with preachers billed as the 'Salvation Midget', the 'Hallelujah Giant' and
the 'Converted Sweep' together initiating what was described as a
'carnival of equality'.[110] The sheer absurdity of this carnival cast its
shadow over even the theatres of the West End; in 1893 the playwright
Henry Arthur Jones speculates what might happen if the Salvation Army
and, indeed, all their co-religionists were put on the secular stage – what
he envisages is a 'great perpetual comedy':

> Here a Bishop of Lincoln judgment . . . there an epileptic dance to General
> Booth's pipes and tabors; here a churchyard riot over a dead Dissenter . . .
> there [a] low comedian Spurgeon railing at the stage; at one moment a
> Church . . . piously imagining that it regulates the weather; at another Mr.
> Gladstone . . . swallowing the whole herd of Gadarene swine with the ease
> of a conjurer swallowing a poker.[111]

Jones goes on to remark, of the prospect of 'religious melodrama', that
'one cannot contemplate such a development of our theatre without a
shudder'. The theatre would also, no doubt, shudder; to adapt Wilde,
'come great *Church,* and shake the stage'.

For Wilde, in Rome just before his conversion, the Church does itself
shake like a bad stage set. Writing in a letter about his new-found passion
for photography, Wilde asks, quite marvellously:

> Can you photograph cows well? I did one of cows in the Borghese . . . Cows
> are very fond of being photographed, and, unlike architecture, don't move.[112]

The architecture that moves is the church-filled city of Rome; in the badly-
photographed world of Wilde's last months even the Holy City is askew.
But then, in these last months God shades into the whole surreal comedy
of modern things, not just cameras, but umbrellas. In another letter Wilde
remarks,

> This time I really must become a Catholic, though I fear that if I went before
> the Holy Father with a blossoming rod it would turn at once into an
> umbrella.[113]

For Wilde, the high seriousness of becoming a Catholic cannot be sepa-
rated from the low comedy of a rod becoming an umbrella. Once dead,
indeed, Wilde is *himself* reduced to an umbrella – when the State comes
looking for money to pay for Wilde's burial, and finds nothing, its rep-
resentative ends up asking after the monetary value of Wilde's
umbrella.[114]

The dead Wilde, though, is an umbrella that might just move; as Robert
Ross records, their friend Maurice Gilbert took a badly-lit photograph of
Wilde's corpse.[115] The dead Wilde thus belongs to the shifting, moving
world of the badly-taken photograph; to adapt again Wilde's own words:
'cows are fond of being photographed and, unlike *dead men and
umbrellas*, don't move'. We should not forget that, for Wilde, 'it is absurd
to say the age of miracles is past'.[116]

The age of miracles has, in fact, always been latent within Wilde's anti-
realism, in particular his anti-Arnoldian insistence that the function of
criticism is 'to see the object as in itself it really is *not*'.[117] Wilde most spec-

tacularly does this when he mistakes the hanging-house of Reading Gaol for a photography booth:

> the shed in which people are hanged is a little shed with a glass roof, like a photographer's studio on the sands at Margate . . . [indeed] for 18 months I thought it *was* the studio for photographing prisoners.[118]

In seeing the hanging-house as the object it really is *not*, Wilde sees dead men move, or at least being photographed. In Reading this is a hideous mistake, in the glass-roofed shed no one is being photographed, only hung; in Paris, however, Wilde is both dead *and* photographed. Given Wilde's comic conviction that photographed things tend to move, there is still the possibility that the dead man might be a *thing* that moves. And indeed, the movement does not necessarily require bad photography, for the dead man that is Wilde *is* a thing that moves: what we learn from the dead Wilde is that the dead man moves *us*. Of course, it is often the thing the dead man leaves behind that moves us most. In this sense, the thing *does* move.

But then we should know this for, in Wilde's case, the thing left behind is an umbrella; and, as we know from 'Lord Arthur Saville's Crime', we inhabit a world shared with both Anarchists and Nihilists – people mad enough to invent not only explosive clocks but the 'explosive umbrella'.[119] This is true Christian dynamite; it is no accident that Lord Arthur speaks of having '*faith* in explosives'.

chapter six

Joycing Derrida, Churching Derrida

Glas, église and *Ulysses*

Before

a riddling sentence to be woven and woven on the church's looms.
(James Joyce, *Ulysses*, 1922)

. . . everything here is woven against a church.
(Jacques Derrida, *Glas*, 1974)[1]

The riddling sentences of *Glas* and *Ulysses* are woven both on and against the church; even when opposing the church, these texts could not exist without it. To follow this particular weaving, my reading will shuttle between *Glas* and *Ulysses*, a movement that is itself churchy or ecclesial, in that the French for 'shuttle', *navette*, is also – as *Glas* reminds us – 'a church term' meaning 'incense vessel'.[2] But then, so many of the seemingly secular words of *Glas* and *Ulysses* double as church terms; they have, as it were, a buried and distant ecclesial life – such words, to use yet another, 'communicate' from *afar*. For this reason, the church in *Glas* and *Ulysses* must *tele*communicate;[3] here, as Derrida observes of Genet's fiction, 'the Gospel [is] . . . violently . . . fragmented . . . as if [it] . . . reached us over . . . an overloaded telephone exchange'.[4]

In *Ulysses* the church literally telecommunicates: the 'archbishop's letter' is 'repeated in the *Telegraph*'; Buck Mulligan cries 'Telegram! A papal bull'; 'the signal for prayer . . . [is] given by megaphone'; and 'His grace [the Bishop] phone[s] . . . twice [in one] . . . morning.'[5] In Dublin, a city full of priests, the church never stops ringing:

. . . a priest round the corner is elevating it. Dringdring! And two streets
off another locking it into a pyx. Dringadring! And in a ladychapel another
taking housel all to his own cheek. Dringdring![6]

It is, of course, the dringdring of the eucharist bell, but Joyce cannot resist
re-imagining the church as a bizarre network of telephone lines: in *Ulysses*
we read not only that 'his grace phoned' but also that, in another place
and time, 'Buck Mulligan antiphoned'.[7] Derrida also antiphones, or rather
anti-phones, for just as *Glas* is woven '*against* the church', so it is wired
against, or in despite of the official church; in Genet's 'overloaded telephone exchange' it is only on 'a wire-tap' that Derrida hears, or rather
overhears the church and its gospel – he is listening in from without. This
is the church inside-*out,* where telecommunication comes close to *ex-*
communication. In *Glas* (the word means 'passing-bell'), we hear not just
the bell that sounds at funerals but 'all the bells of a church' including
both the telephone bell and the 'bell, book and candle' that ex-communi-
cates.[8] It is an illicit and ex-communicated church that *Glas*, through
Genet, seeks to write, or wire-tap.

It is a dangerous wire to tap. When Derrida reads Genet's 'The
Funambulists' the wire in question is a high-wire; here we watch an
'acrobat . . . twenty-five . . . feet from the ground . . . pray[ing] and
cross[ing] himself'.[9] Genet's story shifts, says Derrida, 'from vigil to wire'
and, indeed, back again with those clowns, or 'saltimbanques who . . .
danced in front of . . . cathedrals'.[10] The Genet quote continues, '"I don't
know to what god you will address your feats of dexterity, but you need
one"'; the later Derrida *does*, of course, address his feats of dexterity to
a god – as seen in 'Circumfession': 'I am', writes Derrida, 'addressing
myself here to God.'[11] Addressing God begins, though, in *Glas* where
Derrida himself performs in front of cathedrals. In returning Hegelian
thought to the 'Christianity of which it is the truth',[12] Derrida opens up a
space for philosophy *before* philosophy, a space he calls 'the parvis' – the
enclosed area before a cathedral. Here *Glas* locates a church *before* the
church, a church before what Derrida calls philosophy's 'church of stone',
Hegel's petrified abstraction of Christianity.[13] Derrida, like the whole
theatre of religion – 'advent . . . the cross . . . [and] resurrection play' –
joins the clowning saltimbanques in 'play[ing] on the parvis . . . *before*
philosophy's erect construction'.[14]

Though this 'church of stone' is built of philosopher's stone it also
invokes the stone that is St Peter: as Derrida reminds us, Jesus declares,
'thou art Peter [meaning 'rock'] and upon this rock I will build my
church'.[15] St Peter is also invoked by the word 'parvis', deriving as it does
from *paradisus,* or 'Paradise', the portico in front of St Peter's Church in

Rome. In *Ulysses* Bloom comes across a book called *Why I left the church of Rome*; in *Glas* it sometimes seems as if all roads lead *back* to that church.[16] The word 'parvis' leads, however, to the court where the Pope takes a hammer to the church: in a ceremony performed once every twenty-five years, the Pope knocks down the walled-up Holy Door.[17] It is an act or moment that Derrida chances upon when he predicts, of the church of stone, that 'the stone [*pierre*] itself will give rise . . . to . . . fracture . . . [and] ruin'.[18] The ruining of the walled-up door to which the Pope gives rise marks the beginning of the Roman Year of Jubilee. This is the year of remission from the penal consequences of sin which is named after the Jewish Jubilee, that fifty-yearly remission of debts in which, as Derrida observes, not just 'property [but] . . . the proper is . . . equalized [and] levelled'.[19] For Derrida, the Jewish Jubilee takes a hammer to the very logic of property, the logic of the proper, or self-same.

Glas then is a political text; indeed, though written in 1974, it anticipates the international debt-relief campaign, 'Jubilee 2000'.[20] Concerned as it is with 'the space of debt', *Glas* includes Christ's parable of two forgiven debtors , and dreams of ways to 'escape . . . the operation of . . . debt' through 'the giving of . . . the pure *cadeau* [that] . . . does not let itself be thought by . . . dialectics' – the dialectics of indebtedness.[21] *Glas* comes even closer to jubilee at the level of pure sound, for just as 'the *glas* is first of all [etymologically] . . . the signal of a trumpet' so 'Jubilee' is first of all *yobel,* 'a ram's horn'.[22] The *glas*-trumpet, however, 'is destined to *call* [or] . . . gather together . . . a *class* of the Roman people'; it serves the very *proper*tied class that the jubilee-trumpet sounds *against*. In this sense, *Glas*'s jubilee is ironized, is itself woven against. Though *Glas* performs upon the parvis before the Hegelian church of stone, it does so under the philosophical sign of the proper: 'this work of mourning', writes Derrida, 'is always for/of the proper name'.

In *Glas*, however, the proper name is never simply being mourned; also at work is a jubilee that jubilates at the proper name's passing, celebrating and even hastening the destabilization of names. In cancelling debt every fifty years the Jewish Jubilee redefines not only property but the proper name, the name in which property is held – both become provisional, liable to change. As Derrida puts it, 'jubilee . . . constitutes [or renders] . . . possession as loan [*en prêt*] and . . . the name as [merely] a lent-name [*prête-nom*]'.[23] In so doing, jubilee impacts upon the very name of the church; for here *prêt* becomes *prête*, an anagram of 'Peter', the lent-name which not only founds the church but signals its end as *perte* ('ruin'), another anagram of 'Peter' which appears in the very last line of *Glas*. By scrambling the church's proper name, jubilee – like Genet – leads the church into 'the occulted tradition of anagrammatizing names', a tradition that Derrida identifies with 'the depths of a crypt', that dark church *beneath* a church which, for Derrida, is not only a crypt but cryptic: there are, he writes, 'anagrams . . . in . . . a crypt'.[24] There is also a thief; for Genet here 'moves [like] . . . a thief in the night'; this church beneath a church redistributes property as well as proper names. It is a church made in the im-proper image of jubilee.

Something of this church is also found in *Ulysses*; here the proper name of '*Joyce*' is always-already purloined by a church that en*joys* itself, that is beside itself with laughter.[25] For all the novel's funerals and passing-bells, here 'joybells ring in . . . church' and so, indeed, do 'rams' horns'.[26] As Derrida reminds us, Hegel's friend Niethammer spoke of 'the *comedy* of Christianity' – it is, for Niethammer, a comedy to be avoided, whereas in *Ulysses* we encounter not just 'the ballad of joking Jesus' but the *church* of joking Jesus; as Joyce observes, 'the . . . Church was built on a pun'.[27] What, though, makes all this joking a jubilee is that it is a witness to suffering. When, in November 1906, Joyce is visiting Rome an anarchist bomb goes off in St Peter's. In his letter the next day he remarks, 'it's a bloody funny church';[28] it almost is as if the church is most funny when it is also literally bloody. This irony is repeated when, in *Ulyssses*, we encounter not Simon *Peter* but Simon *Stephen* – namely 'His Eminence Simon Stephen Cardinal Dedalus'.[29] Here, at the moment of high parody, is a church founded not on Peter-the-rock but Stephen-the-stoned, Stephen the church's first martyr stoned to a bloody death. What Stephen himself calls the 'nightmare of history'[30] is, in the case of the church, so bloody it has to be funny; if the terrible crimes of the church are to be communicated at all it must be as a joke. For the Hegelian Niethammer, such mixing of tragedy and comedy is unthinkable: '"[it is only] weak individuals . . . who play the comedy of Christianity with cross, blood . . . and self-degradation"'; Derrida, however, is of a different mind. On the very last page of *Glas* we read that

> the syllogism of spiritual art (epos, tragedy, comedy), leads esthetic religion to revealed religion. Through comedy then.[31]

To arrive at revealed religion – the tragic religion of cross, blood and self-degradation – we must go through comedy. Perhaps Joking Jesus laughs so much that he cries; indeed, according to revealed religion, that is precisely what he does: as the New Testament reveals, 'Jesus wept.'[32] Joyce's Jesus certainly comes close to crying in the very moment of laughter:

> She laughed:
> – O wept! . . .
> With sadness. [33]

For 'Jesus wept' read 'O wept!'; for revealed religion read exclamation. In this case, laughter, or comedy, might appear to lead not so much *towards* revealed religion as *away* from it; in the moment of laughter Jesus vanishes: 'O' is no one. If, though, history is a nightmare, a form of apparition, then the more insubstantial Jesus is the more historical he becomes. We might yet arrive at a historical Jesus through the tricks, apparitions and vanishings of laughter. 'Through comedy then.'

This is certainly the lesson of *Glas*, for here Derrida announces that it is 'time to perfect the resemblance between Dionysus and Christ', to invoke a laughing, carnivalized, drunken Christus;[34] in doing so, Derrida also invokes the violence that so besets the history of Christ, or at least the history of the drugged and dangerous Christ of Christian unreason. Derrida hints at this by speaking of 'Jesus's pharmacy'; for Derrida, the word 'pharmacy' entails not only drug (*pharmakon*), but violence (*pharmakos* meaning 'scapegoat').[35] Here are shades, of course, of the Marxian line that 'religion is . . . the opium of the people'; but whilst Marx presents the church as an hallucinatory escape from history, Derrida knows there is no such escape in Jesus's pharmacy. Indeed, from pharmacy, or chemistry, originates the science behind the most explosive nightmare of history – namely, nuclear fission. The bomb in St Peter's in 1906 is not the only the bomb to go off in the twentieth-century church.

Bomb

I hear the ruin of all space, shattered glass and toppling masonry.

(*Ulysses*)

In *Ulysses*, even as church bells toll, the Second Watch in Nighttown declares, 'The bomb is here.'[36] That bomb is, in one sense, a Fenian bomb; as Fairhall remarks, 'the [1867] Clerkenwell explosion resounds throughout *Ulysses*'.[37] The Fenian bomb particularly resounds in All Hallows Church. It is there Bloom recalls 'that fellow that turned queen's evidence on the Invincibles', the Fenian splinter group that carried out the Phoenix Park murders of 1882:

> That fellow used to receive the, Carey was his name, the communion every morning. This very church.[38]

The Clerkenwell bomb resounds in 'that fellow's very name, for one of the bombers was so nearly called Carey, Casey was his name'. Carey, of course, was by no means the only Fenian within Irish Catholicism; in that sense, All Hallows was not the only turn-of-the-century Dublin church in which the Fenian bomb resounded. That is a simple lesson of history.[39] Indeed, as *Glas* demonstrates, one simple lesson of *the dictionary* is that a bomb resounds in every church:

> *glas* 'ringing of all the bells of a church' . . . *glas* . . . 'noise of a bomb'.[40]

The noise of a bomb is, perhaps, first heard in church by Nietzsche who, in 1888, warns that the doctrine of 'equality of souls' is 'Christian dynamite' capable of 'ignit[ing] a "world conflagration."'[41] In 1888 no explosive is capable of igniting the world; fifty-seven years before Hiroshima, Nietzsche is locating in the church a dynamite that somehow anticipates the far more terrible 'dynamite' of nuclear fission. Twenty-three years before Hiroshima, Joyce does something similar in *Ulysses* – here the Magnificat becomes 'magnificandjewbang' and Boylan cries 'Godblazegrukbrukarchkhrasht!'; in both cases it is as if the church's creed is so outrageous as to somehow split what Molly calls the 'atom of . . . expression'.[42] Such a splitting or fission was already on the way in contemporary physics: in June 1922, Niels Bohr tells Werner Heisenberg that 'electrons . . . [are] not . . . things'.[43] Joyce himself did not, in a sense, need to be told this; did not need to join 'Father Butt in the physics theatre'. Though *Finnegan's Wake* (1939), speaks of 'reading work on German physics', such physics was always already Joycean, or Bloomian. [44] After all, German physics was also known as 'modernist', or 'Jewish' physics, the field being dominated by Jews.[45] There is, it seems, not only Christian dynamite but Jewish dynamite; as *Ulysses* puts it, 'magnificand*jew*bang'.

Glas puts it differently, but it too comes close to the Judaeo-Christian dynamite at work in a nuclear explosion. The word *Sa* that so preoccupies Derrida in *Glas* is certainly explosive; this is true whether we read it as initials for Hegel's *savoir absolu* (absolute knowledge), or, alternatively, as Freud's *ça* (the id, or unconscious). Of Genet we read, 'he is wherever that explodes', wherever '*ça* saute'; here *ça* explodes but so too does the *sa* of '*sa*ute'. Derrida insists that *savoir absolu* arises from a dialectic driven by the 'metaphor . . . of the bomb': as Derrida points out, the first 'moment' of the dialectic, 'the passage into the absolute opposite', is compared by Hegel to the point at which 'a bombshell at its zenith effects a jolt'.[46] Indeed, the *final* 'moment' of Hegel's dialectic, the point at which the opposite reflects the subject, or self, is still more explosive: 'Hiroshima', argues Mark Taylor, 'might be understood' as 'the self affirm[ing] . . . itself through . . . absolute negation.'[47] As Genet writes, and Derrida cites, '"total presence . . . is transformed into a bomb of . . . terrific power."'[48] In this sense, it is always the case that 'the bomb is here'; since what is explosive, what can annihilate the other, is the 'is here', the self-present.

But for Joyce in Rome on November 18, 1906 the bomb in St Peter's is, most crucially, not *here* but *there*; as he writes to his brother, 'I had intended going to the morning service (and would consequently have been in the church at the time of the explosion), but that I waited in for a letter from you.'[49] This letter is unusual; as Carla de Petris observes, 'in [the rest of] his [Rome] letters . . . the hundreds of churches [Joyce] . . . had to pass . . . every day are not even mentioned'; for Joyce in Rome, any bomb in the church was, necessarily, *there* rather than *here*.

There is, though, a bomb in the church that actually derives its terrific power from what is always already *elsewhere*; this is the buried theme of Derrida's declaration that 'the institution, the stone of the Church will provoke another fission'.[50] Fission of the nuclear kind is a chain-reaction of splitting upon splitting of atomic nuclei, a quasi-infinite impossibilizing of the centre of the atom that comes close to deconstruction's critique of self-presence. Witness Mark Taylor's pointedly Derridean remark that, 'atomic fission . . . make[s] . . . centeredness impossible'.[51]

The trace or ghost of nuclear fission may certainly be pursued throughout *Glas*, a text that itself splits and then splits again: here (and there), 'each textual atom . . . bursts'.[52] Paraphrasing Hegel, Derrida writes that 'one divides itself into two, such is the distressing source of philosophy'; if so, *Glas* represents an almost infinite chain-reaction to that philosophical splitting. It is, though, a fission that also comes from the church. For whilst 'the Hegelian reading of Christianity seems', says Derrida, 'to describe a reconciliation . . . Christianity [in fact] opens a new morseling'.[53] This is most conspicuous in the eucharist, when the church is literally morseling – that is, biting and breaking the body of Christ; for Derrida, it is at this moment that 'divinity stands, very precariously, between swallowing and vomiting . . . neither solid nor liquid, neither outside nor in'.[54] Split between two states and two locations, the eucharistic body of Christ is 'here' in crisis; thus giving a new and explosive sense to that Marxian phrase which appears later in *Glas*: namely, 'the "critical Christ."'[55] Derrida writes of a 'religion [that] would have a *critical* effect on *Sa*', but *Glas* has a critical effect on religion, in particular the mass; in *Glas,* as the nuclear physicists say, the mass goes critical.

It is, though, always already critical in that, as the 'perpetual memorial of Christ's sacrifice', the church's breaking of bread is a perpetual process of dividing, or splitting. In the Dublin of *Ulysses* this is obvious: here Stephen imagines himself a priest administering the mass whilst, of course,

> . . . at the same instant perhaps a priest round the corner is elevating it. Dringdring! And two streets off another locking it into a pyx. Dringadring! And in the lady chapel another taking housel all to his own cheek. Dringdring! Down, up, forward, back . . . Dan Occam thought of that.[56]

In a city full of Catholic churches the Real Presence, it seems, is never purely and simply present. Jacques Derrida, in a sense, thought of that; it is what he calls, in *Glas*, the '*not yet* of philosophy', a not yet that echoes the not yet of the mass that is 'a perpetual memorial *until he comes again*'.[57] For Derrida, this Christological not yet is also, however, the not yet of total nuclear war. In 'No Apocalypse: Not Now' (1984), Derrida ends his meditation on the absolute uniqueness of such a war, 'its-being-for-the-first-time-and-perhaps-for-the-last-time', by invoking the Christ of the Apocalypse, he who declares '"I am the first and the last."'[58] This Apocalyptic Christ is akin to the 'non-event' of nuclear war. Once again, there is a metaphorical bomb in the church.

It is, though, perhaps, fear of an actual, anarchist bomb that keeps Joyce passing by the churches of Rome; in so doing, he falls into step with Hegel, who writes (as Derrida cites), '"I never more than pass by churches."'[59] Genet, however, *does* do more, he *does* go in; what Jean Cocteau called 'the Genet bomb' is habitually drawn to churches, his writing is full of them.[60] This, for Genet, is because 'the church [is] . . . a box of surprises'; for Derrida, it is because Genet thought of *that*, of *ça* – 'Genet is wherever *ça* explodes' even, it seems, when *ça* explodes in church.

This is literally true of Genet's play *Blacks*. In September 1963, at the height of the Civil Rights movement, one particular American performance of *Blacks* replaced Genet's line 'One hundred thousand youngsters who died in the dust' with the words 'Four little girls who died in a Birmingham church.' The four girls were black and had been killed by a white supremacist's bomb.[61]

Black

> The white stone becomes black.
>
> (*Glas*)[62]

Unlike Joyce, Genet – or at least his play – *is* there when the bomb goes off in church. But then, as Derrida writes, Genet 'is wherever it explodes [because] he no longer inhabits the . . . Christian West'; 'it explodes', implies Derrida, *outside* the Christian West, and so it does in 1963 in the sense that the church in Birmingham is a Black church; its congregation is African American.[63] It is, though, still a church – the Genet bomb may go off outside the Christian West, but not outside the church. The terrible lesson of 1963 is that there *is* an explosive church outside the Western church: a black church. This is a lesson that Genet himself needed to learn; for though the play seeks to invert all conventional values by declaring black all that is conventionally white, this does not include the church:

> . . . black was the colour of priests. . . . But everything is changing. Whatever
> is gentle and kind and good and tender will be black. Milk will be black,
> sugar, rice, the sky, doves, hope, will be black.[64]

The play dreams of a black that has left behind the black of the priests, a
revolution that takes place without the church: a dream which the bomb
of 1963 explodes. It was no accident that the Black Civil Rights movement of the 1960s was led by Martin Luther King, a pastor, a man of the
church. Black revolution, it seems, does not leave the church.

This can be seen in *Glas;* for here Genet's inverted and absolutely black
world entails a black church – he inhabits 'the depths of a crypt' that is
dedicated to 'a nocturnal God' and thief-in-the-night Christ.[65] In *Glas,* this
crypt operates as the black other of a Hegelian church of stone that proves
to be 'white stone' – literally, a 'white mythology': we are reminded that
'missionary reports' informed Hegel's declaration that 'Africa . . . "has no
history."'[66]

The idea, or conceit, of a black counter-church is also a Joycean one.
Joyce delighted in the fact that in Rome the leader of the Jesuits, that
'church' within the Church, was known as the 'Black Pope'.[67] In *Ulysses*
there is talk of 'the . . . African heresiarch'; 'black candles' are lit for a
black, or 'reversed . . . mass'; and Bloom goes 'through a form of clan-
destine marriage . . . in the shadow of the Black church'.[68] This particular
church is black because it is made of black Dublin rock,[31] but Joyce's black
church is made also of black African souls: 'Father Conmee thought of
. . . the African mission and of the millions of black and brown . . . souls'.
In *Ulysses*, the black church is not only a trope, or a metaphoric dark
continent, it is also simultaneously a specific historical reality wrought by
powerful *white* men.[69] The same may be said of Genet's *Blacks* as
performed in America in September 1963 when the terrible reality of the
Black church in Birmingham, Alabama is that the church is not only black
but *blackened*, bombed, burnt – 'four little girls killed in a church'.

This, though, is not 'just' history; according to Derrida, black children
are still being killed within the church, or at least under the sign of the
church and its code of sacrifice. In *The Gift of Death* the biblical story of
Abraham and Isaac prompts Derrida to return to the theme of jubilee with
the terrible declaration that 'because of . . . external debt . . . [our]
"society" *puts to* death . . . millions of children . . . in [an] . . . incalcu-
lable sacrifice'.[70] It is difficult to think of child-sacrifice happening today;
as Derrida puts it, 'we can hardly imagine a father taking his son to be
sacrificed on the top of . . . Montmartre'. Perhaps not; but the irony of
Derrida's remark is that the city fathers of Paris *did* imagine building *Sacré
Coeur* on the top of Montmartre to commemorate the many sons that

were sacrificed in the Franco-Prussian War of 1871. Built of white stone *Sacré Coeur* is, literally, a white church, but it soon grows symbolically white – a white church for white Isaacs, white Christs – as Derrida reminds us of how easily we forget the millions of Isaacs killed not on European battlefields but through the suffering caused by African debts. These are black Isaacs, black Christs.

Black Christs are, likewise, on the mind, or conscience of Joyce; witness Bloom's reading of the newspaper:

> *Black Beast Burned in Omaha, Ga* [sic] . . . a Sambo strung up in a tree with . . . a bonfire under him. Gob [sic], they ought to . . . crucify him to make sure.[71]

Later, Molly exclaims, 'Jesusjack, that child is a black', but here Jesusjack is himself not only black but blackened. If Genet is wherever *ça* explodes, Joyce is – in this case – where 'Sambo' burns: namely, Georgia or 'Ga' as it is abbreviated by Joyce. 'Ga' is the next state along from the explosive Birmingham, Alabama. It is as if all roads lead to the Deep South and a black and blackened church; that, it seems, is where both Freud's *ça* and Hegel's *Sa* end up. This, of course, is a variation on the familiar themes of contemporary America as the dead-end of psychoanalysis and the end, or telos, of Hegelian history;[72] it is a variation that sees a specifically racist America at the end of the line, at the end of the Freudian and Hegelian line. In Genet and Joyce the blackened church is witness to the fact that the *Sa/ça* in Ameri-*ca* is violently white. So too is the *Sa/ça* in Ireland, for the blackened Christ of 'Ga' is not limited to Georgia but reappears in Dublin, as Bloom in Nighttown; here Bloom stands dressed, like Christ, in 'a seamless garment marked I.H.S'. with a 'bag of gunpowder round his neck', whilst figures 'kneel down and pray. . . . [until he] becomes . . . carbonized . . . black in the face'.[73]

Once again, Jesusjack is a Black. So too was that Jewishjack, Jacques Derrida; as a child in Algeria, Derrida was, in his own words, 'a little black and very Arab Jew'.[74] Indeed, just like Bloom's crucified Sambo, the Derrida of *Glas* finds himself in 'Ga', not the 'Ga' that is Georgia but the 'Ga' that is Galilee: in the Genet column 'we are', writes Derrida, 'in Galilee'.[75] Or, more fully, 'we are in Galilee between 1810 and 1910', the long nineteenth century of European colonialism – the text at this point cuts to '"Frenchmen bombarding Algiers in 1830 . . . "' We are not, however, stuck in a nineteenth-century, Eurocentric Galilee; for in *Glas* we encounter not so much the Victorians' famously 'pale Galilean' as the strange spectre of a dark Galilean.[76] 'Could it be that you are from Galilee too?' The question is first put to Jesus but it also appears in *Glas* and rebounds upon its Algerian author, for *Glas* is published, of course, by

Éditions Galilée.[77] Alluding to this, Geoffrey Hartman declares that '*Glas* is of the House of Galilee'. What we must add is that, in *Glas*, Galilee is by no means a safe house, but rather is identified with bombarded Algiers just as closely as *Glas*'s Galilean author is identified with the figure of a *galerien*, a galley-slave: 'the author', writes Derrida, 'rows with the application of a . . . *galerien*'.[78] *Glas*'s Galilee – its Christianity – is black with the blackness of the North African unconscious of its author.[79]

It is also black because it is blackened or singed by Genet's searing critique, what Derrida calls Genet's 'violent . . . radiographic interpretation . . . of Golgotha'.[80] Another blazing interpretation of Christianity at work in *Glas* is that of Feuerbach, whose name transliterates as 'stream of fire'. With this in mind Marx famously proclaims: 'Christians . . . there is no other road for you to *truth* . . . except that leading through the stream of fire.'[81] There certainly are both Christians and churches who go the way of fire in *Ulysses*: witness the church at Sandymount where 'one of the candles was just going to set fire to the flowers'; or again, 'the Earl of Kildare [who once] . . . set fire to Cashel cathedral'.[82] As it happens, the candle is moved to safety; indeed, the Archbishop whom the Earl intended to kill was not in the cathedral. On this occasion, the church burns and no one is hurt; nevertheless, a terrible potential is glimpsed or encoded in the strangely-phrased reference to '*those* incense they burned in the church'.[83] This fiery potential has found terrible historical realization; *those they burned* in the church has, since 1922, come to include not just heretics but Jews – the church, of course, played a significant part in stoking the flames of the Holocaust (literally, total burning).[84] Genet is mindful of this; as Derrida observes, 'in *Funeral Rites*, the Trinity (the church), represents the eagle of the Reich'.[85] The anti-Semitism that would link church and Reich is brilliantly distilled in *Ulysses* as: 'those jews they said killed the christian boy'.[86] The nightmare in which the *Nazis*'s 'christian boys' would kill Jews is a future that *Ulysses* also distills, or chances upon when Martin Cunningham remarks, 'that will be a great race tomorrow in Germany'. Martin has in mind, of course, a *motor*-race; on his part the prediction is wholly unwitting, he speaks better (or worse), than he knows. So too does Stephen when he declares that 'the blood-boltered shambles in . . . [*Hamlet*] is a forecast of the concentration camp';[87] Stephen has in mind the camps used by the British in the Boer War, but the novel anticipates something even worse. As well it might, in that there is a 'little' holocaust upon the day of *Ulysses*, the day on which the action takes place: 'All those women and children excursion beanfeast burned and drowned in New York. Holocaust.'[88] Bloom here refers to a report that appeared on June 16, 1904 in the *Freeman's Journal*:

> Five hundred persons, mostly children, perished today by the burning of the
> steamer General Slocum . . . in New York Harbour. . . . The annual St
> Mark's German Lutheran Church was proceeding to . . . Long Island.[89]

Coming just fifty pages after 'jews . . . killed the christian boy', this New
York holocaust that killed yet more Christian boys is an uncanny
doubling of both holocaust past (the killing of Christ), and holocaust
future (the killing of the Jews).

One holocaust is, of course, one too many; but in the age of mechanical reproduction, doubling is the fate of even holocaust; the New York
holocaust is itself mechanically reproduced (via telegraphy and printing
press), as a Dublin newspaper report. Equally reproducible is the sacrifice
or holocaust that is the crucifixion; recall Genet's 'violent . . . radiographic
interpretation . . . of Golgotha', an interpretation that Derrida compares
to placing 'relics in a kind of developing bath'.[90] There are shades here of
Bloom's 'Easter number of *Photo Bits*', a phrase charged with the conceit
that, in the age of photographic reproduction, Christ's Easter body (a
body already broken in bits), must endure another dismemberment.
Reading 'Easter number of *Photo Bits*' more closely, it is as if Easter is
itself a kind of photography; in which case photographic reproduction
belongs to the age of the church, not vice versa. Jean-Michel Rabaté
thought of that; in *The Ghosts of Modernity* he reminds us of the story
of St Veronica who, meeting Jesus on his way to Golgotha, wiped his
sweating face with a cloth upon which there was left an image of Christ's
features.[91]

The reproductive magic of photography is, for Roland Barthes, more
specifically related to Easter *Sunday*: 'photography', he writes, 'has something to do with resurrection'.[92] *Glas*, however, maintains the link with
the crucifixion, the Golgothan holocaust. This 'blazing', writes Derrida,
'is not yet philosophy'; but it *is* photography in that a holocaust is so
terrible as to demand reproduction – it *must* be remembered, *must* be
reproduced.[93] In this sense, one holocaust is *not* enough; this riddle lies
buried in Derrida's dark and difficult talk of 'a holocaust of the holocaust'. It is as if, for Derrida, any 'reflection . . . of the holocaust' must be
a *repetition*, must itself *be* a holocaust, as if anything else would not be
faithful to the sheer awfulness of the event. In this sense, holocaust impos-
sibilizes the whole Western logic of representation and verisimilitude.[94]

This is precisely the belief at work in every eucharist in every Catholic
church in *Glas* and *Ulysses*. For Transubstantiation means, of course, that
in breaking the bread these churches break not an *image* of Christ's
holcaust-ed body but the body itself; likewise, in pouring wine they are
pouring out not an *image* of Christ's holocaust-ed blood but the blood

itself. Moreover, moving still closer to Derrida's 'holocaust of a holo-caust', many of the churches of *Glas* and *Ulysses* reproduce the Jewish burnt sacrifice through the actual burning of incense; this is, in a sense, fire for fire.

Boat

Incense, of course, is carried in a symbolic boat: Buck Mulligan's 'boat of incense' or navette is, as Derrida observes, 'a small metal vessel in the form of a boat' – 'they keep', he adds, 'incense in it'.[95] Though it is the incense that is supposed to burn, on June 16, 1904 a German Lutheran church sets out in a boat that itself burns; this is a church that literally burns its boats. But then that is the nature of a Lutheran church, which in breaking from Rome breaks from a past that, as *Ulysses* reminds us, begins at sea. As Joyce recites, 'Peter, on which rock was the holy church . . . founded' is also 'he that holdeth the fisherman's seal' – 'Peter Piscator'.[96] The church of Rome, as the church of Peter, is made in the image of a ship as well as a rock; but a ship cannot be founded on a rock, it can only founder upon it. Once again, Derrida's prediction: 'the stone [of the church of stone] . . . will give rise to another fracture, another ruin'.[97]

The church does, though, survive its own decline – *perte* ('ruin'), being an anagram, or ruin of 'Peter'. In *Ulysses*, Stephen declares that 'Peter Piscator lives . . . in the house that Jack built'; in *Glas* he lives *on* in the house that *Jacques* declares unsafe, a ruin that survives to the last line of the Hegel column: 'elle court à sa perte'.[98] Indeed, this ruin of a church is a sea-going ruin; the last line of the Genet column ends with the word 'debris' – the debris, we presume, of what Derrida has just called 'the machine . . . of writing', a curious and enigmatic machine that seems to double as a ship:

> drop[ping] anchor and ink[ing] in another depth. . . . Pulleys . . . [and] greased ropes grow taut . . . the breathing of slaves bent double. Good for pulling. Proofs ready for printing. The cracking whip of the first mate [*contremaitre*]. . . . So little would have been necessary, the slightest error of calculation . . . The machine is still too simple, the pre-capitalist mode of writing.[99]

This writing-cum-printing machine that is also a kind of ship is, *if anything*, the publishing house of Galilee, the printing machine which recalls the *sea* of Galilee, the sea that is, much earlier, punningly encoded as 'la mère galiléenne', the sea that launched the church.[100]

This final sea of *Glas* is not, though, simply a 'Sea of Faith'; it is also, in a sense, 'the Atlantic Ocean'.[101] For the Genet column runs aground upon the cryptic words: 'what I had dreaded, naturally, already re-edited itself', words which seem to articulate Derrida's fear of the 'natural' re-editing that is *translation* – translation by a transatlantic press; Derrida wrote *Glas* knowing that translation into English, or rather American, was inevitable.[102] In this sense, the ruined ship-machine of *Glas* is bound for America; so too is Derrida. The following year, 1975, he made the first of his annual visits to Yale which, in the wake of *Glas*, inspired that dream of an infinitely playful textuality which went by the name of American deconstruction. What the end of *Glas* seems to 'know', however, is that the late-1970s American dream of deconstruction would be a dream of a *non*-simple, *high*-capitalist writing machine, a machine of infinitely moveable type that was, at the time, fast being realized as the computerized text. This is 'known' to *Glas* if only because the sheer difficulty involved in its typesetting almost necessitates the word-processor, almost requires its invention; computers were not used by European publishers at the time of *Glas* and so Derrida himself had to mock up the individual pages, had himself to act as a kind of computer. This affinity with the computer is tacitly acknowledged in Derrida's 'Circumfession', the essay 'projected after *Glas*'; here Derrida makes several references to word processing and includes a photograph of the text on the screen of his Macintosh computer.[103] To revise Hartman's claim, *Glas* is of the American house of Macintosh.

Or rather, it is of the house of *both* Galilee and Macintosh; for what we enter in *Glas* is a church that, under the impact of modernity, is so 'violently . . . redistributed' as to become an anagram or, in the case of Genet, 'an overloaded telephone exchange' in which not just letters but whole 'lines [are] . . . moved out of place'.[104] In *Ulysses* this dream or nightmare of the modern church as the model of a crazed, and infinitely flexible writing machine is encoded in 'THE CHAPEL OF FREEMAN TYPESETTERS' whose potential to make thinkable a chapel, or church, of free *type* finds comic realization in those five 'sandwichmen' whose lettered hats can spell out not only 'H. E. L. Y. S.' but every other possible combination; they are, for Bloom, a bizarre kind of priesthood: this 'procession of whitesmocked . . . men [with] . . . scarlet sashes . . . Like that priest they are this morning' – like that priest, of course, with 'Letters on his back: I. N. R. I.? No: I. H. S.'[105] In both *Glas* and *Ulysses* the ultimate writing machine is not just high-capitalist and high-tech but also high-church; at times, indeed, the machine *is* the church. Early on in *Glas* there is a bleak vision of a church that is on the side of the philosophical police:

All the police forces in the world can be routed by a surname, but even before they know it, a secret computer, at the moment of baptism, will have kept them up to date.[106]

By the time of 'Circumfession' (1991), however, the high-church computer is a benign and lyrical dream of a self-editing text: an 'angel', writes Derrida, 'last night took hold of my computer, dooming once more invention to dispossession'.[107]

Something, it seems, has changed in Derrida's relation to the high-church writing machine, the machine that *is* writing; but then, for Derrida, the direction of writing has changed course. Whilst *Glas* is finally bound for America, 'Circumfession' is set towards Africa. Here, Derrida is once again preoccupied with *Sa*, or rather SA; this time, though, it is not SA as in *USA* but SA the initials of Saint Augustine, the *Algerian*. In 'Circumfession' Derrida compares his own sailing from Algiers in 1949 to the young Augustine's much earlier voyage out; moreover, the essay ends with a mysterious sea voyage that, inevitably, makes as if to repeat Augustine's return to Algiers:

> you . . . whose life will have been so short, the voyage short, scarcely orga-nized, by you with no lighthouse and no book, you the floating toy at high tide and under the moon, you the crossing between these two phantoms of witnesses who will never come down to the same.[108]

In relation to his first voyage, his voyage out, Derrida writes of 'seasick-ness bad enough to make you give up the ghost', but it seems, at the end of 'Circumfession', that the sea-going Derrida has not given up ghosts. His ship is a ghost ship, or rather a *holy-g*host ship: Derrida's 'phantoms of witnesses' suggest the New Testament's 'great *cloud* of witnesses', the Church Invisible, or communion of saints – the sainted dead.[109]

For Derrida the Church Invisible will never be in*div*isible, the phantoms of witnesses will never come down to the same. For Bloom, however, they *will* – or rather, we all will; regarding mortality, Bloom offers the simple but resounding sentence: 'In the same boat.'[110] Bloom is certainly in a very similar boat to Homer's Ulysses – Bloom is making a journey home that mimics Ulysses's sea journey back to Ithaca; but it is not, of course, the identical boat, not the *same* boat. Bloom is no more in precisely the same returning boat as Ulysses than Derrida is in precisely the same returning boat as Saint Augustine; in fact, it is the *same* difference. Ironically, Derrida and Bloom are in the same boat of *not* being in the same boat.

To absorb difference into a higher order of sameness is, of course, a Hegelian movement, a movement which my comparative reading can never fully escape.[111] Nor, though, can Derrida; for 'those two phantoms of witnesses who will never come down to the same' in so doing *are* – in a sense – the same; they are in the same boat of *not* being the same. Derrida's boat, for all its refusal of sameness, is still in Hegelian waters; but then Derrida predicts this in *Glas* when he foresees not only 'another fracture, [and] another ruin [but also] . . . another relief', another sublation, or resolution of difference.

What *is* different, however, at the sea-going end of 'Circumfession' is that this Hegelian resolution is dramatically reworked in simple and existential terms that precisely echo Bloom's blunt sentence, 'In the same boat.' For here, the same-in-difference phantoms of witnesses answer not to a philosophical problem but to Derrida's overwhelming human fear that he 'will never have had any witness'. This is the fear to which he confesses immediately before going on to express the conviction that, though utterly alone at sea, he *will* somehow be witnessed. Though this is a 'voyage . . . with . . . no lighthouse and no book', and though he is but 'a floating toy at high tide', there *are* 'these . . . phantoms of witnesses'.

Were it not for the Church Invisible, that church of the dead, we the living would ourselves, it seems, be invisible. To quote again the New Testament: 'seeing we are compassed about with so great a cloud of witnesses' *we ourselves are seen.*

'What has not yet happened'

> What has not yet arrived at or happened to Christianity is Christianity.
> (Derrida, *The Gift of Death*)[1]

This book was written in the half-conscious hope that 'what has not yet happened to Christianity' might just happen. This, of course, was a quite unreasonable hope. What has not yet happened to Christianity will never be a book. *Queer Fish*, therefore, is about something that has *still* not yet happened – or at least, *still* not yet happened to me. Had it done so, I would (in a sense) have become a kind of fish. This, though, might still be a possibility; for in this conclusion I find myself speaking in the first person and, as Derrida once pointed out, it is not far from *Ich* to *Ichthus*, from 'I' to the Christ-fish. This is the riddling, cryptic point of these almost unreadable words from *The Truth in Painting*:

> *Ich*, snatched fish body, foreign body of a word . . . in the . . . speculating on the *I* . . . bait for the Christic . . . *Ichthys*.[2]

From a conventional, scholarly perspective such word-playing speculations are suspect, dubious, even fishy. Freud, we might remark, is not the only one who has grown stupid from keeping the company of fish. Derrida, it might be said, should have heeded the advice of Lewis Carroll's Piscator: 'Think not of fish, dear Scholar.'[3] But then Derrida is a scholar who does not so much *think* of fish as dream of becoming one; in his strange, epistolary essay, 'Envois', he writes, to a nameless beloved: 'you becloud me like a fish, I let myself be loved in the water.'[4] This particular fish-dream is a dream of love, or indeed Love.

Poor fellow! He has done his best, but what does a fish's best come to when a fish is out of water?

(Samuel Butler, *The Way of all Flesh*, 1903)

'You are the ultimate uselessness, the laundress of fish.'

(André Breton, 'Soluble Fish', 1924)

Notes

Introduction 'Dover Beached'

1 Michel Foucault, *Madness and Civilisation,* tr. Richard Howard (London: Routledge, 1989), pp. 78–9.

2 Matthew Arnold, *Literature and Dogma* [1873], *The Complete Prose Works of Matthew Arnold*, 11 vols (Ann Arbor: University of Michigan Press, 1960–1977), 6.315.

3 1 Corinthians 1.25. This and all other biblical references are to the 1611 Authorised Version.

4 Søren Kierkegaard, *Papers and Journals: A Selection,* tr. Alistair Hannay (Harmondsworth: Penguin, 1996), p. 307; Gustave Flaubert, *The Temptation of St Anthony* [1874], tr. Kitty Mrosovsky (Harmondsworth: Penguin, 1980), p. 106; J. H. Newman, 'On the introduction of rationalistic principles into revealed religion' [1835], in *Essays Critical and Historical*, 3 vols (London: Basil Montague Pickering, 1875), 1.31.

5 See Bamber Gascoigne, *The Christians* (London: Jonathan Cape, 1977), p. 240.

6 Blaise Pascal, *Pensées* [1670], tr. A. J. Krailsheimer (Harmondsworth: Penguin, 1995), p. 127.

7 Charles Kinglsey, *His Letters and Memories of His Life* [1876], ed. 'his wife' (London: Macmillan, 1890), pp. 303–4.

8 Charles Dickens, *Our Mutual Friend* [1865], ed. Adrian Poole (Harmondsworth: Penguin, 1997), p. 491.

9 Anthony Trollope, *The Way We Live Now* [1875] (London: Oxford University Press, 1951), p. 210; Edmond Gosse, *Father and Son* [1907] (Harmondsworth: Penguin, 1983), pp. 215–16; James Joyce, *Ulysses* [1922] (Harmondsworth: Penguin, 1986), p. 67.

10 Fyodor Dostoyevsky, *The Idiot* [1868], tr. Alan Meyers (Oxford: Oxford University Press, 1992), p. 191.

11 See Elaine Showalter, *Sexual Anarchy: Gender and Culture at the 'Fin de Siècle'* (London: Virago, 1992), pp. 111–12.

12 See Robert Louis Stevenson, *The Strange Case of Dr Jekyll and Mr Hyde*, ed. Jenni Calder (Harmondsworth: Penguin, 1979), p. 33.

13 'The Critic as Artist' [1890], *Oscar Wilde: Plays, Prose Writings and Poems,* ed. Anthony Fothergill (London: Everyman, 1996), p. 139.

14 Friedrich Nietzsche, *Daybreak: Thoughts on the Prejudices of Morality* [1881], tr. R. J. Hollingdale (Cambridge: Cambridge University Press, 1982), aphorism no. 68, p. 40.

15 *The Poems of Matthew Arnold*, ed. Miriam Allott (London: Longman, 1979), p. 256, ll. 21–5.

16 Christina Rossetti, *Time Flies: A Reading Diary* (London: SPCK, 1885), p. 198. The Christian fish is caught, albeit briefly, by Stephen D. Moore in his wonderful *Mark and Luke in Poststructuralist Perspectives: Jesus Begins to Write* (New Haven: Yale University Press, 1992), pp. 56–7.

17 Søren Kierkegaard, *The Point of View* [1859], tr. Howard V. Kong and Edna H. Kong (Princeton: Princeton University Press, 1998), p. 220.

18 Jacques Derrida, *The Gift of Death* [1992], tr. David Wills (Chicago: Chicago University Press, 1995), p. 109.

19 Hélène Cixous, *Readings: the Poetics of Blanchot, Joyce, Kafka, Kleist, Lispector, and Tsveteyeva*, ed. Verena Andermatt Conley (London: Harvester Wheatsheaf, 1992), p. 147.

20 A good example of such alignment is found in Roland Barthes' 'From Work to Text': 'Just as Einsteinian science demands that *the relativity of the frames of reference* be included in the object studied, so the combined action of Marxism, Freudianism and Structuralism demands, in literature, the relativisation of the relations of writer, reader and observer (critic)' – *Image-Music-Text*, ed. Stephen Heath (London: Fontana, 1977), p. 156. Jacques Derrida, 'Faith and Knowledge', in Jacques Derrida and Giani Vattimo (eds), *Religion* [1996], (Cambridge: Polity, 1998), p. 28.

21 Derrida, *The Gift of Death*, pp. 2, 4.

22 Kierkegaard, *Papers and Journals*, p. 103.

23 Wilkie Collins, *The Moonstone* [1968], ed. J. I. M. Stewart (Harmondsworth: Penguin, 1966), p. 454.

24 Flaubert, *St Anthony*, p. 111.

One   Boat Memory

 1 Charles Darwin, *On the Origin of Species by Means of Natural Selection* [1859], ed. John Burrow (Harmondsworth: Penguin, 1968), p. 456. All subsequent references to the *Origin* are, unless otherwise stated, to this first edition.

 2 See *Charles Darwin's Beagle Diary*, ed. Richard Darwin Keynes (Cambridge: Cambridge University Press, 1988), p. 7.

 3 Charles Darwin, *The Voyage of the Beagle* [1839] (London: Dent, 1906), p. 218.

 4 Darwin, *Diary*, p. 137.

 5 Darwin, *Voyage*, p. 218.

 6 N. Barlow (ed.), *Charles Darwin, and the Voyage of the Beagle* (Pilot Press, 1945), p. 223.

 7 The most obvious and well-known example of this trend is perhaps Holman Hunt's 'The Light of the World' (1851–53). George Eliot writes of 'the genteel Christianity of the nineteenth century' – see 'Evangelical Teaching: Dr Cumming' in George Eliot, *Selected Essays, Poems and Other Writings*, ed. A. S. Byatt and Nicholas Warren (Harmondsworth: Penguin, 1990), p. 38.

8 Darwin, *Origin*, pp. 211, 201.
9 Charles Darwin, *The Descent of Man, and Selection in Relation to Sex* [1871], 2 vols (Princeton: Princeton University Press, 1981), 2.386 – my italics.
10 *Ibid.*, 1.127.
11 See Gillian Beer's brilliant chapters on the voyaging Darwin in *Open Fields: Science in Cultural Encounter* (Oxford: Clarendon Press, 1996); my essay obviously owes much to Beer's work. For an excellent discussion of exactly when Darwin 'loses his faith' see James R. Moore, 'Of Love and Death: Why Darwin gave up Christianity', in Moore (ed.), *History, Humanity and Evolution* (Cambridge: Cambridge University Press, 1989).
12 Matthew 3.4.
13 Eliot, *Selected Essays,* p. 38; *Diary*, pp. 272, 293.
14 Quoted in Adrian Desmond and James R. Moore, *Darwin* (Harmondsworth: Penguin,1991), p. 142.
15 See Valentine Cunningham, *Everywhere Spoken Against: Dissent in the Victorian Novel* (Oxford: Clarendon Press, 1975), p. 285; John Chapman, *Christian Revivals: Their History and Natural History* (London, 1860), p. 31; see Royal Rhodes, *The Lion and the Cross: Early Christianity in Victorian Novels* (Columbus: Ohio State University Press, 1996), p. 253; Walter Leonard Arnstein, *The Bradlaugh Case: Studies in Late-Victorian Opinion and Politics* (Oxford: Oxford University Press, 1965), p. 278; see Edward Royle (ed.), *The Infidel Tradition: From Paine to Bradlaugh* (London: Macmillan, 1976), pp. 215–18.
16 George Eliot, *Middlemarch* [1871–2], ed. Rosemary Ashton (Harmondsworth: Penguin, 1994), p. 331; Charles Dickens, *Pickwick Papers* [1836–7], ed. Robert. L. Patten (Harmondsworth: Penguin, 1972), p. 455; Charles Dickens, *Oliver Twist* [1837], ed. Peter Fairclough (Harmondsworth: Penguin, 1966), p. 182; Charles Dickens, *Barnaby Rudge* [1841], ed. Donald Hawes (London: Everyman, 1996), p. 253; Harold Begbie, *The Life of General William Booth*, 2 vols (New York: Macmillan, 1920), 2.17.
17 Friedrich Nietzsche, *Twilight of the Idols* [1889] / *The Anti-Christ* [1895], tr. R. J. Hollingdale (Harmondsworth: Penguin, 1990), p. 190.
18 Charles Kingsley, *Hypatia* [1853] (London: Nelson, n.d.), pp. 445, 436.
19 Quoted in Desmond and Moore, p. 478. There is no evidence that Darwin had read *Hypatia* though Darwin does, of course, cite a letter from Kingsley in the third edition of the *Origin* – see *On the Origin of Species: A Variorum Edition*, ed. Morse Peckham (Philadelphia: University of Pennsylvania Press, 1959), p. 478.
20 I was first prompted to think along these lines by Valentine Cunningham's passing observation that: '1859 was not only the year of . . . the *Origin of Species* but the year of the Ulster Revival . . . and of the birth of Smith Wigglesworth, prophet of the twentieth-century Pentecostal Movement' – *Everywhere*, p. 282; Chapman begins by foot-noting no less than nine books on the subject of the revivals, all published in 1859.
21 Quoted in Desmond and Moore, p. 260.
22 Frederick Burkhardt and Sidney Smith (eds), *The Correspondence of Charles*

Darwin, 7 vols (Cambridge: Cambridge University Press, 1985–91), 1.204, 230, 207.

23   Jacques Derrida, 'Différance' in *Margins of Philosophy* [1972], tr. Alan Bass (London: Harvester Wheatsheaf, 1982), p. 11; Jacques Derrida, *Of Grammatology* [1972], tr. Gayatri Chakravorty Spivak (Baltimore: Johns Hopkins University Press, 1976), p. 313.

24   *Diary*, pp. 84, 257.

25   *Descent*, 1.153.

26   *Ibid.*, 1.203.

27   See *The Oxford Dictionary of the Christian Church*, ed. F. L. Cross (London: Oxford University Press, 1957), p. 506.

28   Lewis Carroll, *Alice's Adventures in Wonderland* [1865] and *Through the Looking Glass* [1872], ed. Roger Lancelyn Green (Oxford: Oxford University Press, 1982), p. 236.

29   *The Swinburne Letters*, ed. C. Y. Lang, 6 vols (Oxford and Yale Universities' Press, 1959–62), 6.176 – I am grateful to Catherine Maxwell for alerting me to this phrase of Swinburne's. As Lang points out, the 'Galilean serpent' is borrowed form Shelley's 'Ode to Liberty' (1820), where, interestingly, it 'forth did creep' from the sea – to be specific, 'its sea of death' (ll. 119–20); Christina Rossetti, *Time Flies: A Reading Diary* (London: SPCK, 1885), p. 198.

30   Stanley Edgar Hyman, *The Tangled Bank: Darwin, Marx and Freud as Imaginative Writers* (New York: Athenaeum, 1974), p. 34 – this is another book to which I am greatly indebted; Matthew 12.39.

31   *Origin*, p. 357.

32   *Correspondence*, 1.231, 1.220.

33   See Desmond and Moore, p. 363; L. Huxley, *Life and Letters of Sir Joseph Dalton Hooker*, 2 vols (Murray, 1918), 1.187; two years later Darwin writes, 'to this day I remember keenly a letter you wrote to me from Oxford, when I was at the Water-cure' – F. Darwin, (ed.), *The Life and Letters of Charles Darwin*, 3 vols (Murray, 1887), 3.270.

34   See Desmond and Moore, pp. 152, 208.

35   *Time Flies*, p. 198.

36   See *The Times Literary Supplement*, Jan 29th 1999, p. 14.

37   Søren Kierkegaard, *Fear and Trembling : Dialectical Lyric by Johannes 'de silentio'* [1843] tr. Alistair Hannay (Harmondsworth: Penguin, 1985), p. 67. Interestingly, Beer does at one point place Darwin alongside Kierkegaard: she links Darwin's chapter on 'Fear' in the *Expression of the Emotions* (1872) to Kierkegaard's *The Concept of Dread* (1844) – see *Darwin's Plots*, p. 230.

38   *Correspondence*, 1.504, 4.159.

39   *Fear and Trembling*, pp. 67–8.

40   *Origin*, p. 217.

41   *Life and Letters of Darwin*, 2.86; *Diary*, p. 94.

42   Kierkegaard describes faith as not only a leap but also a fall.   For Kierkegaard, the 'knight of faith' is distinguished from the mere 'knight of infinity' by how he falls: ' . . . the mass of humans live disheartened lives . . . these are the sitters-out who will not join in the dance. The knights of

infinity are dancers too . . . they make the upward movement and fall down again . . . but when they come down they cannot assume the position straight-away . . . to be able to land in just that way, and in the same second to look as though one was up and walking, to transform the leap in . . . to a gait . . . that is something only the knight of faith can do . . .' (*Fear and Trembling*, p. 70). *The Works of John Ruskin*, ed. E. T. Cook and A. Wedderburn, 39 vols (London: George Allen, 1909), 36.115.

43   *The Autobiography of Charles Darwin*, (ed.) N. Barlow (London: Collins, 1958), pp. 81–2.

44   *Origin*, p. 24.

45   'A feather bed to catch a falling Christian', is how Darwin's grandfather Erasmus described the Unitarian beliefs of Charles' other grandfather, Josiah Wedgwood – see E. Krause, *Erasmus Darwin . . . with a Preliminary Notice by Charles Darwin*, tr. W. S. Dallas (Murray, 1879), p. 45; *Diary*, pp. 371, 67; *Correspondence*, 2.352.

46   *Origin,* p. 66.

47   *Ibid.*, pp. 55, 142.

48   *Ibid.*, p. 126.

49   *Ibid.*, p. 461.

50   Quoted in E. Halévy, *The Triumph of Reform, 1830–1841* (Benn, 1950),p. 56; Friedrich Nietzsche, *Thus Spoke Zarathustra: A Book for Everyone and No One*, tr. R. J. Hollingdale (Harmondsworth: Penguin, 1961), p. 68.

51   Friedrich Nietzsche, *The Gay Science* [1882], tr. W. Kaufman (New York: Random House), p. 357. For a very good discussion of Darwin and Nietzsche see Keith Ansell Pearson, *Viroid Life: Perspectives on Nietzsche and the Transhuman Condition* (London: Routledge, 1997), pp. 85–122.

52   *The Twilight of the Idols*, written in 1888, is subtitled 'How to Philosophise with a Hammer'; *Correspondence*, 1.460.

53   *Diary*, pp. 12, 36.

54   See Robin Gilmour, *The Victorian Period* (London: Longman, 1993), pp. 118–19; *Correspondence*, 1.460; *Autobiography*, p. 77.

55   *Correspondence*, 1.232, 1.418–19 (my italics). Interesting in this connection is Beer's remark that 'for his theory to work Darwin needs the sense of free play, of *jeu*, as much, or even more, than he needs history' – *Darwin's Plots*, p. 97. I am suggesting that, for Darwin, history *is* a kind of play.

56   *Diary*, p. 445; Jacques Derrida, 'Structure, Sign and Play' in *Writing and Difference* [1967], tr. Alan Bass (London: Routledge, 1978), p. 279.

57   *Fear and Trembling*, p. 77.

58   *Origin*, pp. 316, 295.

59   *Diary*, pp. 290, 356, 427–8.

60   See *Correspondence,* 1.245, 1.247, 1.444; *Diary,* p. 152; *Voyage*, p. 122; see Desmond and Moore, pp. 143, 149.

61   *Correspondence*, 3.2.

62   *Diary*, pp. 272–3, 273 n.1.

63   Michel Foucault, *Madness and Civilization: A History of Insanity in the Age of Reason* [1961], tr. Richard Howard (London: Routledge, 1967), p. 79; Jacques Derrida, *The Gift of Death*, tr. David Wills (Chicago: University of Chicago Press, 1995), p. 68.

64 Quoted in Desmond and Moore, p. 569.
65 *Ibid.*, p. 427.
66 *Correspondence*, 5.32.
67 *Descent*, 2.404.
68 *Origin*, p. 246; the phrase 'an image of despair' does not appear in the first edition – see Peckham, p. 401.
69 Quoted in Hyman, p. 41.
70 *Diary*, p. 154.
71 *Descent*, 1.78.
72 Luke 23.24.
73 *Descent*, 1.40; Florence Nightingale, *Cassandra and other selections from Suggestions for Thought*, ed. Mary Poovey (London: Pickering and Chatto, 1991), p. 230; see *Open Fields*, p. 129. Interesting in connection with this is G. W. Foote's question: 'What Christianity ever taught the rights of the lower animals?' see *Christianity or Secularism: Which is True? A Verbatim Report of a Four Nights' Debate Between the Rev. Dr. J. McCann and Mr. G. W. Foote* (London: Progressive Publishing, 1886), p. 14.
74 Algernon Charles Swinburne, *The Poems of Algernon Charles Swinburne*, 6 vols (London: Chatto and Windus, 1904), II. 104.
75 *Origin*, pp. 81, 436, 200, 275, 289.
76 Quoted in Desmond and Moore, p. 645.
77 'Progress' (1852), *Poems*, p. 277, l. 27; Gilmour, p. 95.
78 'As kingfishers catch fire', *The Poems of Gerard Manley Hopkins*, ed. W. H. Gardner and N. H. MacKenzie (Oxford: Oxford University Press, 1967), p. 90.
79 Holman Hunt reminded the Victorians of the figure of the scapegoat in his famous painting of that name in 1857; Mark 1.13 (my italics).
80 *Swinburne*, I. 69; *Correspondence*, 1.525 – Darwin refers to standing in the court of Christ's College, Cambridge after returning to England.
81 Quoted in H. E. Gruber, *Darwin on Man* (London: Wildwood House, 1974), p. 40; see David Amigoni and Jeff Wallace (eds), *Charles Darwin's The Origin of Species: New Interdisciplinary Essays* (Manchester: Manchester University Press, 1995), pp. 1–2; *Correspondence*, 7.368.
82 *Cassandra*, p. 14.
83 *Correspondence*, 3.394; *Origin*, p. 460.
84 *Ibid.*, pp. 65–6.
85 *Origin*, pp. 217, 280, 262, 472.
86 See Jacques Derrida, 'Circumfession', tr. Geoffrey Bennington in Geoffrey Bennington and Jacques Derrida, *Jacques Derrida* [1991] (Chicago: University of Chicago Press, 1993), pp. 3–315; *Origin*, p. 290.
87 *Ibid.*, p. 66 (my italics).
88 *Ibid*, pp. 252, 417.
89 *Autobiography*, p. 122 (my italics).
90 *Origin*, pp. 309, 66; *Correspondence*, 1.180.
91 *Diary*, p. 431.
92 *Correspondence*, 1.493; *Origin*, p. 142.
93 *Diary*, p. 87.
94 *Origin*, pp. 345, 294, 371.

95 *Diary*, p. 442.
96 I Corinthians 10.1–5.
97 *Ibid.*, p. 444.
98 *Correspondence*, 1.432.
99 *Origin,* pp. 458, 122, 128.
100 Psalms 46.9, Isaiah 11.6.
101 *Origin*, pp. 263, 345.
102 *Descent*, 1.170 – in Monte Video he asks, 'whether Despotism is not better than . . . anarchy', *Diary*, p. 91; in August 1835 Darwin witnessed what he called 'Anarchy' in post-revolutionary Peru – see *Correspondence*, 1.462.
103 *Origin*, p. 348.
104 *Voyage*, p. 484.
105 *Diary*, p. 444.
106 William Winwood Reade, *The Martyrdom of Man*, tenth edn (New York, n.d.), p. 514.
107 Quoted in Desmond and Moore, p. 487.
108 *Descent*, 2.122; *Diary*, p. 354.
109 See Richard Adams Locke, *The Moon Hoax* (Boston: G. K Hall and Co., 1975), *passim*, and Russell Freedman, *2000 Years of Space Travel* (New York: Holiday House, 1963), pp. 144–56.
110 *Correspondence*, 1.515.
111 *Diary*, p. 277.
112 P. H. Barrett *et al.*, *Charles Darwin's Notebooks, 1836–1844* (Cambridge: British Museum/Cambridge University Press, 1987), C76.
113 *Correspondence*, 7. Supplement.
114 Quoted in Desmond and Moore, p. 652.
115 For a discussion of Christ's entanglement with the figure and story of the Fisher King, see Jessie Weston, *From Ritual to Romance* (Bath: Chivers Press, 1920), pp. 117–29.
116 Alfred Nutt's *Studies on the Legend of the Holy Grail* (London, 1888), a publication of the Folk-Lore Society, is concerned with no less than seven Victorian editions and translations of medieval Grail romances all published between 1844 and 1884 – see pp. 1–4. Lubbock was a member of the Council of the Folk-Lore Society at the time that Nutt's study was published; his name appears with the others on the reverse of the frontispiece.
117 Darwin quotes from the *Idylls* in *Descent*, p. 101; Asa Gray, *Darwiniana: Essays and Reviews Pertaining to Darwinism*, ed. A. Hunter Dupree (Cambridge, Mass.: Harvard University Press, 1963), p. 74; quoted in Hyman, p. 30.
118 *Origin*, p. 456.
119 *Ibid.*, p. 215.
120 *Voyage*, p. 170.
121 *Origin*, pp. 21, 196; *Descent*, 1.161; in the *Descent* he writes of 'the reappearance of long-lost characters' (1.113).
122 *Correspondence*, 1.432.
123 *Ibid.*, 1.312, 331.
124 *Voyage*, p. 209. Beer hints at Darwin's hint at an interest in the invisible, in particular invisible forces – this she does by beginning *Open Fields* with a

dictionary definition of 'field' as 'a region in which one body experiences force as a result of the presence of some other body.'

125 Asa Gray, *Natural Selection not inconsistent with Natural Theology* (London: Tübner and Co., 1861), p. 12.

Two   Marx and Angels

1   Hebrews 13.2; Jacques Derrida, 'Circumfession', in Jacques Derrida and Geoff Bennington, *Jacques Derrida* [1991] (Chicago: University of Chicago Press, 1993), p. 238; Karl Marx, *Capital: A Critique of Political Economy* [1867], tr. Ben Fowkes, 3 vols (Harmondsworth: Penguin, 1976), / Karl Marx and Friedrich Engels, *Werke*, 39 vols (Berlin: Dietz Verlag, 1956–76), 23.86. As and when I am dealing closely with the particular wording in Marx and/or Engels I shall, as here, supply a reference to the original German text, and always to this edition which will be referred to as MEW. It was Louis Althusser and Etienne Balibar who, back in 1965, wrote that 'some day it is essential to read *Capital* to the letter' – see *Reading Capital* (London: New Left Books, 1970), p. 13; since then many have responded to the challenge to read Marx to the letter, this chapter is my own attempt to do something similar. To my knowledge, only one other critic has written about Marx and angels – see Jean Michel Rabaté, *The Ghost of Modernity* (Gainesville: University Press of Florida, 1996), pp. 105–6, 222–6. Many more have written about Marx, Engels and Christianity – several are mentioned below, but to them I should add Slavoj Žižek, *The Fragile Absolute* (London: Verso, 2000).

2   Matthew Arnold, 'The Study of Poetry' (1880), *The Complete Prose Works of Matthew Arnold*, ed. R. H. Super, 11 vols (Ann Arbor: University of Michigan Press, 1960–77), 9.161.

3   Karl Marx and Friedrich Engels, *The Holy Family or Critique of Critical Criticism* [1845], tr. R. Dixon and C. Dutt, in Karl Marx and Friedrich Engels, *Collected Works*, 47 vols (London: Lawrence and Wishart, 1975–95), 4.211; from hereon this edition will be referred to as MECW.

4   *Economic and Philosophical Manuscripts* [1932], Karl Marx, *Early Writings*, tr. Rodney Livingstone and G. Benton (Harmondsworth: Penguin, 1975), p. 395 – from hereon I shall use the acronym *EPM*; Marx refers to Etienne Cabet's *Voyage en Icarie* (Paris, 1842), a book describing a communist utopia – 'Letters from the *Franco-German Yearbooks*', *Early Writings*, p. 208; 'The Eighteenth Brumaire of Louis Bonaparte' [1852], Karl Marx, *Surveys from Exile, Political Writings: Volume 2* (Harmondsworth: Penguin,1973), p. 248 / MEW 8.206.

5   *Capital* 1.104 / MEW 23.31.

6   *Early Writings*, p. 243 / MEW 1.377; quoted in J. Hillis Miller, *Victorian Subjects* (London: Harvester Wheatsheaf, 1990), p. 284.

7   *EPM, Early Writings*, p. 365.

8   Quoted in David McLellan, *Karl Marx: A Biography* (London: Papermac, 1995), pp. 208, 243.

9   Jacques Derrida, *Specters of Marx: The State of the Debt, the Work of Mourning, & the New International* [1993], tr. P. Kamuf (London:

Routledge, 1994), p. 13. Derrida's remark is discussed by Kevin Hart, see 'Impossible Marx', *Arena* 5 (1995), p. 189; also see Terrell Carver, *The Postmodern Marx* (Manchester: Manchester University Press, 1998), p. 166.

10 'Eighteenth Brumaire', *Surveys from Exile*, p. 245 / MEW 8.204.

11 'The Chartists', *ibid.*, p. 269 / MEW 8.349.

12 See Elizabeth Gaskell, *Cranford / Cousin Phillis*, ed. Peter Keating (Harmondsworth: Penguin, 1976), p. 233; McLellan, p. 208.

13 Willy Maley, 'Specters of Engels' in Peter Buse and Andrew Stott (eds), *Ghosts: Deconstruction, Psychoanalysis, History* (London: Macmillan 1999), p. 25. This chapter was very much triggered by Maley's excellent essay.

14 Quoted in Stanley Edgar Hyman, *The Tangled Bank: Darwin, Marx and Freud as Imaginative Writers* (New York: Athenaeum, 1974), pp. 180, 167n.

15 See Terrell Carver, *Marx and Engels, The Intellectual Relationship* (Brighton: Harvester, 1983), pp. 51–95; quoted in Hyman, p. 180.

16 Engels to Marx, 25–26 October 1847, MECW 38.138–9.

17 Jeffrey Mehlman, *Revolution and Repetition: Marx / Hugo / Balzac* (Berkeley: University of California Press, 1977), p. 5.

18 Preface to *A Contribution to the Critique of Political Economy* (1859), *Early Writings*, p. 426 / MEW 13.10.

19 Marx to Engels, 10 February 1851, MECW 38.283.

20 Carver, *The Postmodern Marx*, p. 171.

21 *Capital*, 1.272 / MEW 23.183; 'Eighteenth Brumaire', *Surveys from Exile*, 149 / MEW 8.117

22 Friedrich Engels, 'On the Early History of Christianity' (1894–95), Karl Marx and Friedrich Engels, *Basic Writings on Politics and Philosophy*, ed. Lewis S. Feuer (Glasgow: Collins, 1959), p. 209; for a fascinating discussion of this essay see Willy Maley, 'Communing with the Church: Revelation and Revolution in Engels' in John Schad (ed.), *Writing the Bodies of Christ: the Church from Carlyle to Derrida* (Aldershot: Ashgate, 2001). It is sometimes argued that Engels was more sensitive to the complexities of religion than Marx – see, for example, Delos B. McKown, *The Classical Marxist Critiques of Religion: Marx, Engels, Lenin, Kautsky* (The Hague: Martinus Nijhoff, 1975), pp. 77–85.

23 Friedrich Engels, 'Natural Science and the Spirit World', *Dialectics of Nature*, tr. Clemens Dutt (Moscow: Progress, 1934), p. 68. Here again I am indebted to Maley's essay 'Specters of Engels.'

24 Engels, 'History of Early Christianity', p. 230.

25 'Speech at the Anniversary of the *People's Paper*' (1856), *Surveys from Exile*, p. 299.

26 Marx and Engels, *The German Ideology* (1846), MECW 5.24/ MEW 3.13.

27 *Capital* 1.168 / MEW 23.89.

28 Friedrich Nietzsche, *Thus Spoke Zarathustra: A Book for Everyone and No-one*, tr. R. J. Hollingdale (Harmondsworth: Penguin, 1961), p. 68 / Friedrich Nietzsche, *Also Sprach Zarathustra: Ein Buch für Alle und Keinen* (Berlin: Walter de Gruyter and Co. 1968), p. 45. For a fine comparative study of Marx and Nietzsche see Nancy S. Love, *Marx, Nietzsche and Modernity* (New York: Columbia University Press,1986).

29   *Capital*, 1.198 / MEW 23.118–19.

30   *Dialectics of Nature*, pp. 243–4 / MEW 20.509.

31   Quoted in Hyman, p. 93.

32   *Capital*, 1.267 / MEW 23. 179.

33   *EPM, Early Writings*, p. 355.

34   For an excellent account of these developments see Gillian Beer, *Open Fields: Science in Cultural Encounter* (Oxford: Oxford University Press, 1996), pp. 243–4, 286–7, 295–318. To my knowledge, the only other critic to discuss this aspect of Engels's writing is Hyman; see his brief but very interesting discussion of 'the modernity of Engels's scientific metaphors' (*Tangled Bank*, p. 176).

35   *Dialectics of Nature*, pp. 238–9.

36   *Ibid.*, pp. 9–10 .

37   *Ibid.*, pp. 270, 265.

38   Karl Marx and Friedrich Engels, *Selected Works*, 2 vols (London: Lawrence & Wishart, 1962), 1.374–5.

39   Quoted in Derrida, *Specters of Marx*, p. 171.

40   Quoted in Robert C. Tucker, *Philosophy and Myth in Karl Marx* (Cambridge: Cambridge University Press, 1972), p. 90.

41   *Dialectics of Nature*, p. 265.

42   Friedrich Engels, 'Schelling and Revelation', MECW 2.201.

43   *Dialectics of Nature,* pp. 45, 39.

44   Karl Marx and Friedrich Engels, *The Communist Manifesto* [1848], tr. Samuel Moore (Harmondsworth: Penguin, 1967), pp. 83, 82.

45   Quoted in Karl Marx, *The Revolutions of 1848 Political Writings Volume 1*, ed. David Fernbach (Harmondsworth: Penguin 1973), p. 315.

46   *Ibid.*, p. 114.

47   Rereading the classical Marxist model of base and superstructure in terms of, simply, 'structure'. Althusser finds cause to be absent in the sense that a structure does not produce its own elements as a cause produces an effect, or as the base is supposed to determine the superstructure; for Althusser, 'the structure is immanent in its effects' – see *Reading Capital*, pp. 189, 188.

48   *Dialectics of Nature*, p. 287.

49   *Communist Manifesto*, p. 103.

50   'Eighteenth Brumaire', *Surveys From Exile*, pp. 149, 148.

51   *Communist Manifesto*, p. 86.

52   *Capital*,p. 143 / MEW 23.66 (my italics).

53   Friedrich Nietzsche, *Twilight of the Idols* [1889] and *The Anti-Christ* [1895], tr. R. J. Hollingdale (Harmondsworth: Penguin, 1968), p. 196.

54   Karl Marx, 'Critique of Hegel's Doctrine of the State' (1843), *Early Writings*, p. 146.

55   *The Revolutions of 1848*, p. 114. As David McLellan writes, 'Marx vigorously opposed those numerous socialists who claimed to find inspiration in . . . Christianity' – *Marxism and Religion* (London: Macmillan, 1982), p. 21.

56   Quoted in Paul Avrich, 'Introduction', in Mikhail Bakunin, *God and the State* [1882] (New York: Dover, 1970), p. vi (my italics).

57   Ernest Jones, 'We are Silent' (1851), Peter Scheckner (ed.), *An Anthology of Chartist Poetry: Poetry of the British Working Class, 1830s–1850s* (London:

Associated University Presses, 1989), p. 199.

58 *The Holy Family*, MECW 4.9.

59 Marx, 'The British Constitution' (1855), *Surveys from Exile*, p. 283 ; *German Ideology*, MECW 5.104; 'Eighteenth Brumaire', *Surveys from Exile*, p. 170; *Holy Family, passim*; Marx to Engels 31 March 1851, MECW 38.323; Marx to Weydemeyer, 27 June 1851, MECW 38.376.

60 Karl Marx, 'Critique of Hegel's Philosophy of Right. Introduction' (1844), *Early Writings*, p. 245 / MEW 1.379; Exodus 33.23.

61 For a brilliantly researched discussion of this specific cartoon and, indeed, the whole counter-culture of Victorian secularism, see Joss Marsh, *Word Crimes: Blasphemy, Culture, and Literature in Nineteenth Century England* (Chicago: University of Chicago Press, 1998), p. 142, *passim*. For a very good discussion of Marx as a parodic writer see Dominick LaCapra, *Rethinking Intellectual History: texts, contexts, language* (Ithaca: Cornell University Press, 1983), p. 281.

62 Friends of Eliot certainly report that she spoke of being 'Strauss-sick' as she expended enormous nervous energy in painstakingly translating his work – particularly difficult was Strauss' account of the crucifixion (see Frederick Karl, *George Eliot: A Biography* (London: Harper Collins, 1995), p. 82); however, there is no evidence that she actually cried. This, though, is still said; it was, for instance, mentioned by A. N. Wilson on Melvyn Bragg's BBC Radio 4 programme 'In Our Time', 16 March 2000; Wilson was discussing his excellent book *God's Funeral* (John Murray, 1999). The comic strip, 'The New Life of Christ' is also discussed in *Word Crimes*, p. 144.

63 'Critique of Hegel's Philosophy', *Early Writings*, pp. 247–8.

64 'Eighteenth Brumaire', *Surveys from Exile*, p. 146.

65 *Communist Manifesto*, p. 110; 'Agitation Against the Sunday Trading Bill', *Surveys from Exile*, p. 289; 'Eighteenth Brumaire', *ibid.*, p. 188; Karl Marx, 'Critical Notes on "The King of Prussia and Social Reform"' (1844), *Early Writings*, p. 404.

66 See Michel Foucault, *Madness and Civilization: A History of Insanity in the Age of Reason* [1961], tr. Richard Howard (London: Routledge, 1967), p. 79.

67 *The Holy Family*, MECW 4.9.

68 Søren Kierkegaard, *The Point of View: On My Work as an Author* [1848] tr. Howard V. Hong and Edna H. Hong (Princeton: Princeton University Press, 1998), pp. 221, 220.

69 Florence Nightingale, *Cassandra and other selections from Suggestions for Thought*, ed. Mary Poovey (London: Pickering and Chatto, 1991), pp. 223, 51.

70 MECW 5.104; Fyodor Dostoyevsky, *The Idiot* [1868], tr. Alan Myers (Oxford: Oxford University Press, 1992), pp. 4, 28.

71 'Eighteenth Brumaire', *Surveys from Exile*, p. 150.

72 Karl Marx, 'On the Jewish Question' (1843), in *Early Writings*, p. 224.

73 Bakunin writes that 'If God is, man is a slave', *God and the State*, p. 25.

74 George Woodcock, *Anarchism: A History of Libertarian Ideas and Movements* (Harmondsworth: Penguin, 1986), p. 186; Nietzsche, *The Anti-*

Christ, pp. 189, 150. For a brief outline of Christianity's relationship to anarchism see Peter Marshall, *Demanding the Impossible: A History of Anarchism* (London: HarperCollins, 1992), pp. 74–85.

75 For full details see Eileen Yeo, 'Christianity in Chartist Struggle 1838–1842', *Past and Present* 91 (1981), 123–39.

76 Quoted in F. C. Mather (ed.), *Chartism and Society: An Anthology of Documents* (London: Bell and Hyman, 1980), p. 280; quoted in Yeo, 130, 130 n.58.

77 'The Sunday Trading Bill' (1855), *Surveys from Exile*, p. 290.

78 *German Ideology*, MECW 5.218.

79 'Early Christianity', p. 233.

80 Karl Marx, 'The "Cologne Revolution,"' *Revolutions of 1848*, pp. 166, 169 / MEW 5.419, 5.421.

81 *Communist Manifesto*, p. 111 / MEW 4.486.

82 It is, indeed, precisely as exiled and fallen angels that the youthful Marx and Engels caricature themselves in Engels's mock-Miltonic epic which depicted their response to Bruno Bauer's dismissal from Bonn University in March 1842: 'The Free [i.e. Marx and Engels] are horror-struck, the Angels filled with glee. The Free take flight, the Host pursues relentlessly [and] the free are driven down to Earth in full confusion' – quoted in Carver, *Marx and Engels*, p. 17.

83 *German Ideology*, MECW 5.125.

84 You may wish to see my discussion of Derrida's *Specters of Marx* in Schad, *Victorians in Theory: Derrida to Browning* (Manchester: Manchester University Press, 1999), p. 108; 'Critical Notes', *Early Writings*, p. 419.

85 Karl Marx, 'Excerpts from James Mill's *Elements of Political Economy*' (1844), *Early Writings*, p. 278.

86 *German Ideology*, MECW 5.47.

87 *EPM*, *Early Writings*, p. 361.

88 For a lively account of the excesses of Marx's life-style see Francis Wheen, *Karl Marx* (London: Fourth Estate, 1999); for an account of the street-lamp breaking, see McLellan, p. 241.

89 *EPM*, *Early Writings*, p. 366.

90 Romans 7.15; Marx to Arnold Ruge, September 1843, *Early Writings*, pp. 209, 208–9.

91 *The Idiot*, p. 584.

92 See William Shakespeare, *The Merchant of Venice*, ed. John Russell Brown (London: Routledge, 1954), I.i.1; Franz Kafka, *The Trial* [1925], tr. Willa and Edwin Muir (London: Secker and Warburg, 1968).

93 Marx to Ruge, November 1842 / *MEW*, 27.412.

94 'Critique of Hegel's Philosophy', *Early Writings*, p. 244 / MEW 1.378. For a nice discussion of the metaphor of the halo in Marx see Marshall Berman, *All that is Solid Melts into Air* (London: Verso, 1983), p. 115.

95 See Raymond Williams, *Modern Tragedy* [1966] (London: Hogarth Press, 1992), pp. 75–6, and George Steiner, *The Death of Tragedy* (London: Faber and Faber, 1961), p. 343. Both are discussed in Nicholas Lash, *A Matter of Hope: A Theologian's Reflections on the Thought of Karl Marx* (London: Darton, Longman and Todd, 1981), p. 268.

96 *Communist Manifesto*, p. 91; 'Eighteenth Brumaire', p. 149; 'Critique of Hegel's Philosophy of Right', *Early Writings*, p. 249.

97 'Jewish Question', *Early Writings*, pp. 211–41; 'The Magyar Struggle', *Revolutions of 1848*, pp. 225–6.

98 Carver, *Postmodern Marx*, p. 156 – Carver is specifically referring to Marx in 'The Eighteenth Brumaire.'

99 'The Russian Note' (1848), *Revolutions of 1848*, p. 147.

100 This claim was, of course, put to the test by Roberto Benignini's 1997 film *Life is Beautiful (La Vita e bella)*, which presents the Holocaust precisely as a farce.

101 *Communist Manifesto*, p. 87.

102 'Critical Notes', *Early Writings*, p. 412; 'Speech at the Anniversary of the People's Paper' (1856), *Surveys from Exile*, p. 299; *Dialectics of Nature*, p. 295.

103 Søren Kierkegaard, *Papers and Journals: A Selection*, tr. A. Hannay (Harmondsworth: Penguin, 1996), p. 44.

104 'Eighteenth Brumaire', *Surveys from Exile*, p. 242 / MEW, 8.201; *Capital*, p. 923.

105 See Yvonne Kapp, *Eleanor Marx*, 2 vols (London: Virago, 1979), 2.696–700.

106 *EPM, Early Writings*, p. 355 ; Emile Durkheim, *Suicide: A Study in Sociology* [1897], tr. John A.Spaulding and ed. George Simpson (London: Routledge and Kegan Paul, 1952); 'Peuchet: On Suicide' (1845), MECW 4.597–612.

107 Dostoyevsky, *The Idiot*, p. 437; Nightingale, p. 46.

108 MECW 4.612 .

109 *The Complete Poems of Christina Rossetti*, ed. R. W. Crump, 3 vols (Baton Rouge: Louisiana State University Press, 1990), 3.166.

110 Kierkegaard, *Fear and Trembling*, p. 70.

111 *Ibid.*, p. 67.

112 *Holy Family*, MECW 4.67; *German Ideology*, MECW 5.147, 104.

113 *Capital*,1.195.

114 *EPM, Early Writings*, p. 377.

115 *Capital*, 1.481; *Early Writings*, p. 406.

116 'Critical Notes', *Early Writings*, p. 415.

117 The Parisian *Journal des Economistes* described Marx as 'a cobbler [who] . . . does [not] proceed beyond abstract formulas' – see MECW 38.67n. Marx was, no doubt, well aware of the long tradition of political radicalism among shoe-makers – see E. J. Hobsbawm and Joan Wallach Scott, 'Political Shoemakers', *Past and Present*, 89 (1980), 86–114.

118 'Eighteenth Brumaire', *Surveys from Exile*, p. 197; Peter Stallybrass, 'Marx and Heterogeneity: Thinking the Lumpenproletariat', *Representations*, 31 (1990), 70.

119 'The Bill for the Abolition of Feudal Burdens' (1848), *Early Writings*, p. 138.

120 Kierkegaard, *Papers and Journals*, p. 116; for a good discussion of Kierkegaard's political conservatism see Terry Eagleton, *Ideology of the Aesthetic* (Oxford: Blackwell, 1990), pp. 190–3.

121 As Stallybrass writes, 'Bakunin lost his early interest in the revolutionary potential of . . . workers when he came to believe that they were irredeemably

tainted with "science," "theory" and "dogma." In their place he put the outlaw, the criminal, the bandit' (Stallybrass, p. 89). For further discussion of Bakunin and the lumpenproletariat see *Bakunin on Anarchy: Selected Works*, ed. and tr. Sam Dolgoff (New York: Knopf, 1972), p. 334.

122 See Frank Paul Bowman, *Le Christ des barricades 1789–1848* (Paris: Les Éditions du Cerf, 1987), p. 11; quoted in Yeo, p. 130.

123 Karl Marx, 'Camphausen's Declaration in the Sitting of 30 May 1848', *Revolutions of 1848*, p. 117.

124 'Jewish Question', *Early Writings*, p. 238.

125 *The German Ideology*, MECW 5.9.

126 'Eighteenth Brumaire', *Surveys from Exile*, p. 181; 'Bill for the Abolition of Feudal Burdens', *Revolutions of 1848*, p. 143; article in the *Neue Rheinische Zeitung* 15 December 1848, *Revolutions of 1848*, 190 / MEW 6.106.

127 Although 'Dover Beach' was not published until 1867, it is thought that Arnold began to compose the poem as early as 1851 – see *The Poems of Matthew Arnold*, ed. Miriam Allott (London: Longman, 1979), p. 256; Marx, *The Class Struggles in France 1848 to 1850*, *Surveys from Exile*, p. 54.

128 Christina Rossetti, *Time Flies: A Reading Diary* (London: SPCK, 1885), p. 198.

129 *The Idiot*, p. 431.

130 *Capital*, p. 90; MECW 5 192; Kierkegaard, *Papers and Journals*, p. 240.

131 Nightingale, p. 61; 'As kingfishers catch fire', *The Poems of Gerard Manley Hopkins*, ed. W. H. Gardner and N. H. MacKenzie (Oxford: Oxford University Press, 1967), p. 90.

132 See Bowman, *passim*.

133 'Sonnet to Liberty' (1881), Oscar Wilde, *Complete Poetry*, ed. Isobel Murray (Oxford: Oxford University Press, 1997), p. 126; Elizabeth Barrett Browning, *Aurora Leigh*, ed. Margaret Reynolds (New York: Norton, 1996), 6.1247–49.

134 *The German Ideology*, MECW 5.42.

135 Marx to Hermann Becker [about 1 February 1851] MECW 38.273 – 'the carpenter' is an ironical allusion to August Willich (1810–1878), a member of the Communist League who resigned from the Prussian army to work as a carpenter.

136 Nietzsche, *The Twilight of the Idols*, written in 1888, is subtitled 'How to Philosophize with a Hammer.' I here allude, of course, to Marx's famous declaration that 'philosophers have only *interpreted* the world . . . the point is to change it' – 'Theses on Feuerbach' (1845), *Early Writings*, p. 423.

137 Quoted in S. S. Prawer, *Karl Marx and World Literature* (Oxford: Clarendon Press, 1976), p. 28; *The Holy Family*, MECW 4.123.

138 *Early Writings*, p. 115; *Capital* 1.461.

139 'The British Rule in India' (1853), *Surveys from Exile*, p. 321.

140 Article from the *N.Rh.Z.*, 18 June 1848, *Revolutions of 1848*, p. 125.

140 See 'Critique of Hegel's Philosophy of Right', *Early Writings*, p. 244.

142 Benjamin Disraeli, Preface to the fifth edition (1849) of *Coningsby*, *The Works of Benjamin Disraeli, Earl of Beaconsfield*, 15 vols (New York: Walter Dunne, 1904), XII. xvi.

143 Derrida, *Specters*, p. 174.
144 *The Holy Family*, MECW 4.23, 22 / MEW 2.23, 22.
145 *Ibid.*, 4.142 / MEW 2.150.
146 Marx refers to that 'abstract country, the European nation' – 'Reviews from the *N.Rh.Z. Revue*' (1850), *Revolutions of 1848*, p. 314.
147 Terry Eagleton, *Saints and Scholars* (London: Verso, 1987), p. 129.

Three Stations

1 *The Complete Letters of Sigmund Freud to Wilhelm Fliess 1887–1904*, tr. Jeffrey Moussaieff Mason (Cambridge, Mass.: Harvard University Press, 1985), p. 274 / *Sigmund Freud: Briefe an Wilhem Fliess 1887–1904*, Herausgegeben von Jeffrey Mouissaieff Masson, Bearbeitung der deutschen Fassung von Michael Schröter; Transkription von Gerhard Fichtner (Frankfurt: S. Fischer, 1985), p. 295. As and when I am dealing closely with the particular wording in Freud's letters to Fliess I shall, as here, supply a reference to the original German text.

2 For discussion of Freud's preoccupation with (not) going to Rome, see Paul C. Witz, *Sigmund Freud's Christian Unconscious* (London: Guilford Press, 1988), pp. 72–100.

3 *The Interpretation of Dreams* [1900], The Penguin Freud Library, 15 vols, tr. James Strachey, ed. Angela Richards and Albert Dickson (Harmondsworth: Penguin, 1973–), 4.283 / Sigmund Freud, *Gesammeltte Werke,*18 vols, ed. Anna Freud (London: Imago, 1940–52), II/III.200. Unless otherwise stated, all subsequent references to Freud will be to this edition, which will always be referred to as PFL; as and when I am dealing closely with the particular wording in Freud I shall, as here, supply a reference to the original German text and always to this edition which will be referred to as *GW*. In Joyce Crick's more recent translation of *The Interpretation of Dreams* (Oxford: Oxford University Press, 1999) *Leidensstationen* is translated literally, as 'stations of his suffering;' but there is, of course, no getting away from Strachey's understanding of the phrase, given that *das Leidensweg* means 'the Way of the Cross' whilst *Stationen* can be used in the context of 'the Stations of the Cross' [*die vierzehn Stationenen*]. For excellent material in relation to the Jew's relationship to the train, see Adam Biro, *Two Jews on a Train,* tr. Catherine Tihanyi (Chicago: Chicago University Press, 2001); Andrew Benjamin, *Art, Mimesis and the Avant-Garde* (London: Routledge, 1991), pp. 89–90; Sidra DeKoven Ezrahi, *Booking Passages: Exile and Homecoming in the Modern Jewish Imagination* (Berkeley: California University Press, 2000), pp. 109–16; Sander L. Gilman, *Freud, Race and Gender* (Princeton: Princeton University Press, 1988), pp. 124–9; and, in passing, Nicholas Daly, 'Sensation Drama, the Railway and the Dark Face of Modernity', *Victorian Studies* 42 (1998–99), 68.

4 The legend, which echoes Christ's own words in John 16.5, appears in the apocryphal 'Acts of Peter' and is also the subject of Annibale Carracci's famous painting 'Christ Appearing to Saint Peter on the Appian Way' (1601–2).

5 Schorske refers to 'th[is] picture of the little-Jew-Christ-Freud reaching

Carlsbad-Rome on a *"via dolorosa"* – Carl E. Schorske, *Fin-de-Siecle Vienna: Politics and Culture* (Cambridge: Cambridge University Press,1981), p. 190; also see Witz, pp. 86–7.

6   Søren Kierkegaard, *Papers and Journals: A Selection*, tr. Alistair Hannay (Harmondsworth: Penguin, 1996), p. 21; Fyodor Dostoyevsky, *The Idiot* [1868], tr. Alan Meyers (Oxford: Oxford University Press, 1992), p. 3. For further interesting writing on the train and Christianity, see Walter Benjamin, *One-Way Street*, tr. Edmund Jephcott and Kingsley Shorter (London: Verso, 1979), p. 82.

7   Gustave Flaubert, *Sentimental Education*, tr. Robert Baldick (Harmondsworth: Penguin, 1964), p. 298.

8   PFL, 4.283 (my italics).

9   Quoted by Witz, p. 86.

10 Quoted by Jean Baudrillard in *Forget Foucault* (New York: Semiotexte, 1987), p. 49.

11 *Psychoanalysis and Faith: The Letters of Sigmund Freud and Oskar Pfister*, ed. Heinrich Meng and Ernst L. Freud, tr. Eric Mosbacher (London: Hogarth Press, 1963), pp. 74–5 (my italics).

12 *Ibid.*, p. 75.

13 Quoted in Wolfgang Schivelbusch, *The Railway Journey: Trains and Travel in the Nineteenth Century,* tr. Anselm Hollo (Oxford: Blackwell, 1980), p. 37; *The Interpretation*, PFL 4.534. Schivelbusch's book is an excellent exploration of the cultural history of the train; also good in this connection are: Nicholas Faith, *The World the Railway Made* (London: Pimlico, 1990); Michael Robbins, *The Railway Age* (Manchester: Mandolin, 1985), and Michael de Certeau, *The Practice of Everyday Life*, tr. Steven Randall (Berkeley: University of California Press, 1984), pp. 111–4.

14 See Albert Einstein, *Relativity: the Special and the General Theory* (London: Methuen, 1962), pp. 25–27. Freud and Einstein were often paired together as famous Jewish intellectuals – see Moshe Gresser, *Dual Allegiance: Freud as a Modern Jew* (Albany: SUNY Press, 1994), p. 185.

15 Quoted by Werner Heisenberg, *Physics and Beyond* (New York: Harper and Row, 1971), p. 80.

16 Sigmund Freud, *New Introductory Lectures* [1933], PFL 2.212.

17 *Letters to Fliess,* p. 307; see F. R. B.Whitehouse, *Table Games of Georgian and Victorian Days* (Royston: Priory Press, 1974). Freud himself refers to the 'chance of an accident when we are on a railway-journey' – *Introductory Lectures on Psychoanalysis* [1916], PFL, 1.447.

18 See Laura Marcus, 'The Oedipus Express', in Warren Chernaik, Martin Swales and Robert Vilain (eds), *The Art of Detective Fiction* (London and Basingstoke: Macmillan, 2000), p. 208; I am much indebted to Marcus's excellent essay.

19 Quoted in Gilman, *Freud, Race and Gender,* p. 126.

20 Sigmund Freud, 'Fragment of an Analysis of a Case of Hysteria' ('Dora'), [1905], PFL 8.100, 108.

21 'He [Freud] seems surprised . . . that the good little boy never seemed to have the idea of pulling the spool behind him and playing at its being a carriage: or rather at its being a wagon (*Wagen*), a train. It is as if one could wager

(*wagen* again) that the speculator . . . would himself have played choo-choo'
– Jacques Derrida, 'Freud's Legacy', *The Post Card: From Socrates to Freud and Beyond* [1980], tr. Alan Bass (London: Chicago University Press, 1987), p. 314. For Pascal's famous wager, see Blaise Pascal, *Pensées* [1670], tr. A. J. Krailsheimer (Harmondsworth: Penguin, 1995), pp. 121–6.

22 Gregory Zilboorg, *Psychoanalysis and Religion* (London: Allen and Unwin, 1967), p. 167.

23 Sigmund Freud, *The Psychopathology of Everyday Life* [1901], PFL 5.47.

24 See Sander L. Gilman, *The Case of Sigmund Freud: Medicine and Identity at the Fin de Siècle* (Baltimore: Johns Hopkins University Press, 1993), p. 33; see Jack Wertheimer, *Unwelcome Strangers: East European Jews in Imperial Germany* (Oxford: Oxford University Press, 1987), pp. 50–51.

25 Schorske, pp. 122, 130; quoted in *ibid.*, p. 172.

26 Sigmund Freud, *Jokes and their Relation to the Unconscious* [1905], PFL 6.121

27 Quoted in Dennis B. Klein, *Jewish Origins of the Psychoanalytic Movement* (Chicago: Chicago University Press, 1985), p. 62.

28 For information on Freud's reading habits see Peter Gay, *Freud: a life for our time* (London: J. M. Dent, 1988), p. 166; see Marcus, pp. 201–21.

29 PFL, 1.233.

30 *Collected Poems of Edward Thomas* (Oxford: Oxford University Press, 1981), p. 24.

31 Quoted in Witz, p. 25; for discussion of this journey see Marcus, p. 208.

32 See Gay, p. 629; *Letters of Sigmund Freud 1873–1939* ed. Ernst L. Freud, tr. Tania and James Stern (London: Hogarth Press, 1961), p. 445.

33 Witz, p. 201.

34 *Letters to Fliess*, pp. 283, 322.

35 Quoted in Yosef Hayim Yerushalmi, *Freud's Moses: Judaism Terminable and Interminable* (New Haven: Yale University Press, 1991), p. 53.

36 Freud, of course, is well aware of this episode in the life of Christ – see his joke about 'Dr Herodes' the child-doctor (PFL 4.574).

37 As Martin Gilbert writes, 'two . . . were murdered at Treblinka, the eighty-two-year-old Marie and the eighty-year-old Pauline. Two others of his sisters also perished, the eighty-four-year-old Rosa in Auschwitz, and the eighty-one-year-old Adolfine in Theresienstadt' – *The Holocaust: the Jewish Tragedy* (London: Fontana, 1986), p. 476.

38 *Letters of Sigmund Freud,* p. 451.

39 *Ibid.*, 202.

40 PFL, 5.47.

41 *Letters to Fliess*, p. 363.

42 Sigmund Freud, *Group Psychology and the Analysis of the Ego* [1921], PFL 12.118.

43 Biro, p.xi.

44 Quoted in Stanley Edgar Hyman, *The Tangled Bank: Darwin, Marx and Freud as Imaginative Writers* (New York: Athenaeum, 1974), p. 407; 'The Psychogenesis of a Case of Homosexuality in a Woman' [1920], PFL 9.377, 390.

45 *Ibid.*, PFL, 9.372; L. N. Tolstoy, *Anna Karenin* [1874–6], tr. Rosemary

Edmonds (Harmondsworth: Penguin, 1954), p. 801.

46 Quoted in Valentine Cunningham's wonderful *British Writers of the Thirties* (Oxford: Oxford University Press, 1989), p. 353.

47 For a discussion of Freud's Anglophilism, see Carl E. Schorske, 'Freud: The Psychoarcheology of Civilization' in Jerome Neu (ed.), *The Cambridge Companion to Freud* (Cambridge: Cambridge University Press, 1997), pp. 10–13. As Schorske points out, Freud 'himself talks of 'England['s] . . . sober industriousness' p. 10; my point is that this explicit and conscious view of England is complicated by an implicit and unconscious sense of England as anything but sober.

48 PFL, 1.148.

49 Lewis Carroll, *The Annotated Alice*, ed. Martin Gardner (Harmondsworth: Penguin, 1960), p. 218.

50 'Introductory Lectures', PFL 1.149.

51 Sigmund Freud, 'From the History of an Infantile Neurosis', PFL 9.242; *Letters of Sigmund Freud*, p. 443.

52 Sigmund Freud, *The Future of an Illusion* [1927], PFL 12.231.

53 *Ibid.*, p. 210; *Alice*, p. 251.

54 PFL, 9.218; this text was cited by Steven Connor in a wonderful series of talks he gave for BBC Radio 4 called *Rough Magic*, January 2000.

55 PFL, 9.146; Florence Nightingale, *Cassandra and other selections from Suggestions for Thought*, ed. Mary Poovey (London: Pickering and Chatto, 1991), p. 230.

56 PFL, 9.151; Oscar Wilde, *De Profundis*, *The Letters of Oscar Wilde*, ed. Rupert Hart-Davis (London: 1962), pp. 490–1.

57 Oscar Wilde, *The Importance of Being Ernest* in *Oscar Wilde: Plays, Prose Writings and Poems*, ed. Anthony Fothergill (London: Everyman, 1996), p. 436.

57 John Ruskin, *The Seven Lamps of Architecture, The Complete Works*, ed. E. T. Cook and A. Wedderburn, 39 vols (London: George Allen, 1903–1912), 8.159.

58 Martin Heidegger, *Basic Writings*, ed. David Farrell Krell (London: Routledge, 1993), p. 347.

59 Jacques Derrida, *Le Toucher, Jean-Luc Nancy* (Paris: Galilée, 2000), p. 274n.

60 *Psychopathology*, PFL, 5.104. The only critic who, to my knowledge, touches on Freud's occasional references to Wilde is Phillip McCaffrey – see 'Freud's Uncanny Women' in Sander L. Gilman *et al.* (eds), *Reading Freud's Reading* (New York: New York University Press, 1994), pp. 92–6.

61 PFL, 5.65.

62 See Gay, pp. 609, 629. Derrida also makes a link between Freud's Ernst and Wilde's Ernest – see *The Post Card*, pp. 301–2.

63 See PFL, 4.552.

64 Sigmund Freud, *Moses and Monotheism* [1939], PFL, 13.286.

65 *The Interpretation,* tr. Crick, p. 271; interestingly, Strachey translates *Inkarnationen* as 're-incarnations' thus losing the especially Christian force of the word – see PFL, 4.552.

66 PFL, 13.286

67 Wilde, *Letters* p. 819; PFL, 5.302.
68 See PFL, 11.284.
69 Derrida, *Post Card*, p. 314.
70 Jacques Lacan, 'The Freudian Thing', *Écrits: A Selection* (London: Routledge, 1977), p. 115.
71 PFL, 11.285.
72 Quoted in José Brunner, *Freud and the Politics of Psychoanalysis* (Oxford: Blackwell, 1995), pp. 121, 111.
73 PFL, 1.215.
74 'From the History of an Infantile Neurosis' [1918], PFL 9.238.
75 PFL, 1.114.
76 Wilfred Owen, 'Strange Meeting', *The Collected Poems*, ed. C. Day Lewis (London: Chatto and Windus, 1964), p. 36.
77 See Luke 22.44.
78 'Some Character-Types Met with in Psychoanalytic Work' [1916], PFL 14.319 / GW X.391.
79 I refer, of course, to 'Hymn to Proserpine', *The Poems of Algernon Charles Swinburne*, 6 vols (London: Chatto and Windus, 1904), 1.69.
80 PFL, 14.319.
81 'Thoughts for the Times on War and Death' [1915], PFL 12.66 . For a good discussion of 'Freud's [early] zeal for his country'-at-war, see Gay, *Freud*, pp. 349–50.
82 Owen, *Collected Poems,* p. 42
83 *The Interpretation*, ed. Crick, p. 325 / PFL, 4.638.
84 I refer, of course, to Kierkegaard's *Fear and Trembling* (1843) 'with which', writes Witz, 'Freud was . . . familiar' (Witz, p. 232, n.76).
85 *The Idiot,* p. 23.
86 For an excellent account of how war, in some ways, increased religious belief, see Annette Becker, *War and Faith: The Religious Imagination in France 1914–1930*, tr. Helen McPhail (Oxford: Berg, 2002), pp. 47–59 and Paul Fussell, *The Great War and Modern Memory* (Oxford: Oxford University Press, 1975), pp. 114–20. The passivity of the soldier-Christ is obvious both in Becker and Fussell respectively, and in Hibberd and Onions, pp. 89–108.
87 *The Idiot,* p. 532.
88 See Fussell, p. 123.
89 Wilfred Owen, *Collected Letters*, ed. Harold Owen and John Bell (London: Oxford University Press, 1967), p. 562.
90 PFL, 12.125.
91 PFL, 9.275.
92 PFL, 9.275 / GW 1.274.
93 *Psychoanalyis and Faith*, p. 140.
94 Quoted in Witz, p. 119.
95 Quoted in Fussell, p. 118.
96 Søren Kierkegaard, *Armed Neutrality*, ed. Howard V. Hong and Edna H. Hong (Bloomington: Indiana University Press, 1968); the phrase was also used, and so given contemporaneous currency, by Woodrow Wilson, in *Message to Congress,* February 26 1917.
97 Owen, *Collected Letters*, p. 461.

98 PFL, 9.238. Early on in the war Freud also describes himself as living in a 'primitive trench' – see Frank J. Sulloway, *Freud: Biologist of the Mind* (Cambridge, Mass.: Harvard University Press, 1992), p. 479.

99 'Psychoanalysis and Telepathy' [1941], *The Standard Edition of The Complete Psychological Works of Sigmund Freud*, 24 vols, tr. James Strachey (London: Hogarth Press, 1953–74), XVIII.180.

100 PFL, 2.88.

101 PFL, 1.53.

102 1 Corinthians 1.23

103 Friedrich Nietzsche, *The Genealogy of Morals*, tr. Walter Kaufmann and R. J. Hollingdale (New York: Vintage, 1989), p. 162.

104 PFL, 13.210 .

105 Quoted in Witz, p. 127.

106 PFL, 11.338.

107 David C. Cassidy, *Uncertainty: The Life and Science of Heisenberg* (New York: W. H. Freeman, 1992), p. 455.

108 *Civilization and its Discontents* [1930], PFL 12.280.

109 See Gay, p. 427; as Ernest Jones remarks, 'from now on Freud's speech was very defective' – *Ernest Jones, Sigmund Freud: Life and Work,* 3 vols (London: Hogarth Press, 1955–7), 3.100.

110 Sigmund Freud, *Totem and Taboo: Some Points of Agreement between the Mental Lives of Savages and Neurotics* [1913], PFL 13.140.

111 PFL, 4.187–8.

112 PFL, 13.299.

113 See 'The Jewish Foot' chapter in Sander L. Gilman, *The Jew's Body* (London: Routledge, 1991), and 'The Degenerate Foot and the Search for Oedipus' chapter in Gilman, *The Case of Sigmund Freud*, pp. 113–57.

114 Kierkegaard, *Fear and Trembling*, tr. Alastair Hannay (Harmondsworth: Penguin, 1985), p. 70. For a rare discussion of Freud in relation to Kierkegaard, see Frederick J. Hacker, 'Freud, Marx and Kierkegaard', in B. Nelson (ed.), *Freud and the Twentieth Century* (London: Allen and Unwin: 1958).

115 Quoted in Jones, 2.466.

116 Quoted in J. B. Pontalis, *Frontiers in Psychoanalysis: Between the Dream and Psychic Pain*, tr. Catherine Cullen and Phillip Cullen (London: Hogarth Press, 1981), p. 49 .

117 Heinrich Heine, *Almansor* [1823], *The Complete Poems* (Boston: Suhrkamp, Inc., 1992), p. 302, l.245; *Freud–Jung Letters*, ed. William McGuire, tr. Ralph Manheim and R. F. C. Hull (Princeton: Princeton University Press, 1974), p. 211.

118 'Delusions and Dreams in Jensen's *Gradiva*' [1907], PFL 14.89. This imprint is pursued in Jacques Derrida, *Archive Fever: A Freudian Impression*, tr. Eric Prenowitz (Chicago: Chicago University Press, 1996), pp. 98–101.

119 PFL, 14.36.

120 Sigmund Freud, 'The Moses of Michelangelo' [1914], PFL 14.256.

121 PFL, 6.121.

122 PFL, 3.333; *The Letters of Sigmund Freud and Arnold Zweig*, ed. Ernst L.

Freud, tr. Elaine and William Robson-Scott (London: Hogarth Press, 1970), p. 77 / *Sigmund Freud, Arnold Zweig, Briefwechsel*, ed. Ernst L. Freud (Frankfurt: S. Fischer Verlag, 1968), p. 87.

123 PFL, 4.677 / GW II/III.535.

124 *The Interpretation*, ed. Crick, p. 159 / GW II/III.212.

125 PFL, 2.212–3.

126 PFL, 4.700.

127 *The Interpretation*, ed. Crick, p. 159.

128 See PFL, 4.274.

129 PFL, 5.316–7.

130 For just one example, see Gilbert, *The Holocaust*, p. 469.

131 *Letters of Sigmund Freud*, p. 299.

132 Quoted in Witz, p. 507.

133 Georg Simmel, 'Money in Modern Culture', in *Simmel on Culture*, eds D. Frisby and M. Featherstone (London: Sage, 1997), p. 250; George Eliot, *Daniel Deronda* (Harmondsworth: Penguin, 1967), p. 557. For a brief discussion of Freud's response to *Daniel Deronda*, see Gresser, pp. 89–90.

134 PFL, 1.233.

135 Owen, *Letters,* p. 461; Edmund Blunden, 'Memoir', in Owen, *Collected Poems*, p. 39.

136 Percy Wyndham Lewis, *Blasting and Bombardiering: An Autobiography 1914–1926* [1927] (London: John Calder Press, 1982), p. 2; *The Complete Poems and Plays of T. S. Eliot* (London: Faber and Faber, 1969), p. 62.

137 PFL, 1.233.

138 PFL, 11.450.

139 *Ibid.*, p. 449.

140 GW 10.328; GW XVI.252 (my italics).

141 Sigmund Freud, *Civilization and its Discontents* [1929], PFL 12.251–2.

142 PFL, 2.35, 112./ GW XV.6

143 PFL, 4.539 – for discussion of Freud's early interest in fish, see Ursula Reidel-Schrewe, 'Freud's Debut in the Sciences', in Gilman, *Reading Freud's Reading*, pp. 1–22.

144 PFL, 1.194.

145 PFL, 1.46.

146 *Letters to Fliess*, pp. 254, 374–5 / 272, 411, 413.

147 *Ibid.*p. 447/ 492.

148 PFL, 4.664–5: my italics.

149 PFL, 11.445; *Letters to Fliess*, p. 393. It is very rare that critics pick up on Freud and the trope of the sea – see, though, Malcolm Bowie, *Freud, Proust and Lacan: Theory as Fiction* (Cambridge: Cambridge University Press, 1987), p. 30 and William J. McGrath, *Freud's Discovery of Psychoanalysis: The Politics of Hysteria* (Ithaca: Cornell University Press, 1986), pp. 130–33, 199. Interestingly, H. D. (Hilda Doolittle), once referred to Freud as 'the Old Man of the Sea' – quoted in John Forrester, *Dispatches from the Freud Wars* (Cambridge, Mass.: Harvard University Press, 1997), p. 121.

150 *Psychoanalysis and Faith*, p. 25.

151 *Letters to Fliess*, p. 219 / 230–1.

152 As the editors to the *Letters to Fliess* observe, Freud often plays on the various meaning of 'constitutions', p. 221, n.1.
153 *The Interpretation*, ed. Crick, p. 283. For an account of Freud's attitudes to Zionism, see Gresser, pp. 201–4.
154 *Psychoanalysis and Faith*, p. 140.
155 See Gilbert, p. 135.
156 PFL, 11.448.
157 *Letters to Fliess*, p. 219.
158 *Ibid.*, p. 269.
159 Quoted in Gilman, *Case of Sigmund Freud*, p. 43.
160 See, for example, *Jokes and their Relation to the Unconscious* [1916], PFL 6.85, 112; see Witz, p. 85.
161 Quoted in Gilman, *Freud, Race and Gender*, p. 110.
162 Friedrich Nietzsche, *Daybreak: Thoughts on the Prejudices of Morality* [1881], tr. R. J. Hollingdale (Cambridge: Cambridge University Press, 1982), aphorism no. 68, p. 40.
163 *Letters to Fliess*, p. 398.
164 PFL, 4.572–3.
165 The reader of the New Testament is reminded of this in Matthew 27.33.
166 PFL, 9.303–4.
167 For a good discussion of Freud's recurring fascination with Easter, see Witz, pp. 73–5.
168 The young Freud was regularly taken to church by his Roman Catholic nanny – see Witz, pp. 1–30.
169 In 1918 Freud's Christian friend, Pfister, wrote to Freud: 'I should say of you: a better Christian there never was . . . ' (*Psychoanalysis and Faith*, p. 63).

Four   **Subterranean Soul**

1   1 Corinthians 12.27; Jacques Derrida, 'Fors', Foreword to N. Abraham and M. Torok, *The Wolf Man's Magic Word: A Cryptonymy*, tr. N. Rand (Minneapolis: University of Minnesota Press, 1986), pp. xi, xxxix.
2   Charles Dickens, *Pictures from Italy* [1846], ed. Kate Flint (Harmondsworth: Penguin, 1998), p. 67.
3   *The Letters of Charles Dickens*, ed. W. Dexter, 3 vols (London: Nonesuch Press, 1938), 3.402.
4   Mrs Trollope, *The Vicar of Wrexhill,* quoted in Valentine Cunningham, *Everywhere Spoken Against: Dissent in the Victorian Novel* (Oxford: Clarendon Press, 1975), p. 22.
5   *Pictures*, pp. 139,137.
6   Dennis Walder, *Dickens and Religion* (London: Allen & Unwin, 1981), p. 25.
7   Charles Dickens, *Great Expectations*, ed. Charlotte Mitchell (Harmondsworth: Penguin, [1860–61] 1996), p. 4; Charles Dickens, *Our Mutual Friend* [1865], ed. Adrian Poole (Harmondsworth: Penguin, 1997), p. 221; Charles Dickens, *Hard Times* [1854], ed. Kate Flint (Harmondsworth: Penguin, 1995), p. 29.
8   Acts 17.6.

9   *Great Expectations*, pp. 4, 45.

10   *Ibid.*, pp. 24, 458 (my italics).

11   Thomas Carlyle, *On Heroes, Hero-Worship and The Heroic in History* [1840] (Cambridge: Cambridge University Press, 1914), p. 166.

12   *Pictures*, p. 137 (my italics); Derrida, 'Fors', p. xxxvi.

13   *Ibid.*, p. 386.

14   'What I like about post cards', writes Derrida, 'is that . . . they are made to circulate like an open but illegible letter' – *The Post Card: From Socrates to Freud and Beyond* [1980], tr. Alan Bass (Chicago: University of Chicago Press, 1987), p. 12.

15   *Pictures*, p. 6.

16   See Fred Kaplan, *Dickens: A Biography* (London: Hodder & Stoughton, 1988), p. 198.

17   Carlyle, *On Heroes*, p. 166.

18   *Pictures*, p. 80; see Jacques Derrida, *Writing and Difference*, tr. Alan Bass (London: Routledge, 1978), p. 278.

19   *Pictures*, p. 119.

20   Charles Dickens, *A Tale of Two Cities* [1859], ed. Richard Maxwell (Harmondsworth: Penguin, 2000), p. 162.

21   Derrida, *The Post Card*, p. 123.

22   *Pictures*, p. 132.

23   See Owen Chadwick, *The Victorian Church* (London: Adam & Charles Black, 1966), p. 327.

24   *Pictures*, p. 138; *Tale of Two Cities*, p. 102; Charles Dickens, *Martin Chuzzlewit* [1833–4], ed. Patricia Ingham (Harmondsworth: Penguin, 1999), p. 79; Charles Dickens, *Dombey and Son* [1849], ed. Peter Fairclough (Harmondsworth: Penguin, 1970), p. 887.

25   Charles Dickens, *The Old Curiosity Shop* [1841], ed. Norman Page (Harmondsworth: Penguin, 2000), p. 403.

26   'The system of "hearing (understanding)-oneself-speak" [*s'entendre parler*] through the phonic substance – which *presents itself* as the nonexterior . . . noncontingent signifier – has necessarily dominated the history of the world during an entire epoch' – Jacques Derrida, *Of Grammatology*, tr. Gayatri Chakravorty (London: Johns Hopkins University Press, 1974), pp. 7–8.

27   Charles Dickens, *Little Dorrit* [1857], ed. Stephen Wall and Helen Small (Harmondsworth: Penguin, 1998), p. 41.

28   John P. Leavey, *Glassary* (Lincoln: University of Nebraska Press, 1986), p. 104c – Leavey is here attempting to describe the place and significance of bells in *Glas* (which means, of course, 'passing-bell'). As Leavey remarks, 'the movement of the bell-clapper swinging one way, barrel the other, is the motion of Derrida's [own] text' and indeed 'an emblem for the . . . movement of . . . his theory of writing as difference' (pp. 93a, 89c); *Hard Times*, p. 66; *Little Dorrit*, p. 40; *Pictures*, p. 45.

29   *Little Dorrit*, p. 15; *Dombey and Son*, p. 888; *The Uncommercial Traveller* (Oxford: Oxford University Press, 1958), p. 87; *Little Dorrit*, p. 40.

30   *Hard Times*, p. 118.

31   *Little Dorrit*, p. 583 (my italics).

32   *A Tale of Two Cities*, p. 194.

33 *Little Dorrit*, p. 198.
34 Charles Dickens, *Bleak House* [1853], ed. Nicola Bradbury (Harmondsworth: Penguin, 1996), pp. 257, 256.
35 *Ibid.*, p. 411; Hebrews 13.14.
36 *Pictures*, pp. 68, 119, 139.
37 Derrida, 'Fors', p. xxxvi; J. Hillis Miller, for example, writes that 'life in the city is the way in which many men have experienced most directly what it means to live without God in the world' – *The Disappearance of God* (Cambridge, Mass.: Harvard University Press, 1963), p. 5.
38 *Pictures*, p. 137.
39 Victor Hugo, *Les Miserables*, tr. N. Denny (Harmondsworth: Penguin, 1980), vol. 2, p. 368; quoted in A. S. Wohl, *Endangered Lives: Public Health in Victorian Britain* (London: Methuen, 1983), p. 101.
40 Friedrich Nietzsche, *Twilight of the Idols* [1889] / *The Anti-Christ* [1895], tr. R. J. Hollingdale (Harmondsworth: Penguin, 1990), p. 178.
41 Terry Eagleton, *The Body as Language: Outline of a 'New Left' Theology* (London: Sheed & Ward, 1970), p. 70.
42 *Bleak House*, p. 180; *Martin Chuzzlewit*, p. 132.
43 This phrase appears in an essay published in 1853 and is quoted by David Trotter in *Circulation: Defoe, Dickens, and the Economics of the Novel* (London: Macmillan, 1988), p. 73.
44 *Pictures*, p. 67.
45 See Trotter, p. 105.
46 *Little Dorrit*, p. 41.
47 Nietzsche, *Twilight*, p. 177.
48 *Letters*, 3.402.
49 *Pictures*, pp. 80, 46.
50 *Bleak House*, pp. 415; Charles Dickens, *David Copperfield* [1850], ed. Jeremy Tambling (Harmondsworth: Penguin, 1996), p. 582.
51 *Dombey and Son*, p. 901.
52 *Ibid.*, pp. 887–8.
53 *Great Expectations*, p. 115.
54 See Jacques Lacan, *Écrits: A Selection,* tr. Alan Sheridan (London: Routledge, 1977), p. 4; *Pictures*, p. 67.
55 John Henry Newman, *Apologia Pro Vita Sua* [1864], (London: Fontana, 1959), p. 326.
56 *The Old Curiosity Shop*, p. 365 (my italics).
57 *Little Dorrit*, pp. 15; the 'Church Invisible' is an ancient theological phrase describing 'those who are known to God alone as His sons and daughters by adoption and grace' – E. Cobham Brewer, *The Dictionary of Phrase and Fable* (Leicester: Blitz, 1990), p. 253.
58 Quoted in Simon During, *Foucault and Literature* (London: Routledge, 1992), p. 5.
59 *Pictures*, p. 67.
60 Michel Foucault, *Madness and Civilisation* [1861], tr. Richard Howard (London: Routledge, 1989), pp. 78–9.
61 *Pictures,* p. 67.
62 *Tale of Two Cities*, p. 385.

63 *The Old Curiosity Shop*, p. 405.
64 Charles Dickens, *Oliver Twist* [1838], ed. Philip Horne (Harmondsworth: Penguin, 2002), p. 144.
65 Alistair Hannay (ed.), *Søren Kierkegaard: Papers and Journals* (Harmondsworth: Penguin, 1996), p. 475 – I am grateful to Jeremy Tambling for bringing this passage to my attention.
66 Nietzsche, *Twilight,* p. 141.
67 *Pictures*, pp. 138, 137.
68 *Great Expectations*, p. 34; 2 Corinthians 11.24–5 – this Pauline allusion was first observed by Joseph A. Hynes, see 'Image and Symbol in *Great Expectations*', *ELH*, 30 (1963), 260–1.
69 Foucault, *Madness*, p. 63; *Little Dorrit*, p. 41.
70 *Pictures*, pp. 120, 186.
71 *Little Dorrit*, p. 68; *Great Expectations*, p. 165; *Pictures*, p. 137.
72 Quoted in John Forster, *The Life of Charles Dickens*, 3 vols, ed. A. J. Hoppé (London: Dent, 1966), 1.24. As Forster observes, at this time in Dickens's life, when he was living in lodgings, 'at home' meant Marshalsca (1.26).
73 *Pictures*, p. 133.
74 *Great Expectations*, p. 454.
75 *David Copperfield*, p. 582.
76 See Michel Foucault, *Discipline and Punish* [1975], tr. Alan Sheridan (Harmondsworth: Penguin, 1991), pp. 6–7.
77 *Hard Times*, pp. 122–3.
78 See Natalie McKnight, *Idiots, Madmen, and Other Prisoners in Dickens* (New York: St Martin's Press, 1993), pp. 18–21, 22–3.
79 *David Copperfield*, p. 784.
80 John 4.2.
81 *Uncommercial Traveller*, p. 85.
82 Michel Foucault, *The History of Sexuality,* tr. Robert Hurley (Harmondsworth: Penguin, 1990), pp. 58–9.
83 Foucault, *Discipline,* p. 202.
84 *Oliver Twist*, p. 146.
85 *Dombey and Son*, pp. 887–8.
86 Charlotte Brönte, *Villette* [1853], ed. M. Lilly (Harmondsworth: Penguin, 1979), p. 109; E. P. Thompson and Eileen Yeo, *The Unknown Mayhew: Selections from the 'Morning Chronicle' 1849–50* (London: Merlin Press, 1971), pp. 97–8; see James Grant, *The Great Metropolis,* 3 vols (New York, 1837), I.19.
87 See the *Examiner,* 4 July 1849, cited in Robert Partlow (ed.), *Dickens the Craftsman* (Carbondale: Southern Illinois University Press, 1970), p. 119.
88 *Martin Chuzzlewit*, p. 662; *Great Expectations*, p. 165; *Little Dorrit*, p. 680.
89 Foucault, *Discipline,* p. 205.
90 *David Copperfield*, p. 25.
91 *Tale of Two Cities*, p. 110.
92 *Bleak House*, p. 290.
93 *Tale of Two Cities*, p. 204; throughout *Bleak House* Lady Dedlock is referred to as 'my Lady' by the anonymous narrator.
94 The 'assumption of his specular image', writes Lacan, takes place whilst the

child is 'still sunk in his . . . nursling dependence' – *Écrits*, p. 2; *Bleak House*, pp. 290–1.

95 For a fuller discussion of the subversive significance of the Virgin Mary, in a Victorian context, see my *Victorians in Theory: from Derrida to Browning*, (Manchester: Manchester University Press, 1999), pp. 120–4.

96 *Little Dorrit*, p. 491.

97 See Harry Stone, *The Night Side of Dickens: Cannibalism, Passion, Necessity* (Columbus: Ohio State University Press, 1994), pp. 240–5; *Little Dorrit*, p. 16.

98 Sigmund Freud, 'The "Uncanny"' in *Art and Literature,* The Penguin Freud Library, 15 vols, tr. James Strachey, ed. Angela Richards and Albert Dickson (Harmondsworth: Penguin, 1973–), 14.345.

99 *Little Dorrit*, pp. 219–20.

100 Freud, 'The Uncanny', p. 364.

101 Foucault argues that since the nineteenth century our society, with respect to sex, 'speaks verbosely of its own silence' – *History*, p. 8.

102 Freud, 'The Uncanny', p. 346; 1 Corinthians 12.23; for a good discussion of carnivalesque inversion see Peter Stallybrass and Allon White, *The Politics and Poetics of Transgression* (London: Methuen, 1986), p. 185.

103 Charlotte A. Eaton, *Rome, in the Nineteenth Century*, 2 vols (London: Henry G. Bohn, 1852), 1.408.

104 *Tale of Two Cities*, pp. 136–7.

105 John Henry Newman, *The Oxford University Sermons* (1892), p. 341.

106 Friedrich Nietzsche, *Beyond Good and Evil* [1886], tr. R. J. Hollingdale (Harmondsworth: Penguin, 1990), p. 31.

107 John Ruskin, *Unto This Last and Other Writings,* ed. Clive Wilmer (Harmondsworth: Penguin, 1985), pp. 107–8.

108 *Little Dorrit*, p. 43; *Uncommercial Traveller*, p. 92; *Dombey and Son*, p. 889.

109 *Pictures*, p. 119.

110 *Ibid.*, p. 99.

111 Elizabeth Barrett Browning, *Aurora Leigh* [1856], ed. Margaret Reynolds (Athens: Ohio University Press, 1992), 9.947.

112 Charles Dickens, 'Please to Leave Your Umbrella', in *Charles Dickens: Selected Journalism 1850–1870*, ed. David Pascoe (Harmondsworth: Penguin, 1997), pp. 589–90.

113 Comte de Lautréamont, quoted in Maurice Nadeau, *The History of Surrealism* (Harmondsworth: Penguin, 1973), p. 25. For a discussion of the importance of Lautréamont's conceit to Surrealism see J. H. Matthews, *An Introduction to Surrealism* (Pennsylvania: Pennsylvania State University Press, 1965), p. 105.

114 Quoted in George Steiner, *Real Presence* (London: Faber, 1989), p. 222.

115 Jacques Derrida, *Spurs: Nietzsche's Styles / Éperons: Les Styles de Nietzsche*, tr. Barbara Harlow (London: University of Chicago Press, 1978), pp. 123–43. Recalling the literary-cum-philosophical scene of his youth, Derrida once observed that 'the memory of surrealism was still alive' – 'This Strange Institution Called Literature' in Jacques Derrida, *Acts of Literature*, ed. Derek Attridge (London: Routledge, 1992), p. 34.

116 Edmond Gosse, *Father and Son* [1907], (Harmondsworth: Penguin, 1983), p. 205.
117 To Robert Ross, late March 1900, *The Letters of Oscar Wilde*, ed. Rupert Hart-Davis (London: Rupert Hart-Davis Ltd, 1962), p. 819.
118 *Uncommercial Traveller*, p. 7.
119 *Ibid.*, pp. 8–9.
120 'Please to Leave Your Umbrella', p. 586.
121 Friedrich Nietzsche, *Will to Power* [1895], tr. Walter Kaufmann and R. J. Hollingdale (New York: Vintage, 1968), pp. 124–5.

Five   The Love that Dare Not Speak its Christian Name

1   J. Cumming, *Ritualism, the Highway to Rome* [1867] – quoted in Ellis Hanson, *Decadence and Catholicism* (Cambridge, Mass.: Harvard University Press, 1997), p. 253.
2   Austin Farrer, *Saint Paul* (London, 1879), 1. 329; Havelock Ellis, *Sexual Inversion: Studies in the Psychology of Sex*, 7 vols (New York: Random House, 1936), I.i.11. I am, of course, indebted to Jonathan Dollimore's seminal work on the cultural history of perversion, in particular his insistence that this history must be traced back to its Christian beginnings – see *Sexual Dissidence: Augustine to Wilde, Freud to Foucault* (Oxford: Clarendon Press, p. 130). Also very important in this connection is Kenneth Burke who, in his own words, 'approach[es] . . . the subject of conversion in terms of perversity' – see *The Rhetoric of Religion: Studies in Logology* (Berkeley: University of California Press, 1970), p. 105 n., and 'Version, Con – , Per – , and In – ', in *Language as Symbolic Action: Essays on Life, Literature and Method* (Berkeley: University of California Press, 1966), pp. 240–53.
3   For a wonderful study of the complex relationship between Catholicism and homosexuality in the late-nineteenth century see, of course, Hanson's *Decadence and Catholicism*. Equally pertinent, albeit concerned with Early Modern texts, is Richard Rambuss's excellent *Closet Devotions* (Durham, NC: Duke University Press, 1998).
4   William Hogan, quoted in *The Confessional Unmasked* (Protestant Evangelical Mission and Electoral Union, 1867), p. 37.
5   Hanson, *passim*; Oscar Wilde, *The Picture of Dorian Gray* [1891], ed. Peter Faulkener (London: Everyman, 1993), p. 105.
6   To Mrs. Lathbury, [? Summer 1890], *The Letters of Oscar Wilde*, ed. Rupert Hart-Davis (London: 1962), p. 265.
7   To Robert Ross, 16 April [1990], *ibid.*, p. 821.
8   Jacques Derrida , 'Circumfession', in Geoff Bennington and Jacques Derrida, *Jacques Derrida* [1991], tr. Geoffrey Bennington (Chicago: University of Chicago Press, 1993), p. 124. When it comes to thinking through the complex relationship between 'being' and 'being Christian' Derrida does, in fact, turn to Oscar Wilde, albeit via *Hamlet*: 'être ou ne pas être chrétien ou, plus sauvagement', *The Importance of (not) Being Christian*' – Jacques Derrida, *Le Toucher, Jean-Luc Nancy* (Paris: Galilée, 2000), p. 274n.
9   Oscar Wilde, *The Importance of Being Ernest* in *Oscar Wilde: Plays, Prose*

Writings and Poems, ed. Anthony Fothergill (London: Everyman, 1996), p. 480.

10   *The Ideal Husband* in *Plays, Prose Writings and Poems*, p. 335; Richard Pine speaks of 'Wilde['s] . . . continual fascination with the act of baptism – and thus of naming' – *The Thief of Reason: Oscar Wilde and Modern Ireland* (Dublin: Gill and Macmillan, 1995), p. 13.

11   *Lady Windermere's Fan* in *Plays, Prose Writings and Poems*, p. 224.

12   To Robert Ross, Thursday [late March 1900], *Letters*, p. 819.

13   *De Profundis, ibid.*, p. 478; the ancient theory that John was a lover of Christ is mentioned by Wilde in a letter to Robert Ross, [July 1898] *ibid.*, p. 756, and developed in *Teleny, or the Reverse of the Medal* [1893] (Ware: Wordsworth, 1995), the anonymous homosexual novel that Wilde is rumoured to have co-written – see p. 111; *Letters*, p. 490.

14   *Plays, Prose Writings and Poems*, p. 432.

15   Quoted in Hesketh Pearson, *The Life of Oscar Wilde* (Harmondsworth: Penguin, 1954), p. 19.

16   I refer, of course, to Douglas's famous line, 'The love that dare not speak its name', which appears in his poem 'Two Loves' and is quoted in *De Profundis* – see *Letters,* p. 441.

17   *Dorian Gray*, p. 162. There has been a tendency to limit the significance of religion in Wilde to the Catholic-Decadent scene; there are, though, exceptions to this rule – in particular, Stephen Arata's excellent unpublished essay on Wilde's representation of Christ; Regenia Gagnier's discussion of Wilde's Christ-inspired opposition to the 'formalism of economic rationality' – see *The Insatiability of Human Wants: Economics and Aesthetics in Market Society* (Chicago: University of Chicago Press, 2000), pp. 146–75; and, above all, Jonathan Dollimore's striking claim that 'some of Wilde's earlier remarks about Christ suggested what might just have been the most daring of all transgressive reinscriptions – an oppositional Christ for our own time which would blast the pieties of the conservatively religious into kingdom come and rescue Christ from his adherents' (Dollimore, p. 96).

18   Galatians 5.11.

19   Michel Foucault, *Madness and Civilisation: A History of Insanity in the Age of Reason* [1961], tr. Richard Howard (London: Routledge, 1967), p. 79; Friedrich Nietzsche , *The Anti-Christ* [1895] in *The Twilight of the Idols / The Anti-Christ* (Harmondsworth: Penguin, 1968), p. 159. Nietzsche and Wilde are also brought together by Eve Kosofsky Sedgwick – see *Epistemology of the Closet* (London: Harvester Wheatsheaf, 1991), pp. 131–81; Kosofsky notes that both writers know that Christianity is not necessarily prohibitive of homosexual desire, p. 140.

20   'The Ballad of Reading Gaol', in *Oscar Wilde: Complete Poetry*, ed. Isobel Murray (Harmondsworth: Penguin, 1997), p. 153.

21   'The Burden of Itys', *ibid.*, p. 48.

22   *An Ideal Husband* in *Plays, Prose Writings and Poems*, p. 378 – the whole play is riddled with intriguing stage directions that very obviously seek to draw attention to themselves.

23   Quoted in Hanson, p. 139.

24   Quoted in *ibid.*, p. 148 – Hanson's own translation.

25 *Salome* in *Plays, Prose Writings and Poems*, pp. 238, 237; Matthew 16.23.

26 'The Sphinx' in *Complete Poetry*, pp. 146–7.

27 Stephen Knight, *The Brotherhood: The Secret World of the Freemasons* (London: Granada, 1984), p. 247 – Catholicism's disapproval of Freemasonry is clearly reflected in Robert Ross's attitude, see *Letters*, p. 565. See Karl Beckson, *The Oscar Wilde Encyclopedia* (New York: AMS Press, 1998), p. 106; Richard Ellmann gathers together the few details that exist of Wilde's Masonic life – see *Oscar Wilde* (Harmondsworth: Penguin, pp. 38–9). Even though these details are so few it is still remarkable how little attention is paid to Freemasonry in Wilde; the only critic, to my knowledge, who mentions it is Regenia Gagnier in *Idylls of the Marketplace: Oscar Wilde and the Victorian Public* (Stanford: Stanford University Press, 1986), p. 195.

28 *Plays, Prose Writings and Poems*, p. 356 – as Fothergill points out, Wilde here echoes Othello as he is about to kill Desdemona, p. 566 n; this echo only adds, of course, to the gravity of Sir Robert Chiltern's words.

29 See Joss Marsh, *Word Crimes: Blasphemy, Culture, and Literature in Nineteenth Century England* (Chicago: University of Chicago Press, 1998), p. 142. I am enormously indebted to this excellent study. Freud also writes about a Dr Schreber, an almost exact contemporary of Wilde's, whose religio-sexual mania includes the notion 'that God lets himself be f——' – see 'Psychoanalytic Notes on an Autobiographical Account of a Case of Paranoia' [1911], The Penguin Freud Library, 15 vols, tr. James Strachey, ed. Angela Richards and Albert Dickson (Harmondsworth: Penguin, 1973), 9.159.

30 Edward Carpenter, *Angels' Wings: A Series on Art and its Relation to Life* [1898] (London: George Allen and Unwin, 1917), p. 26.

31 Genesis 19.11.

32 1 Corinthians 13.12.

33 See Plato, *The Republic*, tr. H. D. P. Lee (Harmondsworth: Penguin, 1955), pp. 278–86.

34 Emmanuel Levinas, 'Ethics as First Philosophy', in *The Levinas Reader*, ed. Sean Hand (Oxford: Blackwell, 1989), p. 82; Thomas Paine, *The Age of Reason, Part the Second, being an Investigation of True and Fabulous Theology* (London, 1795), p. 103; see G. W. F. Hegel, *Phenomenology of Spirit* [1807], tr. A. V. Miller (Oxford: Oxford University Press, 1977), p. 111; Nietzsche, *The Anti-Christ*, p. 125.

35 *The Duchess of Padua* [1891], *The Complete Plays, Poems, Novels and Stories of Oscar Wilde* (London: Magpie, 1993), p. 586. Oliver S. Buckton's excellent essay on *De Profundis* touches upon the way that, in this long letter to Douglas, Wilde effectively avoids a face-to-face encounter with his addressee – see 'Desire without Limits: Dissident Confession in Oscar Wilde's *De Profundis*', in Richard Dellamora (ed.), *Victorian Sexual Dissidence* (Chicago: University of Chicago Press, 1999).

36 *Lady Windemere's Fan* in *Plays, Prose Writings and Poems*, p. 174; see also *An Ideal Husband*, ibid., p. 404, and *Dorian Gray*, p. 149.

37 'The Grave of Keats' in *Complete Poetry*, p. 23; 'Rome Unvisited', ibid., p. 7; *Salome* in *Plays, Prose Writings and Poems*, p. 244.

38 *Dorian Gray*, pp. 44, 68, 45, 68.

39 See *De Profundis, Letters*, pp. 483, 756.

40 *Dorian Gray*, p. 42.

41 See Wladyslaw Szpilman, *The Pianist* [1945], tr. Anthea Bell (New York: Picador, 1999). The importance of this book to our remembering of the Holocaust is reflected by the fact that it was recently made into a popular film by Roman Polanski.

42 *Dorian Gray*, pp. 63, 76.

43 Leo Bersani, *Homos* (Cambridge, Mass.: Harvard University Press, 1995), pp. 165–6.

44 There was much discussion, even within medical circles, of the homosexual-predisposition of Jewish males – see Sander L. Gilman, *Freud, Race and Gender* (Princeton: Princeton University Press, 1988), pp. 42, 159, 162.

45 *De Profundis, Letters*, p. 483; 'Humanitad', in *Complete Poetry*, p. 87.

46 'E Tenebris', *Complete Poetry*, p. 26; 'Rome Unvisited', *ibid.*, p. 7 – both poems appear in the 'Rosa Mystica' section of *Poems* (1881).

47 'The Burden of Itys', *ibid.*, p. 48.

48 'Sonnet to Liberty', *ibid.*, p. 126; *Dorian Gray*, p. 155.

49 *An Ideal Husband* in *Plays, Prose Writings and Poems*, p. 340.

50 *Dorian Gray*, p. 74.

51 *Ibid.*, pp. 75–6, 80.

52 *Ibid.*, p. 164; 'At Verona', *Complete Poetry*, p. 30.

53 *The Importance of Being Ernest* in *Plays, Prose Writings and Poems*, p. 436; 'The Burden of Itys', *Complete Poetry*, p. 47.

54 'Sonnet on the Massacre of the Christians in Bulgaria', *Complete Poetry*, p. 23; *Vera, or the Nihilists* in *The Complete Plays*, p. 656; 'Ave Imperatrix', *Complete Poetry*, pp. 118–9.

55 *An Ideal Husband* in *Plays, Prose Writings and Poems*, p. 339.

56 *De Profundis, Letters*, pp. 457, 477 (my italics); *The Waste Land* in *The Complete Poems and Plays of T. S. Eliot* (London: Faber, 1969), p. 69.

57 'Humanitad', *Complete Poetry*, pp. 77, 83, 86 (my italics).

58 Philip Hoare, *Wilde's Last Stand: Decadence, Conspiracy and the First World War* (London: Duckworth, 1997), p. 9.

59 *The Duchess of Padua* in *The Complete Plays*, p. 621.

60 See Hoare, pp. 26–7.

61 *Ibid.*, pp. 91–3.

62 'Humanitad', *Complete Poetry*, p. 87.

63 To Susan Owen [?16] May 1917, *Wilfred Owen: Collected Letters*, ed. Harold Owen and John Bell (London: Oxford University Press), p. 512. The connection between Oscar Wilde and Wilfred Owen is a fascinating one – as Hoare points out, Owen not only had 'vague Uranian sensibilities' and an early interest in Decadence and Aestheticism but was, on one occasion, entertained by Wilde's lover, Robbie Ross (p. 24).

64 Luke 23.2.

65 To Susan Owen, 22 February 1918, *Collected Letters*, p. 536; *De Profundis, Letters*, p. 487.

66 Nietzsche, *Anti-Christ*, p. 161 – though published in 1895, it was written in 1888; see Richard von Krafft-Ebing, *Psychopathia Sexualis* [1893], tr. Harry Wedeck, ed. Ernest van den Haag (New York: G. P. Putnam's Sons, 1965)

– first published, in Latin, in 1891. For a seminal discussion of the nine-teenth-century emergence of the homosexual as a 'personality type' see Michel Foucault, *The History of Sexuality*, vol. 1, tr. Robert Hurley (Harmondsworth: Penguin, 1979), p. 43.

67 Søren Kierkegaard, *Papers and Journals: A Selection,* tr. Alistair Hannay (Harmondsworth: Penguin, 1996), p. 610.

68 Friedrich Nietzsche, *Beyond Good and Evil: Prelude to a Philosophy of the Future*, tr. R. J. Hollingdale (Harmondsworth: Penguin, 1990), pp. 77, 76; see, for example, Max Nordau, *Degeneration* (New York: Appleton,1895), – a book dedicated to 'Carl Lombroso, Professor of Forensic Medicine' and which includes several chapters on what Nordau calls 'The Psychology of Mysticism'; under this heading he pathologises a whole miscellany of Christians ranging from Tolstoy and the pre-Raphaelites to the Salvation Army and neo-Catholics; *Oscar Wilde's Oxford Notebooks: A Portrait of the Mind in the Making*, ed. Philip E. Smith II and Michael S. Helfland (Oxford: Oxford University Press, 1989), pp. 125–6; *The Importance of Being Ernest* in *Plays, Prose Writings and Poems*, p. 472.

69 On April 25 1895, the day before the first trial opened, Queensberry wrote 'were I the authority that had to mete out to him his punishment, I would treat him with all possible consideration as a sexual pervert of utterly diseased mind, not as a sane criminal' – see *Letters*, p. 450n; quoted in H. Montgomery Hyde (ed.), *The Trials of Oscar Wilde* (London: William Hedge, 1948), p. 361.

70 For an account of the 1533 Act of Henry VIII in relation to Section 11 of the Criminal Law Amendment Act of 1885, see Jeffrey Weeks, *Sex, Politics and Society* (London: Longman, 1989), pp. 99–117; for an account of Labouchère's atheism see Hesketh Pearson, *Labby: The Life and Character of Henry Labouchère* (London: Hamish Hamilton, 1936), pp. 162–3.

71 Quoted in Joseph Pearce, *Literary Converts: Spiritual Inspiration in an Age of Unbelief* (London: Hodder and Stoughton, 1999), p. 3; for details of Queensberry's support for the *Freethinker* see Marsh, p. 153; *ibid.*, p. 129.

72 Quoted in John Stokes, *Oscar Wilde: Myths, Miracles and Imitations* (Cambridge: Cambridge University Press, 1996), p. 56.

73 Quoted in Edward Royle (ed.), *The Infidel Tradition from Paine to Bradlaugh* (London: Macmillan, 1976), p. 130; quoted in Edward Royle, *Radical Politics 1790–1900: Religion and Unbelief* (London: Longman, 1971), p. 116.

74 As Weeks points out, 'in the first third of the nineteenth century . . . more than 50 men were hanged for sodomy' p. 100; *Christianity or Secularism: Which is True? A Verbatim Report of a Four Nights' Debate Between the Rev. Dr. J. McCann and Mr. G. W. Foote* (London: Progressive Publishing, 1886), p. 53.

75 *De Profundis, Letters*, pp. 490–1.

76 *Dorian Gray*, p. 180.

77 James Joyce, *Ulysses,* ed. Hans Walter Gabler (Harmondsworth: Penguin, 1986), pp. 395–6.

78 Virginia Woolf, *Mrs. Dalloway*, ed. Stella McNichol and Elaine Showalter (Harmondsworth: Penguin, 1992), pp. 134–5.

79   'Circumfession', pp. 282–3; Derrida also makes a point of mentioning that his computer is a 'Macintosh' in *Archive Fever* [1995], tr. Eric Prenowitz (Chicago: Chicago University Press, 1996), p. 25; *Mrs Dalloway*, p. 84.

80   *Ibid.*, p. 130. 'As a number of scholars have noted, the homosexual signifi-cance of "queer" had entered English slang by 1900' – Elaine Showalter, *Sexual Anarchy: Gender and Culture at the 'Fin de Siècle'* (London: Virago, 1992), p. 111.

81   Frank Kermode, *The Genesis of Secrecy: On the Interpretation of Narrative* (Cambridge, Mass.: Harvard University Press, 1979), p. 55. For wonderful, post-Kermodean discussions of the 'boy in the shirt' episode see Stephen D. Moore, *Mark and Luke in Poststructuralist Perspectives: Jesus Begins to Write* (New Haven: Yale University Press, 1992), pp. 30–37; and Valentine Cunningham, 'The Best Stories in the Best Order? Canons, Apocryphas and (Post)modern Reading', *Literature and Theology*, 14 (2000), 69–80.

82   See Kermode, p. 58.

83   See Emmanuel Vernadikis, 'Wilde's Reading of Clemens Alexandrinus', in C. George Sandulescu (ed.), *Rediscovering Oscar Wilde* (Gerrards Cross: Colin Smythe, 1994), pp. 421–31; interestingly, the Carpocration version enlarges the part played by Salome – see Morton Smith, *Clement of Alexandria and a Secret Gospel of Mark* (Cambridge, Mass.: Harvard University Press, 1970), p. 34.

84   *Letters* p. 479; 'I hope before I die to write the epic of the Cross, the Iliad of Christianity' – 'Oscar Wilde' in *Oscar Wilde: Interviews and Recollections*, ed. E. H. Mikhail, 2 vols (London: Macmillan, 1979), 2.316; Dollimore, pp. 96–7; see also Stokes, p. 24 and Richard Ellmann, *Golden Codgers: Biographical Speculations* (London: Oxford University Press, 1973), pp. 96–7 – Ellmann quotes Gide's recollection that 'Wilde . . . projected a book to be entitled *Christianisme contre le Christ.*'

85   See Daniel L. Pals, *The Victorian 'Lives' of Christ* (San Antonio, Texas: Trinity University Press, 1972), *passim*; Vernadikis, p. 422.

86   'The Soul of Man Under Socialism', *Plays, Prose Writings and Poems*, p. 22.

87   *De Profundis, Letters*, pp. 483, 485.

88   *Plays, Prose Writings and Poems*, p. 479.

89   See Ellmann, p. 351.

90   *De Profundis, Letters*, p. 477; *Plays, Prose Writings and Poems*, p. 254; Psalm 69.3,21.

91   *Complete Poetry*, p. 87.

92   *Plays, Prose Writings and Poems*, p. 85.

93   *Letters*, p. 825.

94   *Ibid.*, p. 488; the black flag of Anarchism emerged after the Black International was held in 1881, to distinguish it from the Red International – see Peter Marshall, *Demanding the Impossible: A History of Anarchism* (London: HarperCollins, 1992), p. 498.

95   *Plays, Prose Writings and Poems*, p. 46.

96   Quoted in Showalter, p. 3; see Edward W. Said, *Orientalism: Western Conceptions of the Orient* (Harmondsworth: Penguin,1995), p. 190.

97   *Plays, Prose Writings and Poems*, p. 245.

98   *Letters*, p. 478; *Complete Poetry*, pp. 144, 146, 148.

99 Oscar Wilde, *Complete Shorter Fiction*, ed. Isobel Murray (Oxford: Oxford University Press, 1979), p. 27.

100 *Complete Poetry*, p. 129.

101 *Plays, Prose Writings and Poems*, p. 391.

102 See Henry Arthur Jones's essay 'Religion and the Stage' (1885), in *The Renascence of the English Drama: Essays, Lectures, Fragments* (London: Macmillan, 1895), – if Jones is to be believed, the absence of biblical characters on the late-Victorian stage has to do with not so much religious sensibilities as increasing secularism: 'the ordinary English[men]', he writes, 'feel uneasy if religion is broached on the stage, because, having conveniently dispensed with it to a great extent in regulating their everyday lives, they think it may be very well allowed to remain in its present condition of honoured and respectable superannuation' (p. 35).

103 *Complete Fiction*, p. 57.

104 George Eliot, 'Evangelical Teaching: Dr. Cumming'(1855), in *George Eliot: Selected Essays, Poems and Other Writings*, ed. A. S. Byatt and Nicholas Warren (Harmondsworth: Penguin, 1990), p. 38; Samuel Butler, *The Way of All Flesh* [1903], ed. James Cochrane (Harmondsworth: Penguin, 1966), p. 251; Alfred Tennyson, 'The Palace of Art' (1832), *The Poems of Tennyson*, ed. Christopher Ricks, 3 vols (London: Longman, 1987), 1.452.

105 *Plays, Prose Writings and Poems*, p. 471; Friedrich Nietzsche, *Thus Spoke Zarathustra: A Book for Everyone and No One*, tr. R. J. Hollingdale (Harmondsworth: Penguin, 1969), p. 125; *The Complete Poems of Thomas Hardy*, ed. James Gibson (London: Macmillan, 1976), pp. 326–7.

106 *The Anti-Christ*, p. 196.

107 Quoted in Ellmann, p. 273.

108 *Plays, Prose Writings and Poems*, p. 479.

109 'Lord Arthur Savile's Crime', in *Complete Fiction*, pp. 46–7.

110 See Pamela J. Walker, '"A Carnival of Equality": The Salvation Army and the Politics of Religion in Working-Class Communities', *Journal of Victorian Culture*, 5 (2000), 73, 75, 68.

111 Jones, pp. 120–1.

112 To Robert Ross, 21 April 1900, *Letters*, p. 824.

113 To Robert Ross, late March 1900, *Letters*, p. 819. Note Walter Benjamin's claim that 'surrealism . . . in France . . . fed on the . . . last trickle of French decadence' – *One Way Street and Other Writings*, tr. Edmund Jephcott and Kingsley Shorter (London: Verso, 1979), p. 225; the last section of my chapter would very much echo Benjamin's claim, only adding that the Christian aspects of Decadence are crucial to his genealogy.

114 'Then arrived some . . . revolting official; he asked how many collars Oscar had, and the value of his umbrella. (This is quite true and not a mere exaggeration of mine)' – Robert Ross to More Adey, 14 December, 1900, *Letters*, p. 855.

115 'An unsuccessful photograph of Oscar was taken by Maurice Gilbert at my request, the flashlight did not work properly' – *ibid.*, p. 855.

116 To Robert Ross, late March 1900, *Letters*, p. 819.

117 'The Critic as Artist', *Plays, Prose Writings and Poems*, p. 124.

118 To Robert Ross, 8 October 1897, *Letters*, p. 654.
119 *Complete Fiction*, pp. 48, 45 (my italics).

Six Joycing Derrida, Churching Derrida

1   James Joyce, *Ulysses* [1922] (Harmondsworth: Penguin, 1986), p. 2; Jacques Derrida, *Glas* [1974], tr. John P. Leavey and Richard Rand (Lincoln: University of Nebraska Press, 1986), p. 208b – translation modified. When I quote *Glas* in French the page reference is to the original edition published by Éditions Galilée in 1974. I am not, of course, the first to write on Derrida and Joyce – this is done most extensively by Alan Roughley in *Reading Derrida, Reading Joyce* (Gainesville: University Press of Florida, 1999).
2   *Glas*, p. 208b.
3   Derrida returns to this connection between church and modern communication systems in *The Post Card: From Socrates to Freud and Beyond* [1980], tr. Alan Bass (Chicago: University of Chicago Press, 1987), where he writes that: 'for me the post office is a church in which secret rendez-vous are given, Notre-Dame on Sunday afternoon in the crowd' (p. 69). It is, of course, intriguing that when Derrida writes about *Ulysses* he ends up talking on the phone: in 'Ulysses Gramophone' he declares 'In the beginning was the telephone' – Jacques Derrida, *Acts of Literature*, ed. Derek Attrridge (London: Routledge, 1992), p. 270.
4   *Glas,* p. 196b.
5   *Ulysses,* pp. 100, 163, 253, 97.
6   *Ibid.*, p. 33.
7   *Ibid.*, p. 169.
8   *Glas*, p. 89b; *Ulysses*, p. 280. 'To curse "by bell, book and candle" is to pronounce "major excommunication." The bell calls attention; the book contains the sentence to be pronounced; the candle is extinguished to symbolise the spiritual darkness into which the excommunicant is cast' – Don Gifford and Robert J. Seidman, *Notes for Joyce* (New York: E. P. Dutton, 1974), p. 308.
9   *Glas*, p. 101b.
10 *Ibid.*, p. 102b.
11 Jacques Derrida, 'Circumfession' in Jacques Derrida and Geoffrey Bennington, *Jacques Derrida* [1991] (Chicago: Chicago University Press, 1993), p. 56.
12 *Glas*, p. 95a.
13 *Ibid.*, p. 72a.
14 *Ibid.*, p. 96a.
15 *Ibid.*, p. 86a; Matt 16.18.
16 *Ulysses*, p. 148.
17 For full details see Herbert Thurston, S.J., *The Holy Year of Jubilee: An Account of the History and Ceremonial of the Roman Jubilee* (London: Sands and Co., 1900). Fascinating in this connection is the claim that, following the Roman jubilee of 1775, Voltaire declared, 'another such jubilee and it would be all over with philosophy' – Thurston, p. 128.
18 *Glas*, p. 72a.

19 *Ibid.*, p. 52a.
20 Interestingly, *Glas*'s own jubilee year – the year of its twenty-fifth anniversary, 1999 – inspired some to plan a celebratory conference to be held at Cornell University; unfortunately, it never took place.
21 *Glas*, pp. 243a, 62a, 101a.
22 *Ibid.*, p. 86b.
23 *Ibid.*, p. 52a. – translation modified.
24 *Ibid.*, p. 41b. For further discussion of Derrida, crypts and the church see the chapter on Dickens.
25 As Richard Ellmann writes, 'the name of Joyce is derived . . . from the French *joyeux* and Latin *jocax*, and Joyce . . . accepted his name as an omen' – *James Joyce* (Oxford: Oxford University Press, 1982), p. 12.
26 *Ulysses,*pp. 393, 397.
27 *Glas*, pp. 177a; *Ulysses*, p. 16; quoted in Frank Budgen, *James Joyce and the Making of Ulysses and Other Writings* (London: Oxford University Press, 1972), p. 347. For an excellent guide to the pre-modern tradition of comic Christianity see M. A. Screech, *Laughter at the Foot of the Cross* (Harmondsworth: Penguin, 1997); for an excellent guide to its modern development see Robert M. Polhemus, *Comic Faith: The Great Tradition from Austen to Joyce* (Chicago: University of Chicago Press, 1980).
28 *The Letters of James Joyce*, 3 vols, ed. Richard Ellmann (London: Faber and Faber, 1966), 2.196.
29 *Ulysses*, p. 427.
30 *Ibid.*, p. 28.
31 *Glas*, p. 177a.
32 John 11.35.
33 *Ulysses*, p. 212.
34 *Glas*, p. 262a; see Friedrich Nietzsche, *Twilight of the Idols* [1889] / *The Anti-Christ* [1895], tr. R. J. Hollingdale (Harmondsworth: Penguin, 1968).
35 *Glas*, p. 104b; see 'Plato's Pharmacy' in Jacques Derrida, *Dissemination* [1972], tr. Barbara Johnson (London: Athlone Press, 1981), pp. 61–172; Karl Marx, 'A Contribution to the Critique of Hegel's Philosophy of Right. Introduction' [1843–4], in Karl Marx, *Early Writings*, tr. Rodney Livingstone and Gregor Benton (Harmondsworth: Penguin, 1975), p. 244.
36 *Ulysses*, pp. 20, 385.
37 James Fairhall, *James Joyce and the Question of History* (Cambridge: Cambridge University Press, 1993), p. 46 – the bomb was set off by a Fenian splinter group called the Dynamitards in an attempt to free imprisoned comrades from Clerkenwell Prison.
38 *Ulysses*, p. 66.
39 'That fellow' to whom Bloom refers is James Carey (1845–83), one of the Invincibles involved in the Phoenix Park murders; the Clerkenwell bomber is Joseph Casey. Although the Catholic Church in Ireland was, on the whole, opposed to the violent republicanism of the Fenians, there were some priests who were very sympathetic – most famously, Father Lavelle – see Fairhall, pp. 129–31.
40 *Glas,*p. 89b.
41 Nietzsche, pp. 196, 191.

42 *Ulysses*, p. 88, 462.

43 Werner Heisenberg, *Physics and Beyond: Encounters and Conversations,* tr. A. J. Pomerans (New York: Harper and Row, 1971), p. 41. There has been much fierce debate on the relationship between Joyce and contemporary science – see, in particular, Phillip F. Herring, *Joyce's Uncertainty Principle* (Princeton: Princeton University Press, 1987); M. Keith Booker, 'Joyce, Planck, Einstein, and Heisenberg: a Relativistic Quantum Mechanical Discussion of *Ulysses*', *James Joyce Quarterly* 27 (1990), 577–86; Thomas Jackson Rice, *Joyce, Chaos and Complexity* (Urbana: University of Illinois Press, 1997). Whatever the final verdict on Joyce's relationship to nuclear physics we cannot forget Jung's claim that '*Ulysses* . . . is the book that . . . destroys the world' – see Umberto Eco, *The Aesthetics of Chaosmos: The Middle Ages of James Joyce*, tr. Ellen Esrock (Cambridge, Mass.: Harvard University Press, 1989), p. 44.

44 *Ulysses 548;* James Joyce, *Finnegan's Wake* [1939] (Harmondsworth: Penguin, 1992) p. 225.

45 See Gillian Beer's excellent '"Wireless": Popular Physics, Radio and Modernism' in B. Spufford and J. Uglow (eds), *Cultural Babbage: Technology, Time and Innovation* (London: Faber and Faber, 1996), p. 160; and Cassidy, p. 455.

46 *Glas*, pp. 207b, 106–7a.

47 Mark C. Taylor, *Tears* (Albany: SUNY Press, 1990), p. 42.

48 *Glas*, p. 174a.

49 *James Joyce Letters*, II.195; Carla de Petris, 'Exiles or Emigrants', in Giorgio Melchiori (ed.), *Joyce in Rome: The Genesis of Ulysses* (Rome: Bulzoni Editore, 1972), p. 80.

50 *Ulysses*, p. 71a.

51 Taylor, p. 42.

52 *Glas*, pp. 172b, 95a.

53 *Ibid.*, p. 91a.

54 *Ibid.*, p. 71a.

55 *Ibid.*, pp. 203a, 221a.

56 *Ulysses,*p. 33

57 *Glas*, p. 95a.

58 Jacques Derrida, 'No Apocalypse, Not Now (full speed ahead, seven missiles, seven missives)', *Diacritics* 14 (1984), 26, 31, 23.

59 *Glas*, p. 153a.

60 Quoted in Edmund White, *Genet* (London: Picador, 1993), pp. 228, 229.

61 *Ibid.*, p. 507.

62 *Glas*, p. 255a.

63 *Ibid.*, p. 207b.

64 Jean Genet, *The Blacks: A Clown Show* [1959], tr. Bernard Frechtman (London: Faber and Faber, 1967), p. 81.

65 *Glas*, p. 214a.

66 *Ibid.*, p. 255a, 207–9a; I refer, of course, to 'White Mythology: Metaphor in the Text of Philosophy' in Jacques Derrida, *Margins of Philosophy* [1972], tr. Alan Bass (London: Harvester Wheatsheaf, 1982); this title is, of course, given a literal, or post-colonial twist by Robert Young in his celebrated *White*

Mythologies: Writing History and the West (London: Routledge, 1990).

67 See Carlo Bigazzi, 'Joyce and the Italian Press', in Melchiori, p. 59.

68 *Ulysses*, pp. 17, 489, 438.

69 The church is St. Mary's Chapel of Ease (Church of Ireland) – see Gifford and Seidman, p. 413; *Ulysses*, p. 183.

70 Jacques Derrida, *The Gift of Death* [1992], tr. David Wills (Chicago: Chicago University Press, 1995), pp. 86, 85.

71 *Ulysses,* pp. 269, 611.

72 See, for example, Jane Gallop, *Reading Lacan* (Ithaca: Cornell University Press, 1985), pp. 58–9; and Francis Fukuyama, *The End of History and the Last Man* (New York: The Free Press, 1992).

73 *Ulysses*, pp. 406–7.

74 Bennington and Derrida, p. 58.

75 *Glas*, p. 106a.

76 I refer, of course, to Swinburne's 'Hymn to Proserpine' (1867) – *The Poems of Algernon Charles Swinburne*, 6 vols (London: Chatto and Windus, 1904), 1.69; Geoffrey H. Hartman, *Saving the Text: Literature / Derrida / Philosophy* (London: Johns Hopkins University Press, 1981), p. 19.

77 *Glas*, p. 197b.

78 *Ibid.*, pp. 69–70b.

79 For a very interesting discussion of the African, or Algerian Derrida see Lee Morrissey, 'Derrida, Algeria, and "Structure, Sign and Play,"' http://jefferson.village.virginia.edu/pmc/current.issue/9.2morrissey.html.

80 *Glas*, p. 147b.

81 Quoted in Valentine Cunningham, *Everywhere Spoken Against: Dissent in the Victorian Novel* (Oxford: Clarendon Press, 1975), p. 143.

82 *Ulysses,* p. 190 (my italics).

83 *Ibid.*, p. 293.

84 As Hans Kung writes, 'Nazi anti-Semitism . . . would have been impossible without the preceding two thousand years of "Christian" hostility to the Jews' – *The Church* (London: Burns and Oates, 1968), p. 137. I am very aware that to refer to the extermination of the Jews not as 'the Shoah' but in terms of the Greco-Christian ecclesiastical notion of *to holocauston* (burnt offering), may well constitute a Christianisation of the event – but that, in a sense, is precisely what I mean to do, or rather reflect. Interestingly, Simon Critchley raises this issue specifically in relation to *Glas* – see 'A Commentary on Derrida's Reading of Hegel in *Glas*', *Bulletin of the Hegel Society of Great* (1988), 32.n.17.

85 *Glas*, p. 121b.

86 *Ulysses*, p. 89.

87 *Ulysses*, p. 80, 154; these extremely harsh camps were set up to imprison Boer civilians, including women and children – see Gifford and Seidman, pp. 163–4. For an excellent discussion of Judaism and *Ulysses* see Ira B. Nadel, *Joyce and the Jews: Culture and Texts* (Gainesville: University Press of Florida, 1989).

88 *Ulysses*, p. 149.

89 See Gifford and Seidman, p. 150.

90 *Glas*, pp. 196b.

91 'If photography is both . . . a resurrection and a haunting . . . could we not say – as Beckett once said, jokingly – that the inventor of photograph was not Niepce or Talbot but [St.] Veronica' – Jean Michel Rabaté, *The Ghosts of Modernity* (Gainesville: University Press of Florida, 1996), p. 82.

92 Roland Barthes, *Camera Lucida*, tr. Richard Howard (New York: Noonday Press, 1981), p. 82.

93 *Glas*, pp. 242a.

94 Shoshana Felman and Dori Laub explore a related question in writing of the Holocaust as 'an event without a witness'; they argue that the 'the inherently incomprehensible and deceptive psychological structure of the event precluded its own witnessing, even by its very victims' – *Testimony: Crises of Witnessing in Literature, Psychoanalysis and History* (London: Routledge, 1992), p. 80.

95 *Ulysses*, p. 10; *Glas*, p. 208a.

96 *Ulysses*, pp. 319–20.

97 *Glas*, p. 72a.

98 *Ulysses*, p. 320; I am acutely conscious that this line constitutes a decidedly feminine ending; unfortunately, I did not feel able to develop this line of thought within the confines of this chapter.

99 Translation modified.

100 *Glas*, p. 181b. *Glas* meets Christianity in the sea, there they converge; as Gayatri Chakravorty Spivak points out, in *Glas* there is an 'expansion of . . . IC (Immaculate Conception as well as Categorical Imperative), into the ego (ICH), and Christ the Fish (ICHTHYOS)' – 'Glas-Piece: A *Compte Rendu*', *Diacritics* 7 (1977), 27. Hartman makes a similar point – see *Saving the Text*, p. 62.

101 *Glas*, p. 246b.

102 For Derrida there is, of course, a sense in which translation *per se* is always inevitable, even in the case of the untranslatable – see, in particular, the translator's note in 'Living On.'

103 Derrida, 'Circumfession', p. 97 – see pp. 35, 11. It was John P. Leavey – co-translator of *Glas*, of course – who told me about Derrida mocking up the individual pages using photocopies. Leavey also mentioned that Derrida first started using an electric typewriter in the mid-'70s and only began using a computer in the mid-to-late '80s.

104 *Glas*, p. 169b.

105 *Ulysses*, pp. 395, 127, 66.

106 It is this vision of the church that John D. Caputo picks up on when he writes that 'the Church . . . [in the end] calls the police' – *The Prayers and Tears of Jacques Derrida: Religion without Religion* (Bloomington: Indiana University Press, 1997), p. 91; *Glas*, p. 7b.

107 Derrida, 'Circumfession', p. 238.

108 *Ibid.*, pp. 177–80.

109 Hebrews 12.1.

110 *Ulysses*, p. 87.

111 As Mark C. Taylor writes, 'Hegelian philosophy can be understood as a systematic attempt to secure the identity of identity and nonidentity . . . By revealing the Logos of everything to be the logical structure of identity-in-

difference, speculative philosophy is supposed to reconcile opposites without destroying difference(s)' – *Altarity* (Chicago: University of Chicago Press, 1987).

Conclusion 'What has not yet happened'

1   Jacques Derrida, *The Gift of Death* [1992], tr. David Wills (Chicago: University of Chicago Press, 1995), p. 28.
2   Jacques Derrida, *The Truth in Painting* [1978], tr. Geoff Bennington and Ian Mcleod (Chicago: University of Chicago Press, 1987), p. 157.
3   'The Vision of the Three T's: A Threnody', *The Complete Works of Lewis Carroll* (Harmondsworth: Penguin,1982), p. 1051.
4   Jacques Derrida, 'Envois', *The Post Card: from Socrates to Freud and Beyond* [1980], tr. Alan Bass (Chicago: Chicago University Press, 1987), p. 56.

Index